Germany Today

Germany Today

A Student's Dictionary

Edited by

Charlie Jeffery
Deputy Director, Institute of German Studies
University of Birmingham

and

Ruth Whittle
Lecturer, Department of German Studies
University of Birmingham

A member of the Hodder Headline Group
LONDON • NEW YORK • SYDNEY • AUCKLAND

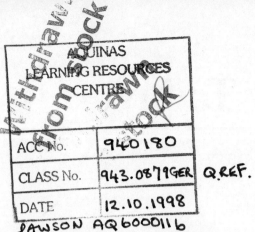

First published in Great Britain in 1997 by
Arnold, a member of the Hodder Headline Group
338 Euston Road, London NW1 3BH
175 Fifth Avenue, New York, NY 10010

Distributed exclusively in the USA by
St Martin's Press Inc.,
175 Fifth Avenue,
New York, NY10010

British Library Cataloguing in Publication Data
A catalogue entry for this book is available from the British Library

Library of Congress Cataloging-in-Publication Data
Germany today: a student's d. tionary/edited by Charlie Jeffery and Ruth Whittle.
    p.   cm.
Includes bibliographical references and index.
ISBN 0–340–66306–5. — ISBN 0–340–66305–7 (pbk.)
    1. Germany—Politics and government—1990— —Dictionaries.
2. Germany—Civilization—20th century—Dictionaries. 3. Germany—Economic con-
ditions—1990— —Dictionaries. I. Jeffery, Charlie. II. Whittle, Ruth.
DD290.29.G496 1997
943.087'9—dc21   97–8833
                                                                               CIP

ISBN 0 340 66306 5 (hb)
ISBN 0 340 66305 7 (pb)

Composition by Saxon Graphics Ltd, Derby
Printed and bound in Great Britain by JW Arrowsmith Ltd, Bristol

Preface

Germany Today is an alphabetical dictionary focusing on the politics, economy, history and culture of contemporary Germany. It will be an invaluable tool for students studying German language and *Landeskunde* in the sixth form or at university, for those embarking on a year abroad in Germany, and for those seeking a more general reference guide to help them understand contemporary German affairs.

Germany Today has cross-referenced entries providing a wealth of in-depth information on contemporary institutions, individuals and concepts. Where necessary for the understanding of contemporary affairs, historical information extending back to the beginning of the twentieth century has also been included.

Headwords were generally chosen to match the terms which the reader is most likely to look up. Where this was not appropriate, references to the entry where the information can be found are given, for example, *ZDF* (*Zweites Deutsches Fernsehen*) is cross-referred to *Rundfunk und Fernsehen*. Where an entry mentions a term more fully dealt with in a separate entry, this is indicated by the term being written in small capitals. Supplementary cross-references are often also given at the end of an entry to enable the reader to explore further related material. German terms are generally given in italics and translations are provided where necessary.

The selection of entries was made with A-level syllabi, university reading lists for German and European Studies and the needs of business users in mind. The dictionary was conceived both as an aid for formal study as well as a guide to steering a way successfully through German newspapers, news broadcasts, discussions with friends and business partners, and so on. It was decided not to include terms which can be looked up in a bilingual dictionary but, rather, to concentrate on terms describing particular aspects of contemporary Germany whose full meaning is not conveyed by literal translation.

All the entries have been written by specialists in the field, who are involved in either the Institute for German Studies or the Department of German Studies at the University of Birmingham, one of the leading centres for the study of contemporary Germany in the UK. We hope that, by drawing on the expertise of German studies at Birmingham, we have assembled a reliable, authoritative and, above all, interesting study tool.

Charlie Jeffery
Ruth Whittle
Birmingham, 1997

Contributors

Charlie Jeffery (CJ), Deputy Director of the Institute for German Studies (IGS), Birmingham
Ruth Whittle (RW), Lecturer, Department of German Studies, University of Birmingham
Mike Dennis (MD), Visiting Fellow to the IGS (University of Wolverhampton)
Eric Owen Smith (EOS), Visiting Fellow to the IGS (Loughborough University)
Rebecca Owen Smith (ROS), European Sales Executive, Boosey & Hawkes
Achill Wenzel (AW), Professor for Teacher Training, Universität Koblenz–Landau
Michael Butler (MGB), Head of the Department of German Studies, University of Birmingham
Nisha Malham (NM), Research Fellow at the IGS, Birmingham

Postgraduate students at the IGS, Birmingham:

Charles Lees (CL)
Penny Henson (PH)
Shlomo Shpiro (SS)
Kerry Langston (KL)
Eike Mennerich (EM)
Simon Green (SG)
Steve French (SRF)

Initials in brackets at the end of each entry in the dictionary indicate the author of that entry.

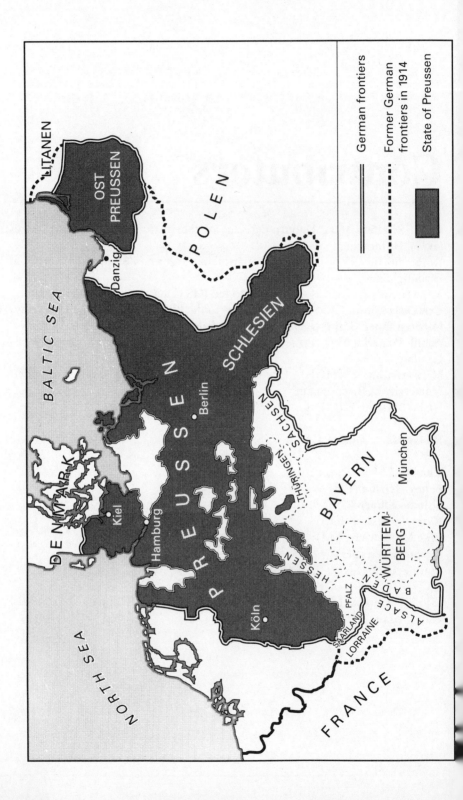

German frontiers

Former German
frontiers in 1914

State of Preussen

LITANEN

OST
PREUSSEN

POLEN

BALTIC SEA

Danzig

SCHLESIEN

DENMARK

Berlin

SACHSEN

Kiel

THÜRINGEN

BAYERN

München

Hamburg

PREUSSEN

HESSEN

WÜRTTEM-
BERG

PFALZ

BADEN

SAARLAND

ALSACE

NORTH SEA

Köln

LORRAINE

FRANCE

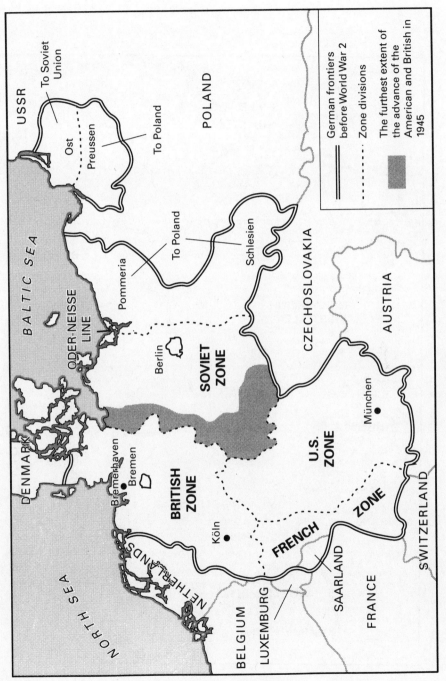

Map 2 Germany in 1945

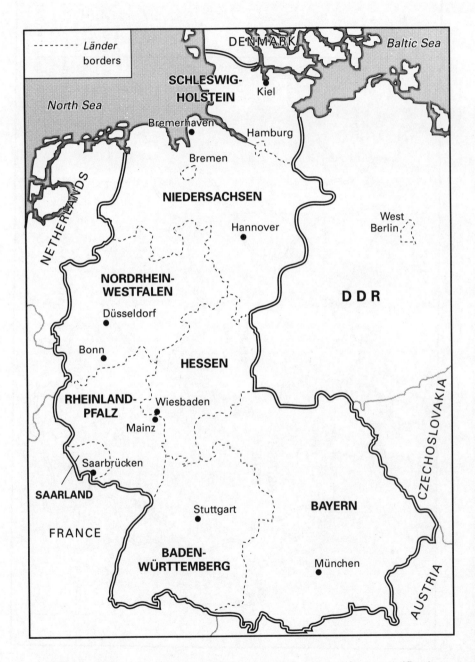

Map 3 The *Länder* of the Federal Republic of Germany prior to reunification

Map 4 The Federal Republic of Germany in 1990

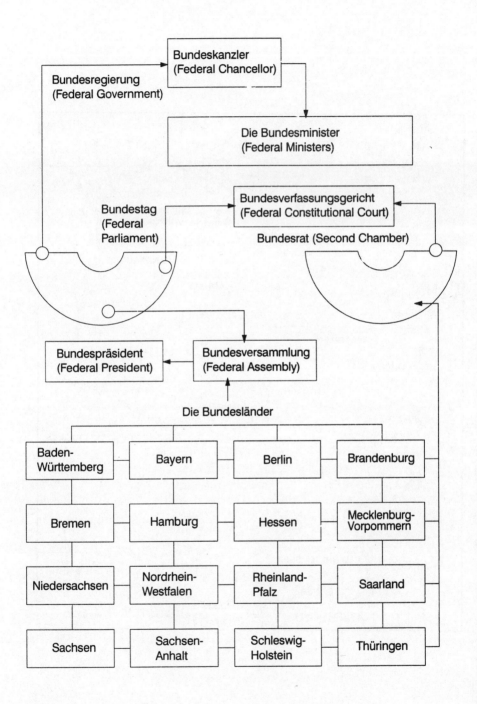

Germany's federal structure

A

Abgeordnete Deputies are elected MPs in the Federal Republic, either of the BUNDESTAG (*Mitglied des Bundestags*, or MdB) or of a LANDTAG (*Mitglied des Landtags*, or MdL). MdBs and MdLs have a 'free mandate' in representing the interests of their voters, i.e. they may not be bound by instructions from any other body or person. The free mandate is protected by two principles: (a) indemnity against professional or judicial penalisation for activities undertaken in parliament; and (b) immunity from prosecution or other restrictions on personal freedom which might arise in connection with parliamentary activity. The principle of free mandate is, however, in practice restricted by deputies typically being members of political parties and therefore subject to the pressures of party discipline.

The role of deputy has become increasingly professionalised in Germany through the award of parliamentary salaries. This has necessitated the public declaration of extra-parliamentary business or other financial interests. German deputies at all levels of government have been strongly criticised in recent years for awarding themselves what many have deemed over-generous salaries and in some cases for maintaining improper extra-parliamentary financial interests. This criticism has contributed to the sense of alienation many Germans have with party politics and the wider political system (POLITIKVERDROSSENHEIT).

(CJ)

Abitur See WEITERFÜHRENDE SCHULEN.

Abrüstung The issue of disarmament has played a significant role in the history of post-war Germany, given the historical context of Germany's role in World War II and its precarious geographical and political position during the Cold War.

The issue proved to be especially controversial in the Federal Republic in the case of the deployment of nuclear weapons by the Western Allies. During the Cold War the Federal Republic contained the largest concentration of nuclear weapons per square mile anywhere in the world, all of which were under the control of external powers. An equivalent situation existed in the GDR in respect of Warsaw Pact nuclear weaponry.

The centrality of Germany in the arms race in Europe helped to spawn a powerful peace movement (FRIEDENSBEWEGUNG) focused in particular on the apocalyptic consequences of the use of nuclear weapons.

The end of the Cold War which came with the demise of the Soviet Union and the downsizing of military capacity across both Western and Eastern Europe has meant that disarmament has become less of a sensitive political issue in Germany.

See NATO-DOPPELBESCHLUß; WARSCHAUER PAKT.

(PH)

Abtreibungsrecht   The right to abortion, regulated in the now notorious Paragraph 218 of the German Penal Code (*Strafgesetzbuch*), has long been a controversial issue in the Federal Republic. It cuts across two fields which each produce conflicting positions on the abortion issue: that of policy on equal opportunities (GLEICHBERECHTIGUNG) for men and women (women should have the right themselves to decide when to bear a child); and that of wider public ethics (the right to life of the unborn should be protected).

Abortion law in the Federal Republic has traditionally tilted towards the latter position. An attempt to reform and liberalise the law in 1974, following long-standing pressure by the Women's Movement (FRAUENBEWEGUNG) was struck down on appeal by the CDU/CSU to the Federal Constitutional Court. A new Abortion Reform Law in 1976 confirmed a restricted right to abortion, only allowable in certain clearly defined circumstances. The issue came to prominence again following unification. The abortion law in the former GDR had been much more open, allowing abortion more or less on demand in the first twelve weeks of pregnancy. The clash of legal regulations was singled out in the Treaty on Unification (EINIGUNGSVERTRAG) as an area which required special consideration and a new solution for a united Germany. A new law was passed in 1992 which sought a compromise between the two legal traditions, allowing abortion in the first twelve weeks of pregnancy, but only after intensive medical, social and legal counselling. This was, however, again rejected by the Constitutional Court on appeal by the LANDESREGIERUNG in Bavaria and 248 CDU/CSU MPs. The Court insisted that the counselling should stress the objective of protecting the life of the unborn (*Schutz des ungeborenen Lebens*).

This stipulation was incorporated into law with effect from 1996, much to the dissatisfaction of women in Eastern Germany, who have seen their legal rights severely narrowed, and of those who felt that the Constitutional Court had made an unjustifiably political intervention in a matter which had legitimately been passed by a majority in the BUNDESTAG.

See FRAUENPOLITIK; VEREINIGUNG.

(CJ)

Abwicklung 'Winding up' is the term widely used to refer to the dismantling of GDR institutions, the removal of staff in public sector employment tainted by close association with the GDR regime, and more broadly to the dismantling of GDR state industries and sometimes even the GDR itself.

Abwicklung was conducted across the board in the years following German unification in 1990. It took place in cultural and medical institutions including the army and the education sector. The term is associated not only with massive restructuring and heavy job losses but it is also applied to what many East Germans perceive to be the high-minded attitude and actions of those Westerners responsible for carrying out the winding-up process.

See KOMBINAT; OSSI; TREUHANDANSTALT; WESSI.

(MD)

Adenauer, Konrad Konrad Adenauer (1876–1967) was the first Chancellor of the Federal Republic of Germany and remained in office from 1949 until 1963. From 1951–55 he also held the office of Foreign Minister. From 1917 he had been Lord Mayor of Cologne but was forced out of this and other offices by the Nazis in 1933. Following the collapse of the Third Reich, Adenauer was one of the founder members of the CDU, representing the Rhineland–Catholic wing which decisively shaped the CDU's political and social message. This integrated Catholics and Protestants under a single party banner and offered a policy platform of the social market economy and western–oriented foreign policy. As chairman of the Parliamentary Council in 1948–49, he also wielded significant influence on the formulation of the GRUNDGESETZ. He became Chancellor following the first elections to the *Bundestag* in 1949.

Adenauer was the dominant political personality in the early years of the Federal Republic. His foreign policy of Western integration did much to rehabilitate Germany in the eyes of the international community. His commitment to Franco-German reconciliation provided a force for the early initiatives in European integration in the 1950s. The wider commitment to the Western Alliance and NATO was reflected in the Federal Republic's accession to NATO and rearmament in 1955. In the same year he managed to negotiate the release of the remaining German prisoners of war with the Soviet Union.

The years of Adenauer's Chancellorship were also those of the 'economic miracle' (WIRTSCHAFTSWUNDER). The combination of international rehabilitation and economic success invested Adenauer with tremendous popularity reflected in increasingly decisive electoral victories for the CDU through the 1950s. However, his style was frequently autocratic and by the late 1950s he was leading an increasingly fractious government. His wider popularity with the German electorate also began to ebb. He resigned on 15 October 1963.

Adenauer's legacy has remained important in the Federal Republic right up to the present. The CDU remains a cross-confessional party and its subsequent leaders, notably Helmut KOHL, have continued to pursue his vision of a united Europe.

See BUNDESKANZLER; PARLAMENTARISCHER RAT.

(SG)

Akademische Freiheit   The academic freedom of research and teaching is a traditional right of university teachers in general and professors in particular. The term refers to the subject to be researched or taught as well as to the methods.

Freedom of teaching is considered necessary to prevent unwanted interference, e.g. from the state or political ideologies. Course regulations imposed by the state limit such freedom but it is still up to the individual teacher to choose his/her methods. In German HOCHSCHULEN, teaching and research are linked. Research results must inform teaching and support the development of the academic disciplines. It has been argued that the best progress can be achieved if freedom of choice by the experts is guaranteed. This kind of freedom is a privilege shared by hardly any other profession and therefore demands responsibility on the part of academic staff.

For students, academic freedom used to mean choosing what, where and how to study. With today's limitations on access to universities in general, and (through NUMERUS CLAUSUS) to particular fields of study, this is hardly the case any more. Once admitted to university, students are, however, still free to choose between courses and to some extent can choose their examiner.

(AW)

Akademische Selbstverwaltung   Academic self-administration is intended to give practical effect to academic freedom (AKADEMISCHE FREIHEIT). It has several aspects. First and foremost it concerns the right of universities (HOCHSCHULEN) to confer degrees (*Diplom, Magister*, PROMOTION, HABILITATION). Not all HOCHSCHULEN confer all forms of degree. Self-administration also refers to the right of the university to appoint new staff and of the individual member of academic staff to choose his/her field of research. The most important institution of self-administration is the university's senate.

Government intervention can limit these rights both at a general level through budgetary policy and more specifically through establishing rules such as exam regulations.

See STUDIENABSCHLÜSSE.

(AW)

Akademisches Auslandsamt   The *Akademisches Auslandsamt* is the university office which deals with all aspects of foreign students studying at a German university.

Those needing information about studying at a specific German university should write to this office in the first place. It can give details on admission, language courses, accommodation and particular courses. The *Akademisches Auslandsamt* also usually organises summer language schools for foreign students.
See IMMATRIKULATION.
(RW)

Allgemeiner Deutscher Automobil Club The Allgemeiner Deutscher Automobil Club, or ADAC, is the German counterpart to the British Automobile Association (AA). It is an organisation of 13 million members offering a wide range of services such as roadside assistance, legal advice, journals and books, information on camping, travel, traffic, cars and motorbikes, and the testing of new cars. It also deals in the second-hand car market.

The ADAC is both a powerful lobby for motorists and has played a prominent role in developing wider environmental awareness in German society. The members' magazine is *Motorwelt*, one of the best-selling journals in Germany.
See UMWELTBEWEGUNG; VERBÄNDE.
(ECM)

Allianz *Allianz* is Europe's and one of the world's largest insurance companies, and also Germany's largest quoted company. Almost DM70 billion in premiums had been underwritten by the mid-1990s. The world-wide labour force stands at around 70 000, over half of whom work in Germany. International expansion has been a key feature in the company's growth. For example, it owns Cornhill in Britain – the sponsor of English test cricket. More recently, about 40 per cent of the Hungarian insurance market was acquired.

The world's largest reinsurer (*Münchner Rückversicherungsgesellschaft AG*) owns 25 per cent of the share capital of *Allianz*. *Allianz* in turn has stakes in a number of other German insurance companies, banks and industrial companies.

The acquisition of the East German *Deutsche Versicherungen* in 1990 was costly in terms of the extensive restructuring required. However, profits have been expected to rise gradually since 1994.
See FINANZWESEN.
(EOS)

Allianz für Deutschland The Alliance for Germany was the conservative coalition of the GDR-CDU with the Democratic Awakening (*Demokratischer Aufbruch*, or DA) and German Social Union (*Deutsche Soziale Union*, or DSU). Chancellor KOHL encouraged its formation in early February 1990 to provide the West German CDU/CSU coalition with a vehicle for mobilising support in the March VOLKSKAMMER election behind Kohl's policy of swift economic and monetary union.

The incorporation of two new groups, the DA and DSU, into the Alliance was intended to dilute criticism of the West German CDU's cohabitation with a former block party (BLOCKPARTEIEN), the GDR-CDU, as well as providing a broader base of support. The Alliance's advocacy of rapid union between the GDR and the Federal Republic was the key to its momentous success in the March election. It obtained 48 per cent of the vote (of which the CDU received 40.8 per cent) and 163 out of 400 seats in the new *Volkskammer*. The Alliance recruited heavily among confessionally oriented voters and among disenchanted manual workers in SACHSEN, SACHSEN-ANHALT and THÜRINGEN. In August 1990, the DA merged with the East German CDU and the latter with its Western partner two days before unification.

See BÜRGERBEWEGUNGEN.

(MD)

Amnesty International   The German section of the international human rights organisation supports the universal aims of Amnesty International: the treatment and release of (non-violent) prisoners of conscience, fair and swift legal processes for all prisoners and opposition to the death penalty and torture. In March 1994 the German section had 10 421 active members and 16 284 supporters.

Although the organisation's own rules mean that a national section of Amnesty International is not allowed to become involved in human rights issues in that country, Amnesty International clearly plays an important role as a pressure group, highlighting those countries which do not abide by the 1948 United Nations declaration on human rights. Moreover, with the changes to the German Constitution limiting the numbers of asylum seekers accepted into the Federal Republic and attempts to limit immigration into the European Union, the role of Amnesty International outside Germany in providing evidence of abuses of human rights and 'justifiable' asylum applications will become increasingly important in protecting the rights of asylum seekers in both Germany and Europe as a whole.

See ASYLRECHT.

(SRF)

Ampelkoalition   See KOALITION.

Antisemitismus   Anti-Semitism, the hatred of Jews, has long been a feature of German and European history. Its most extreme manifestation was in the genocidal anti-Jewish policies of the Third Reich, the HOLOCAUST, in which over 6 million Jews were murdered.

Anti-Semitism has long roots stretching back into Christian prejudices against Jews as the supposed murderers of Christ. These were later supplemented by new prejudices arising from the concentration of Jews in certain professions in Europe, especially banking and money-lending, which were generally held in low regard. In the nineteenth century, such religious and economic prejudices were overlain by new racial prejudices, wrapped up in a scientific terminology which asserted that a Jewish presence was harmful to the health of the host nation. Racial anti-Semitism, though present throughout Europe, became most deeply rooted in German-speaking central Europe. It was an ideological theme taken up by Adolf HITLER and his National Socialist Party in Germany after World War I, and was turned into policy practice after 1933 following the establishment of the Third Reich.

The anti-Jewish policy of the Third Reich passed through a number of phases, each more radical, reflecting the chaotic and competitive decision-making structures of the Nazi state. These were broadly as follows: periodic boycotts of Jewish businesses (1933–34); removal of legal rights, above all in the 1935 Nuremberg Laws; a nationwide organised pogrom in the so-called REICHSKRISTALLNACHT (Night of the Broken Glass) of 1938; forced emigration (1938–39); ghettoisation, with a view to forced deportation to a 'reservation' abroad, for which, for example, Siberia and Madagascar were both considered (1940–41); sporadic mass murder under the cover of the increasingly brutal campaign on the eastern front of World War II (1941); and ultimately, the Nazi's 'Final Solution' (*Endlösung*), consisting of industrialised mass murder in the extermination camps of occupied Eastern Europe, the most notorious of which was Auschwitz (1942 onwards). In total, in the worst genocide in world history, some 6 million Jews were murdered in the name of the anti-Semitism of the Third Reich.

See DRITTES REICH; HOLOCAUST; KONZENTRATIONSLAGER; NATIONAL-SOZIALISMUS; NÜRNBERGER GESETZE.

(CJ)

APO See AUßERPARLAMENTARISCHE OPPOSITION.

Arbeiterwohlfahrt The Workers' Welfare Association is a member of the *Bundesarbeitsgemeinschaft der Freien Wohlfahrtspflege* (the Federal Association of Welfare Groups). It is funded through private contributions and public funds. It concentrates, amongst other things, on providing help for mothers and their families, the disabled and old people as well as the integration of foreign workers, refugees, and *Aussiedler* (settlers from former German territories).

Membership stands at 640 000 with 61 400 full-time employees. These are often supplemented by volunteers and by those opting to perform *Zivildienst* (the alternative to military service).

See DEUTSCHES ROTES KREUZ; EVANGELISCHE KIRCHE DEUTSCHLANDS.

(SRF)

Arbeitslosenversicherung Unemployment insurance is designed to limit the material problems caused by unemployment by financing the payment of unemployment support.

As in the other main branches of social insurance (SOZIALVER-SICHERUNG) in Germany, half the contributions to the insurance fund are made by the employee concerned and half by the employer. Payments from the fund are of a number of types. In case of unemployment, individuals with a sufficient record of contribution to the fund initially receive *Arbeitslosengeld* (unemployment payments). The level of payment is set at around two-thirds of the person's previous income level (with variations in respect of family status). If no new employment has been found after one year, *Arbeitslosenhilfe* (unemployment assistance) is paid, which is set at a lower level than *Arbeitslosengeld*. Payments can also be made if employees are placed on short-time work (*Kurzarbeit*) or are prevented from working by poor weather conditions (*Schlechtwettergeld*), for example, in the building industry. Those who do not qualify for support through insufficient past contributions have an entitlement to SOZIALHILFE (social assistance).

Unemployment insurance is administered by the BUNDESANSTALT FÜR ARBEIT (the Federal Labour Office), which also conducts measures to improve the wider labour market situation.

Like the other branches of social insurance, the unemployment insurance system is facing considerable strain. A relatively high level of unemployment has become the norm in Germany, due to the decline of traditional high employment industries, the introduction of new, labour-saving industrial technologies and wider problems of competitiveness (arising in part from the high cost of maintaining the German social welfare system). The situation has worsened since unification given the substantially higher unemployment levels recorded in the East, causing the expenditures of the *Bundesanstalt* to treble between 1990 and 1993 and to remain at unprecedentedly high levels since.

See KRANKENVERSICHERUNG; RENTENVERSICHERUNG; SOZIALES NETZ.

(CJ)

Arbeitslosigkeit   The Federal Republic had a track record of relatively low unemployment rates until the 1990s. During the 1950s unemployment fell by over 1.3 million, while the number of jobs (*Arbeitsplätze*) increased by 7 million. Between 1960 and 1973, apart from the relatively minor recession in 1967, there were more unfilled vacancies (*offene Stellen*) than registered unemployed. Unemployment rose sharply following the two oil-price shocks (*Ölkrisen*) in 1974–75 and 1981–85. In the first half of the 1990s, amid the post-unification adjustment process, it reached record heights, with East Germany accounting for 25 per cent of the total. For each unfilled vacancy, ten persons were unemployed. The rising value of the DM, domestic recession in the West and an industrial collapse in the East all contributed to the rise in unemployment.

Reducing unemployment has therefore become a major policy problem since unification. A number of approaches have been put forward. Creating part-time jobs in the service sector (*Dienstleistungssektor*) is sometimes seen as one means of creating employment. Extending shopping hours became the best example of this approach. Others see the reduction of working time as a method of creating more jobs. The creation of more low-paid jobs is a third strand to the debate. This would be achieved by either allowing the wage structure to widen or 'topping up' benefits so that total pay always equals the minimum which is socially acceptable. All three approaches envisage different forms of 'flexibility' in the labour market and have been, in general, not welcomed by the trade unions. Changes would have profound implications in both East and West Germany. The quest to reduce unemployment may make it impossible for East German living standards to match those in West Germany, and it will simultaneously be necessary for West Germans to accept radical adjustments in the nature of the labour market.

See ARBEITSLOSENVERSICHERUNG; BUNDESANSTALT FÜR ARBEIT; GEWERKSCHAFTEN; SOZIALE MARKTWIRTSCHAFT; WIRTSCHAFTS-, WÄHRUNGS- UND SOZIALUNION; WIRTSCHAFTSPOLITIK; ZAHLUNGSBILANZ.

(EOS)

ARD (Arbeitsgemeinschaft der öffentlich-rechtlichen Rundfunkanstalten Deutschlands) See RUNDFUNK UND FERNSEHEN.

ASta (Allgemeiner Studentenausschuß) See VERFAßTE STUDENTENSCHAFT.

Asylrecht The right of political asylum in Germany of any individual who is persecuted on political grounds elsewhere is guaranteed in Article 16 of the GRUNDGESETZ. This relatively liberal policy on asylum was introduced to the *Grundgesetz* as a means of redressing the persecution of Jews and other then undesired people under the Nazi regime. Article 16 went beyond the usual conventions of international law and was worded generously in order to insure that no individual would come to harm in their country of origin because they had been refused asylum in Germany. It thus gave individuals arriving in Germany the right to a proper investigation into their claim for asylum. The law put the onus on the German government to disprove the claim for asylum.

The influx of asylum seekers into the Federal Republic during the 1980s and particularly after 1989 brought pressure to change the country's liberal policy. Given the absence of an immigration law, the asylum procedure was increasingly open to abuse and utilised by some as a *de facto* means of immigration. In 1992 the level of applications peaked at 438 191. After heated discussions and prolonged political struggle the *Grundgesetz* was amended with the so-called 'Asylum Compromise' of December 1992. This confirms the right of asylum for all persons who are deemed to be persecuted in their country of origin. The new legislation, however, excludes those arriving in Germany from a EU state or any other state which is deemed to be free of political persecution.

See AUSLÄNDERFEINDLICHKEIT; AUSLÄNDERPOLITIK; VERFASSUNGS-
ÄNDERUNG.

(NM)

Aufschwung Ost See GEMEINSCHAFTSWERK 'AUFSCHWUNG OST'.

Aufstand (1953) The June 1953 uprising in the GDR was the first major
revolt against a communist regime in the Soviet bloc. The acceleration in
applying socialist policies from 1952 onwards was instrumental in trigger-
ing off the uprising. Not only were these policies highly unpopular among
expropriated factory owners and collectivised farmers, but they also
imposed so heavy a financial burden that the SED was obliged to increase
food prices and, in May 1953, to raise work norms by at least 10 per cent
without a commensurate increase in pay. Opposition to the SED's policy
flared up in the countryside and in the factories and emigration levels rose
rapidly from about 22 000 in December 1952 to 58 000 in March 1953.
Stalin's successors in Moscow forced a reluctant Ulbricht to introduce the
so-called 'New Course'. While making significant concessions to farmers,
members of the intelligentsia and craftsmen, the regime failed to revoke
the new work norms of the industrial workers.

On 16 June, a demonstration against the work norms by construction
workers on the Stalinallee in East Berlin sparked off strikes and demonstrations elsewhere in the GDR on the following day. Apart from East Berlin,
the centres of the revolt were the industrial areas of the GDR: Bitterfeld,
Merseburg, Halle, Leipzig, Magdeburg and Gera. About 270 towns and over
370 000 workers, it is estimated, were involved in the protests. Although the
industrial workers spearheaded the revolt, significant contributions were
also made in the countryside and among the intelligentsia.

The demands of the demonstrators, though mainly concerned with
increases in wages and the lowering of work norms, extended to calls for
the release of political prisoners, the dismissal of Ulbricht and free and
secret elections. However, before the demonstrations could gather further
momentum and an effective organisational structure be put in place, the
imposition of martial law and the introduction of Soviet tank patrols on 17
June soon quelled the unrest on the streets. Despite the rapid collapse of
open revolt, the struggle continued within the factories for several weeks
with demands being made for improvements in working conditions and
protests being directed at the lack of democracy in the workplace.

See DEUTSCHE DEMOKRATISCHE REPUBLIK; ULBRICHT, WALTER.

(MD)

Auschwitz See HOLOCAUST; KONZENTRATIONSLAGER.

Ausländerfeindlichkeit Xenophobia in Germany has political, criminal and
social dimensions. Political expressions of xenophobia have mainly been

limited to the parties of the far Right, the NPD, DVU and REPUBLIKANER, particularly in periods when large numbers of asylum seekers have sought entry to the Federal Republic (periodically in the 1980s and especially in the early 1990s). Following unification, there was also a sharp increase in the number of attacks on foreigners. The police were often accused of not reacting as vigorously as they had done against left-wing radicals. Discrimination on a social level is more difficult to assess. Although most Germans are not xenophobic, foreigners, usually those from southern Europe, Turkey and Africa, are frequently the victims of overt or indirect discrimination. Such discrimination is difficult to combat, because Germany has no distinct anti-discrimination legislation.

The post-unification wave of *Ausländerfeindlichkeit* culminated in 1991–93, with anti-foreigner riots in Rostock and Hoyerswerda, as well as the arson attacks on Turkish homes in Mölln and Solingen, resulting in the deaths of nine people. The subsequent public outcry saw hundreds of thousands of people demonstrating against xenophobia. The issue of 'foreigners' continues to be seen as a considerable problem area by the population, typically ranking second in voters' minds after unemployment.

See ASYLRECHT; AUSLÄNDERPOLITIK.

(SG)

Ausländerpolitik 'Foreigners' policy' deals with the rights of non-Germans living in Germany, of whom there are currently 7 million. Over half have lived there for 10 or more years. The need for a specific *Ausländerpolitik* arises from the official line that the Federal Republic is not a country of immigration (*Deutschland ist kein Einwanderungsland*). Citizenship laws are restrictive and do not easily allow the adoption of German nationality. A particular legal regulation for those foreigners living and working in Germany was therefore necessary, especially with the recruitment of large numbers of so-called 'guest workers' (GASTARBEITER) from Turkey and southern Europe during the 1950s and 1960s in order to overcome the Federal Republic's labour shortage of that period. Although the overriding assumption was that these workers would eventually return to their home countries, many instead settled more permanently, in many cases bringing over their families. This situation has led to the passing of a number of *Ausländergesetze* (foreigners' laws) since 1965.

In 1982, the newly installed CDU/CSU-FDP government laid down the three pillars for *Ausländerpolitik* still in force today: (a) no more immigration from non-EU countries; (b) integration of existing foreigners into German society; and (c) increased incentives to encourage voluntary repatriation. Such incentives, introduced in the mid-1980s, largely failed and the new *Ausländergesetz*, passed in 1990, focused on clarifying arrangements under the first two pillars.

Although consensus on the nature and aims of *Ausländerpolitik* was initially broad, considerable differences have developed since 1982, with the SPD, GRÜNE and FDP favouring a more open approach, particularly with regard to the adoption of German nationality, and the CDU/CSU favouring more restrictive policies.

See ASYLRECHT; AUSLÄNDERFEINDLICHKEIT; AUSSIEDLER; STAATSAN-GEHÖRIGKEITSECHT.

(SG)

Ausschüsse   Parliamentary committees play an important role both at the federal level and in the BUNDESLÄNDER.

They are indispensable in performing the classic parliamentary functions of legislation (GESETZGEBUNG) and of scrutinising government activities. In the BUNDESTAG, a range of Standing Committees (*Fachausschüsse*) are established for each four-year parliamentary session in order to consider in detail legislative proposals, and where appropriate to propose amendments. *Bundestag* Standing Committees are typically established in each of the policy areas which fall under the responsibility of federal ministries (BUNDESMINISTERIEN). There are currently twenty-three. Committees of Enquiry (*Untersuchungsausschüsse*) can also be established on an *ad hoc* basis on the motion of one-quarter of the *Bundestag*'s members. All these committees are composed party-politically in proportion to wider party-political strengths in the *Bundestag*. Committee Chairs are appointed in the same way.

A further form of Committee of Enquiry, *Enquete-Kommissionen*, can be established to investigate especially complex problem areas, and, unlike the committees noted above, can consist partly of experts from outside the *Bundestag*. Joint committees of the *Bundestag* and BUNDESRAT may also be established, for example, the Joint Constitutional Commission (*Gemeinsame Verfassungskommission*) of 1991–93, which met to deliberate on any constitutional changes (VERFASSUNGSÄNDERUNG) made necessary by unification. The Mediation Committee (VERMITTLUNGSAUSSCHUß) of the *Bundestag* and *Bundesrat* exists to resolve differences the two chambers may have over proposed legislation.

A standing committee structure similar to, though less extensive than, that of the *Bundestag* also exists in the *Bundesrat* in order to generate its opinions on legislative proposals at the federal level. Equally, standing committees dedicated to particular policy fields and committees of enquiry exist to assist the LANDTAGE in the conduct of their parliamentary functions in the *Bundesländer*.

(CJ)

Außenpolitik   Foreign policy was, for many years an unusual policy field in the Federal Republic. As a consequence of Germany's actions during World War II, and its defeat and occupation in 1945, the Federal Republic was prohibited from developing an independent foreign policy after its establishment in 1949. The Allied Occupying Powers kept a firm control over the content and orientation of German foreign policy and only agreed to the establishment of the Federal Foreign Ministry in 1952. With the support and guidance of the Western Allies, Chancellor Konrad ADENAUER's vision for the Federal Republic's foreign policy led to the development and consolidation of a resolute 'western' orientation throughout the post-war period. The most potent symbol of this has been the Federal Republic's key role in the development of European integration. The preoccupation of foreign policy with the West accelerated the rehabilitation of the Federal Republic, allowing it to regain its legitimacy and sovereignty as an international actor. However, even after the Federal Republic became a fully sovereign state in 1955 and the constraints on foreign policy resulting directly from defeat and occupation were lifted, foreign policy continued to be dictated by the reality of the division of Europe and Germany by the Cold War. It was not until the 1970s and a period of Cold War *détente* that the preoccupation with the West was matched with an active foreign policy interest in Eastern Europe and the Federal Government under the leadership of Willy BRANDT could develop OSTPOLITIK as a key element of West German foreign policy.

Following the unification of Germany there were widely expressed fears that Germany would cease to follow its post-war foreign policy path and would become a more assertive, less predictable actor in the international system. These fears have proved unfounded and although Germany may now talk with a stronger voice in the world and acts more autonomously than previously, its post-war foreign policy alignment has remained essentially unchanged and it remains a central member of the European Union. Furthermore, the introduction of a foreign policy role for the EU by the Maastricht Treaty could potentially act as a further constraint on the content and direction of German foreign policy.

See DEUTSCHLANDVERTRAG; EUROPAPOLITIK; KALTER KRIEG.

(PH)

Außerparliamentarische Opposition (APO)   The 'extra-parliamentary opposition' was a loose alliance of largely middle-class, left-wing radicals, associated with the student movement of the late 1960s (although its roots go back to the 1950s), and focused to some extent on West Berlin. Within the APO, two groups were particularly prominent: first, the 'Easter March' movement (which later became the Campaign for Democracy and Disarmament) and, second, the Social Democratic Students' League (SDS).

The history of the APO can be divided up into three phases. First, the period from the late 1950s until the mid-1960s, when the APO emerged as a left–radical force independent of organised labour or the existing parties. Second, the period of student unrest from 1966–68, characterised by sit-ins and demonstrations. Third, the period from the late 1960s until the early 1970s, in which the APO's tactics became increasingly confrontational, leading to its eventual fragmentation. The APO is most closely associated in the public mind with the phase of student unrest of 1966–68, especially in West Berlin where its figurehead was the controversial SDS leader Rudi Dutschke. This was the 'Grand Coalition' period in Bonn, and the absence of a significant opposition party on the Left allowed the movement to claim that they were the only – albeit extra-parliamentary – opposition in the Federal Republic. In early 1968, Dutschke was shot on the Kurfürstendamm (Berlin's Oxford Street), sparking off major political violence and heralding the APO's final and most confrontational phase.

The ultimate 'failure' of the APO to change the political fabric of the Federal Republic led to its fragmentation in the early 1970s. Orthodox left-wingers retreated into the *K-Gruppen* (ultra-communist groupings), whilst the more extreme elements drifted into terrorism. However, the main legacy of the APO was establishing a culture of civic participation in politics, which was to nurture the New Social Movements and eventually the German Green Party.

See GROßE KOALITION; GRÜNE; NEUE SOZIALE BEWEGUNGEN; STUDEN-TENBEWEGUNG; TERRORISMUS.

(CL)

Aussiedler   *Aussiedler* are ethnic German migrants to the Federal Republic, who have lived in Eastern Europe and the former Soviet Union, often for many generations. Ethnic Germans are admitted into Germany on the basis of Article 116 of the GRUNDGESETZ. This article has its roots in the post-war division of Germany. It made provisions for those Germans who found themselves outside the smaller Federal Republic after 1949, but had nevertheless lived within the boundaries of Germany of 1937. The Federal Republic assumed special responsibility for these groups. The legislation was based on the assumption that all ethnic Germans and their descendants had lived under persecution, and had to be given the right to live in a free country.

Aussiedler are unlike other groups of migrants in that they are considered to be German, and therefore receive full social benefits and language training. More importantly, ethnic Germans have automatic access to German citizenship.

The number of ethnic Germans returning to Germany remained relatively small despite the conclusion of agreements with Poland under Chancellors BRANDT in 1970 and SCHMIDT in 1977 making repatriation of ethnic Germans easier. However, the numbers exploded with the easing of travel restrictions first in the Soviet Union and later in Eastern Europe in the late 1980s and early 1990s.

In response, a more restrictive approach has been adopted. The so-called German Reception Law, regulating the entry of ethnic Germans, was enacted in 1991, and attempts to stem the influx of ethnic Germans by encouraging them to stay in their adopted country largely through providing support of a financial and cultural nature.

See AUSLÄNDERPOLITIK.
(NM)

Aussperrung   The lock-out is a means by which employers can respond to a strike, by closing factories down and stopping employees from working. It is important to differentiate between so-called hot and cold lock-outs. Hot lock-outs affect those plants in a bargaining region where there is a strike. A cold lock-out is used to shut other plants owned by an employer outside the bargaining region on strike.

The lock-out is one of the most controversial areas of labour law. Employers maintain that is a necessary form of defence against industrial action mounted by trade unions, while unions claim that this weapon gives the employers unfair advantages during strikes and should be declared unconstitutional. Legal pronouncements support the use of the lock-out to balance the power of trade unions and employers, but state that employers can only use it in equal proportion to the extent of a strike.

Following a bitter two-week dispute in the metal-working industry in 1984, the CDU/CSU-FDP Federal Government amended the Work Promotion Law to ensure that employees locked out during a strike could not receive benefit payments. This means that unions now have to give financial support to any members locked out, imposing large burdens on their strike funds. The unions claimed this was unconstitutional, but the Federal Constitutional Court upheld the legislation in a judgement in 1995.

The lock-out does not terminate, but merely suspends an employee's contract of employment. This means that entitlements related to the length of service are not lost.

See STREIK.
(SRF)

B

Baader-Meinhof-Bande See TERRORISMUS.

Baden-Württemberg Baden-Württemberg is one of the constituent BUN-DESLÄNDER of the Federal Republic. It was created in 1952 as an amalgamation of the then *Bundesländer* of Württemberg-Baden, Württemberg-Hohenzollern and Baden.

Its capital city is Stuttgart and it is the third largest *Bundesland* in size (35 752km^2) and population (10.27m in 1996). It is one of the strongest *Bundesländer* economically with a GDP per head of 47 980DM and a low rate (7.4 per cent) of unemployment (1995). Its economic strength is based on a large and dynamic MITTELSTAND and a number of major companies, in particular in the car industry (DAIMLER-BENZ, Porsche, Audi).

Baden-Württemberg has been dominated party-politically by the CDU, which has provided the MINISTERPRÄSIDENT (since 1991, Erwin Teufel) after every LANDTAG election since 1953. The most recent election in 1996 produced a coalition of CDU and FDP. The Baden-Württemberg *Landtag* was the first in which the GRÜNE were represented (from 1980) and has seen the strongest representation of the far-Right REPUBLIKANER in the *Bundesländer* since 1992.

(CJ)

BAföG The *Bundesausbildungsförderungsgesetz* (called *BAföG*) is a law stipulating that students from the age of 15 whose parents are not able to support them financially can claim a scholarship from the state in order to pursue their education.

The level of *BAföG* is index-linked to the inflation rate. How much exactly a student receives is subject to a means test. The maximum amount in 1996 was 960DM per month; half the money is awarded as a grant and the other half is an interest-free loan which needs to be paid back in instalments starting five years after graduation. Students need to show evidence of achievement each semester to qualify for continued payment. Provided satisfactory evidence is produced, the maximum duration of payment (*Förderungshöchstdauer*) is the minimum number of semesters required in

the relevant degree regulations (*Regelstudienzeit*) plus, where appropriate, additional semesters. At present around 33 per cent of all students in the old BUNDESLÄNDER and 90 per cent in the new *Bundesländer* receive funds from *BAföG*.
See STUDIENDAUER.
(AW)

Barock See STILE.

BASF BASF was the seventh largest industrial company in Germany in 1995 with a turnover of DM46 billion, employing 106 565 people and with a net income of DM2.47 billion. The *B*adische *A*nilin- und *S*oda-*F*abrik was founded in 1865 and is located in Ludwigshafen. In 1925, BASF formed Interessengemeinschaft Farbenindustrie AG (IG Farben) with five other companies, including BAYER and HOECHST. Thereafter, BASF operated for the next 26 years as Betriebsgemeinschaft Oberrhein – the upper Rhein unit of IG Farben. (A similar organisational approach – *Betriebsgesellschaften* – was ultimately adopted in the steel industry in the same era.) Chemist Carl Bosch (1874–1940), who was chief executive of BASF between 1919–25, became head of IG Farben between 1925–35. Along with Friedrich Bergius, he received a Nobel Prize for chemistry in 1931. IG Farben used forced labour during World War II.

Following the war, BASF has displayed all the characteristic features of the German chemical industry: high export earnings, the ownership of subsidiaries abroad, an appreciable research and development effort and close domestic co-operation. It acquired Boots' pharmaceutical division in 1995 for £850 million, a move analogous to BMW's takeover of Rover, DEUTSCHE BANK's purchase of Morgan Grenfell and DRESDNER BANK's addition of Kleinwort Benson. The acquisition of the Boots' operation, which develops and manufactures prescription drugs, was a significant boost to BASF's pharmaceutical division, increasing its sales by 50 per cent. In 1996, BASF similarly acquired GNR-pharma of Paris from the Stuttgart-based Gehe. The latter company took the view that its manufacturing operations were not large enough to compete in the rapidly consolidating pharmaceuticals market. In addition, BASF has established strengths in audio and video magnetic recording materials.

A slump in the chemicals industry caused profits to fall to DM615 million in 1992 compared to a previous peak of DM2 billion in 1989. Compared to its main rivals, Bayer and Hoechst, both of which have sales outside of Europe bordering on half of total output, BASF lags behind with 36 per cent. At BASF, Western European markets were expected to stagnate. Business in the USA was expected to be 'satisfactory', whereas growth rates in south and east Asia were expected to be 'vigorous'. Capital expenditure has accordingly been characterised by a further shift in emphasis towards Asia.
(EOS)

Bauhaus   The *Bauhaus* was founded in Weimar in 1919 as a school for architecture, crafts and the arts. It moved to Dessau in 1925 and then to Berlin where Hitler dissolved it in 1933.

The main inspiration for *Bauhaus* came from two of its directors, Walter Gropius (1883–1969) and Ludwig Mies van der Rohe (1886–1969) (both architects). Although the *Bauhaus* experimented in all the arts and in new teaching methods, the *Bauhaus* style became world famous – mainly for its buildings. These, like all other works in the genre, drew on the latest technological advances in combination with a careful analysis of future utility. They were inspired by aesthetic concerns and cost-consciousness. This so-called functionalist approach to design was highly influential on subsequent architectural trends in many parts of the world in the twentieth century.

Leading exponents of modern painting, including Kandinsky, Feininger, Klee and Schlemmer, along with the sculptor Marcks also taught there.

See DER BLAUE REITER; ENTARTETE KUNST; JUGENDSTIL.

(RW)

Bayer   Bayer was the ninth largest industrial company in Germany in 1995 with a turnover of DM44.6 billion, employing 142 900 people and with a net income of DM2.42 billion. Founded in 1863, Bayer's reputation under chief executive Carl Duisberg (1861–1935) had become, by 1912, that of 'founder and leader of (Germany's) large-scale chemical industry'. In 1925, Bayer formed IG Farben with five other companies, including BASF and HOECHST. IG Farben was to use forced labour during World War II. At the founding of IG Farben, Duisberg became chair of the non-executive board and Bayer became the Lower Rhine operating division of the conglomerate.

Since the war, Agfa (*A*ktiengesellschaft für Anilin*fa*brikation) and a whole range of proprietary-brand medicinal products have been built up. As a result of a mounting competitive disadvantage, sales in textile dyes were lower in 1995 than in 1994. To safeguard the German production base, a joint venture with Hoechst was formed. The targeted improvement in efficiency was predicted to result in a break-even position by 1996.

The reform of the EU's Common Agricultural Policy and health-care changes in Germany contributed to falls in demand for chemicals in the early 1990s. Because of its large and modern pharmaceutical division, however, the slump in chemicals did not affect Bayer quite as badly as BASF and Hoechst. Profits fell to DM1.4 billion in 1993, compared to a previous peak of DM2.1 billion in 1989. In fact, German chemical production had lagged markedly behind growth in the USA and Japan. On the other hand, in environmental technology, which is partially chemical-industry-based, Germany leads the world.

In contrast to BASF and Hoechst, Bayer has set itself an explicit profitability target. The aim is to boost the return on sales to more than 10 per cent. In both the medium and long term, new jobs will be created primarily in North America and Asia. In Europe – and especially in Germany – the far more modest, even ominous, aim is one of 'consolidation'. Processes and products will continue to be optimised in accordance with consumer needs.
    (EOS)

Bayern Bavaria is one of the constituent BUNDESLÄNDER of the Federal Republic. Its capital city is Munich (München) and it is the largest *Bundesland* in size (70 544km²) and second largest in population with 11.9 million inhabitants (1996). It is one of the strongest *Bundesländer* economically with a GDP per head of 48 640DM and the lowest rate (7 per cent) of unemployment (1995). Formerly an important agricultural region, Bayern now possesses important and productive high-tech industries in electronics, armaments and space research and is also strong in cars, financial services and tourism.
    Bavarian politics have traditionally been dominated by the CSU, a party allied in federal-level politics to the CDU. The CSU has provided the MINISTERPRÄSIDENT since 1946 with the exception of a short SPD interlude from 1954–57. Edmund Stoiber has been *Ministerpräsident* since 1993. The most recent election in 1994 renewed the absolute majority of LANDTAG seats the CSU has enjoyed since 1962.
    (CJ)

Beamte See ÖFFENTLICHER DIENST.

Begabtenförderung See STIFTUNGEN.

Berlin Berlin is one of the constituent BUNDESLÄNDER of the Federal Republic and at the same time is the capital city of Germany.
    Berlin was an evocative symbol of the Cold War and the post-war division of Germany. Following the Berlin Blockade in 1948–49 and, even more so, the building of the Berlin Wall in 1961, Berlin was split in half. Although the city remained formally under the administration of the post-war occupying powers until 1990, West Berlin in practice was integrated as a *Bundesland* into the Federal Republic while East Berlin formed the capital city of the GDR. In 1989, the breaching of the Berlin Wall was a dramatic symbol of the forthcoming collapse of the GDR and the move towards German unification. Following intense discussion of the location of the capital city (HAUPTSTADTFRAGE) after unification, it was decided to re-establish Berlin as Germany's capital city and seat of government. As a result, Berlin is experiencing a massive rebuilding programme in preparation for the transfer of the seat of government from Bonn to Berlin in 1999.

West and East Berlin were unified to form a single *Bundesland* upon German unification in 1990. Proposals to merge Berlin with the surrounding *Bundesland* of BRANDENBURG were rejected in a referendum in 1996. Berlin therefore remains one of the three city-states (*Stadtstaaten*), alongside BREMEN and HAMBURG, among the sixteen *Bundesländer*. It is 833km² in size and has a population of 3.47m (1994). Economically, Berlin displays strong east–west disparities, with a GDP per head of 48 600DM in West Berlin and just 19 400 in East Berlin (1993), although unemployment is higher in the western part of the city (14.3 per cent) than the east (12.4 per cent) on 1995 figures. Important industries are electronics, engineering and chemicals, though these are in decline. The service sector is increasingly important as is – in light of the post-unification rebuilding programme – the construction industry.

Politically, Berlin was a traditional stronghold of the Left. The LANDESREGIERUNG in West Berlin was led by the SPD for all but two years of the period 1951–81. The CDU, however, became the largest party in 1975, and has provided the MINISTERPRÄSIDENT (*regierender Bürgermeister*, since 1990 Eberhard Diepgen) from 1983, apart from the short interlude of an SPD–Green coalition in 1989–90. The CDU has retained its leading position in LANDTAG (*Abgeordnetenhaus*) elections since unification, forming a coalition with the SPD from 1990. The PDS is the leading opposition party by virtue of its strength in East Berlin, while the GRÜNE are also strongly represented.

See BERLINER BLOCKADE; BERLINER MAUER; BESATZUNG; KALTER KRIEG.

(CJ)

Berlinabkommen The Four-Power Agreement on Berlin was signed in September 1971 and came into force in June 1972. It was essentially a means of regularising and improving the situation of the divided city of Berlin.

The Four-Power Agreement was significant because it was the first treaty of its kind involving the GDR and the Federal Republic, although neither were party to the negotiations. An accord was reached about the status of Berlin between the World War II allies. Due to the continuous disagreements between the Soviet Union and the Western powers, the Berlin Agreement avoided a definition of Berlin, referring to it instead as 'the area in question'. The Western powers endorsed their view that West Berlin did not constitute a part of the Federal Republic. However, they also declared that the ties between West Berlin and the Federal Republic ought to be strengthened. Sovereign rights over West Berlin would remain with the three Western powers according to wartime and post-war agreements. The Soviet Union abandoned its claim that West Berlin lay within the territory of the GDR and therefore under its authority. The Agreement clarified that the Federal Republic could represent West

Berlin internationally and therefore extend diplomatic protection to its citizens. It granted West Berliners access rights to the GDR, which had been prohibited since the building of the Berlin Wall in 1961. It also facilitated the transit of people and goods between the GDR, West Berlin and the Federal Republic.

The legal status of Berlin was fully regularised only with the unification of Germany, when the wartime powers relinquished their residual rights in the city, allowing it to emerge as the capital of united Germany and a united BUNDESLAND.

See BESATZUNG; ENTSPANNUNG; MOSKAUER VERTRAG; OSTPOLITIK.

(NM)

Berliner Blockade　The Soviet blockade of Berlin lasted from June 1948 to May 1949. It was motivated by the attempt of the Soviet occupation authorities to prevent the emergence of a powerful market economy in the Western zones, or at the very least to insulate its own occupation zone from market economic principles. The catalyst for the blockade was the currency reform in the Western zones of 20 June 1948. The prospect of the new Western currency also being introduced in the Western sectors of occupation in Berlin, deep inside the Soviet occupation zone, threatened to undermine the command economy the Soviet authorities were seeking to build. When the currency reform was extended to West Berlin on 23 June, the Soviet authorities responded by closing off all land communications between West Berlin and the Western zones and to the surrounding Soviet zone. Travel between the Western and Soviet sectors of the city was still possible in some cases, particularly in the cases of the so-called 'border crossers' who lived in the West but worked in the East. Food, electricity and all other supplies from the countryside were cut off. Maintaining a Western presence in Berlin became a symbol of the Western will to guarantee democracy amid the deepening tensions of the Cold War.

The people of West Berlin survived thanks to the remarkable Allied effort known as the airlift. The planes of the British and US forces set up an airlift operation (*Luftbrücke*), bringing into Berlin virtually everything that was consumed on a daily basis, including milk, meat, fruits and vegetables, medical supplies as well as coal. During the 322 days of the blockade the Western Allies flew in over 2 million tons of goods. The Soviets lifted the blockade on 12 May 1949, opening access to West Berlin via road, railway and canal. The blockade accelerated the decision of the Western Allies to establish a separate West German state.

See BERLINABKOMMEN; BESATZUNG; WÄHRUNGSREFORM.

(NM)

Berliner Mauer　The Berlin Wall was erected on the night of 12 to 13 August 1961 and was re-opened on the night of 9 to 10 November 1989. Dubbed in the West the 'Wall of Shame' and by the SED as the 'anti-fascist protection barrier', the Berlin Wall was the main physical symbol of the post-war division of Europe. Originally consisting of low barbed-wire fencing, the Wall grew into an edifice of concrete slabs 4 metres high and 165 kilometres long completely encircling West Berlin. It was furbished with dog-patrolled tracks, observation towers, minefields, trip wires and booby trap guns. The construction of the Wall was prompted by the mass exodus of East Germans: about 200 000 in 1960 and with monthly totals rising towards 50 000 in 1961. As the flow was destabilising the GDR, the SED leader Walter Ulbricht pressed the Soviet Union and his Warsaw Pact allies to have the borders between East and West Berlin sealed. Their approval was delayed until the Warsaw Pact meeting in early August as they were fearful of Western reactions and reluctant to accept a propaganda defeat of such magnitude. Ironically, it was the demographic haemorrhage of East Germans in 1989 as well as the Soviet President's permission which persuaded the then SED General Secretary Egon Krenz to re-open the Wall in a confused and desperate attempt to prop up the SED's rapidly declining authority.

The official demolition of the Wall began in June 1990 after the accession to power of Lothar de Maizière. A long stretch was left along the River Spree in Friedrichshain in order to remind people of what the Wall was like.

Trials of former border guards and high-ranking SED politicians connected with the shootings at the Wall have acted since German unification as reminders of the harshness of Germany's division.

See DDR; KRENZ, EGON; SCHIEßBEFEHL.

(MD)

Berufsverbote   See RADIKALENERLAß.

Besatzung   The occupation of Germany lasted from Germany's defeat in 1945 until the formation of the GDR and the Federal Republic in 1949. Defeated Germany was divided into four occupation zones (*Besatzungszonen*), each under the authority of one of the four major victorious Allies in their function as occupying powers (*Besatzungsmächte*). The British zone comprised the industrial north-west including the Ruhr, the US occupied the South, including Bavaria, and also the northern port of Bremen. The French zone comprised two strips of land close to their own borders including the SAARLAND. Eastern Germany comprised the Soviet zone. Berlin was administered separately, split into four sectors each under Allied control.

As the defeat of Germany had approached in 1944–45, there still existed no coherent Allied strategy for Germany beyond the vague aims of denazification, demilitarisation and democratisation. At the Potsdam Conference (July–August 1945) the Allies agreed that Germany should be treated as a singular economic entity with an Allied Control Council as a form of government. Despite this proclamation the Eastern and Western zones increasingly pursued very different economic and political paths, arising in part from their divergent views on reparations. Whereas the Soviets favoured dismantling the German industrial base and relocating plant in the Soviet Union, the US came to realise that a weak German economy would only be a hindrance in the future.

In May 1946 dismantling ended in the US zone, shortly after US Secretary of State Byrnes spoke of the US aim to restore self-government and a full economy to Germany. Towards this end the US and British zones were merged in December 1946 to create the 'Bi-zone'. The Bi-zone was further consolidated by the currency reform (WÄHRUNGSREFORM) of 20 June 1948, which also extended to the French zone.

The currency reform set out a clear intention of re-establishing a Western-style, market economy in Western Germany. Unsurprisingly, it provoked strong opposition from the Soviet Union, whose response was to block all land access to the western sectors of BERLIN. This blockade of Berlin accelerated the trend towards separate development in the Western and the Soviet zones and towards the division of post-war Germany. In June 1948 the Western Allies authorised a Parliamentary Council of West German politicians to prepare a Western-style democratic constitution for Western Germany. At the same time, steps were intensified in the Soviet zone to establish an economic and political system based on the Soviet model.

The logical conclusion of these developments was the establishment of two separate German states, with the Federal Republic of Germany formally being established in the West on 23 May 1949, and the German Democratic Republic in the East following suit on 7 October of that year.

See BERLINER BLOCKADE; BUNDESREPUBLIK DEUTSCHLAND; DDR; ENT-NAZIFIZIERUNG; PARLAMENTARISCHER RAT.

(KL)

Besatzungsmächte   See BESATZUNG.

Besatzungszone   See BESATZUNG.

Betriebsrat   Works councils are bodies which represent employees, and can be elected by all employees in any firm or plant employing five people or more. They are responsible for implementing collective agreements agreed by trade unions and employers' associations and possess rights of codetermination (MITBESTIMMUNG) granted by the Works Constitution Law (*Betriebsverfassungsgesetz*) in plant level negotiations.

Works councils legally guarantee employee representation at work. Although independent bodies, works councils have traditionally had good relationships with trade unions. While unions provide information and training for the works councillors, the works councils help to recruit new members to the union. Union members constitute up to 80 per cent of members of works councils.

With changes in the organisation of work and the introduction of new technology, works councils have seen their role as negotiators increase, particularly over qualitative issues not covered in collective agreements. There has consequently been a rise in the number of *Betriebsvereinbarungen* (plant level agreements) concluded by works councils. However, works councils and management are not legally allowed to conclude agreements at plant level which undermine the conditions set out in collective agreements. Furthermore, works councils are legally required to promote the success of a firm and are not permitted to initiate strike action.

With economic collapse in the new BUNDESLÄNDER, there has been a tendency for works councils newly created in the East to concentrate on a firm's survival, even if this means contravening the conditions set out in collective agreements. With economic recession in the West there has also been pressure for such deviations with employers seeking to achieve more flexibility in working conditions. Such examples of plant-focused negotiations tend to undermine the industry-wide minimum pay and working conditions set by collective agreements.

See GEWERKSCHAFTEN; TARIFAUTONOMIE.

(SRF)

Bildungsurlaub   Every employee has the right to volunteer for a (paid) educational holiday of up to ten working days every two years. The time taken off work is voluntary and must be used for further professional training away from the workplace, including courses on political or social issues.

Businesses with fewer than 50 employees can claim some of their salary costs related to *Bildungsurlaub* back from their *Land* authorities. Teachers can only take up rights to *Bildungsurlaub* during school holidays.

(AW)

Binnenmarkt   The Internal Market of the European Community was created by the Single Market programme completed in 1993. The Federal Republic has consistently been one of the European Community's most committed Member States. The Single Market project received wide support from within Germany, reflecting significant aspects of the German Federal Government's free-trading approach to economic policy. The project envisaged the creation of a Single Market within the EC by 1993 which would allow the free movement of goods, capital, services and persons across all internal frontiers of all EC member states. In 1985 the European Commission produced a timetabled list of 300 measures which would need to be implemented for the Internal Market to function. The plan for the Internal Market was agreed by the Heads of Government of the member states in the Single European Act of 1985.

The Single Market Project is in many respects an ongoing enterprise and a number of measures are still awaiting implementation. The free movement of persons has perhaps caused the most problems for the EC, as although Germany has been at the vanguard of attempts to make progress in this particularly sensitive area, other member states have refused to lift border controls with their EC partners. A further problem area is the question of Economic and Monetary Union (EMU), which is seen as a complement to the Single Market, but which is controversial in Germany as well as in a number of other member states.

Despite Germany's enthusiasm for the Internal Market project, its record for the implementation of the necessary measures has not been unblemished, and it has often lagged behind the performance of other member states.

Although the Internal Market is nearing completion it is likely that EMU and the free movement of persons will continue to be the source of some controversy both within Germany and the EU as a whole.

See EUROPAPOLITIK; WIRTSCHAFTS- UND WÄHRUNGSUNION

(PH)

Blaue Reiter, Der The 'Blue Rider' was an association of artists which was formed in Munich in 1911 around the painters Franz Marc and Wassily Kandinsky. It came to an end at the beginning of World War I. The name reflects both the artists' predilection for the colour blue and their interest in riders (Kandinsky) and horses (Marc).

They and their most important associates (Gabriele Münter, Werefkin, Jawlensky and Paul Klee) were deeply influenced by Russian modern painting, on the one hand (Kandinsky, Marianne von Werefkin and Jawlensky all came from Russia) and French impressionism and the *Fauves*, on the other hand. Their aim was to get away from a more superficial '*Naturabmalen*' (naturalism) by 'feeling oneself into the object of painting' (Gabriele Münter). The Alps and particularly Murnau provided the scenery for their work during their most creative years. As their art deviated completely from any classical models it was seen as anarchist from the time when the group first held an exhibition in München in 1909. They published a manifesto in 1912 and held two further exhibitions. During the Third Reich the work of this group together with all other modern artists working in Germany was declared *entartet* (ENTARTETE KUNST). Thus, 1949 saw the first big exhibition of the *Blaue Reiter*. An important permanent collection of the group is now kept in the München *Lehnbachhaus*.

The ideas of the *Blaue Reiter* formed the basis of thought in twentieth-century painting. Kandinsky and Klee continued their co-operation at the BAUHAUS.

(RW)

Blauhelm-Einsätze The question of Federal Republic participation in multinational military operations and observer forces acting under the authority of the UN Security Council in areas of conflict, and aimed at maintaining international peace and security emerged after unification amid considerable controversy.

Peace-keeping/peace-making operations have evolved as one of the main tools for the UN to use in resolving conflicts and wars in many different parts of the world. However, throughout the Cold War Federal Republic forces were unable to participate, due to constitutional restrictions on deployment of military forces outside of NATO's areas of operation. These restrictions, for example, limited Germany's participation in the Gulf War coalition in 1990, bringing Germany under heavy international pressure to participate in international security operations from which it benefited. In 1993 a ruling of the Federal Constitutional Court eased the way to German forces being sent overseas as part of multinational UN missions.

The issue of participation in *Blauhelm-Einsätze* is hotly debated in Germany. A distinction is made between peace-*keeping* missions, designed to stabilise an accord struck by previously warring parties, and peace-*making* missions, in which actual fighting may be involved. While participation in such missions is viewed by the CDU/CSU as desirable, the SPD maintains strong opposition to German forces engaging in active combat overseas, even as part of UN operations.

In 1995 Germany deployed over 4 000 German ground troops in Bosnia and Croatia. The BUNDESWEHR is training special units for future *Blauhelm-Einsätze* world-wide.

(SS)

Blockparteien   Four political parties – CDU, DBD, NDPD and LDPD – were allied with the SED in the 'Democratic Block of Parties and Mass Organisations' founded in 1949. For most of the GDR's history the four block parties were relatively tame adjuncts of the ruling SED and accepted unreservedly its leadership claim. Initially, this was not, however, the case with the CDU (Christian Democratic Union) and the LDPD (Liberal Democratic Party of Germany). Until the early 1950s both sought to pursue an independent line, the CDU chairman, Jakob Kaiser, for example, proclaiming his party to be the 'breakwater of dogmatic Marxism and its totalitarian tendencies'. The LDPD originally advocated the primacy of private over state ownership of the means of production. By 1952, both had been 'tamed' by the SED and together with the NDPD (National Democratic Party of Germany) and the DBD (Democratic Farmers' Party of Germany) performed a so-called 'transmission' function, that is, they transmitted the policies and decisions of the SED to groups of people not under its control. Despite the predominance of the SED, the preservation of the outward appearance of a multi-party system was regarded as a useful legitimising device both at home and abroad.

The CDU, the largest block party, was supposed to act as the political voice of Christians in the GDR and recruited supporters among farmers, artisans, academics, artists and other middle-class groups. In 1972, several CDU deputies opposed the abortion law. The LDPD sought to appeal primarily to white-collar employees, artisans, tradespeople and sections of the intelligentsia. The NDPD and the DBD were both founded in 1948 as a deliberate ploy by SMAD and the SED to weaken the CDU and the LDPD. The NDPD was originally conceived of as a political home for former National Socialists and soldiers. From 1952 onwards in particular, it sought to mobilise groups such as white-collar workers and like the CDU and LDPD recruited from among tradespeople and artisans.

See ALLIANZ FÜR DEUTSCHLAND; BUND FREIER DEMOKRATEN.

(MD)

BMW (Bayerische Motoren Werke)   BMW has traditionally focused on producing premium motor vehicles with a high level of technical excellence at relatively low volumes and in relatively high price ranges.

BMW was established in 1916 to make aero engines, moving to motorcycles in 1923 and cars in 1928. In 1959 the company was rescued from serious financial and marketing difficulties by the Quandt family, who now own almost half the ordinary shares. By the early 1990s, BMW had over 70 000 employees who produced almost 600 000 units and sales had reached DM30 billion.

In 1994 Rover, the largest motor vehicles manufacturer in Britain, was purchased by BMW. A year later, production had consequently risen to over 1 million units, number of employees had risen to over 100 000 and sales by over 50 per cent to DM46 billion. At one fell swoop, BMW secured a fast route into established small car and four-wheel drive markets. BMW's plant in the US also came on-stream in 1994. In addition, an agreement was reached to supply engines for Rolls-Royce and Bentley cars (owned by Vickers). Finally, in a joint venture with Rolls-Royce PLC, BMW has won an order to supply aero engines for small jets, thus enabling the company to resume its original production line.

BMW has developed into a multinational and diversified company in a relatively short period of time. But this process has been characterised by a continued emphasis on products embodying both medium and high technology.

(EOS/ROS)

Böll, Heinrich   Heinrich Böll (1917–1985) is one of the best-known and most controversial writers to have emerged in Germany since 1945. His unremitting criticism of his countrymen's moral amnesia and obsession with affluence brought him admiration and vilification in equal measure. He was awarded the Nobel Prize for Literature in 1972.

Böll's main targets were the Catholic Church, principally for its shameful Concordat with HITLER in 1933, and the politicians of the

ADENAUER era who had restored the values of capitalism on the ruins of the Third Reich. In his view, a unique opportunity to construct a radically new society was thus lost. After some years of poverty, he won recognition for satirical short stories and radio plays, but his literary breakthrough came with his novel *Und sagte kein einziges Wort* (1953). There followed a string of major works, including *Billard um halb zehn* (1959), *Ansichten eines Clowns* (1963), *Gruppenbild mit Dame* (1971), *Fürsorgliche Belagerung* (1979) and the posthumously published *Frauen vor Flußlandschaft* (1985). Despite the critical realism of these texts, Böll's work retained a mythological/theological dimension which was rooted in his Rhineland Catholicism and in an unshaken belief in the values of family life.

Although Böll avoided expressing allegiance to any political party, he was constantly involved in the issues of the day. He was an indefatigable writer of political essays and newspaper articles attacking the power elites of West German society (including the Church). His fearless defence of democratic rights and oppressed minorities, particularly at the height of the public hysteria aroused by urban terrorism in the 1970s, exposed him to fierce attack from the right-wing press. On the other hand, his vigorous support for the opponents of nuclear weapons and power stations and for the Greens won him a loyal following, especially among the young. Dubbed 'the conscience of the nation' – a label he disliked intensely – Böll belonged to a significant generation of left-wing writers and intellectuals in the Federal Republic. He differed from them by his adherence to an idiosyncratic brand of Christian socialism.

See DRITTES REICH; FRIEDENSBEWEGUNG; GRASS, GÜNTER; GRÜNE; TERRORISMUS.

(MGB)

Bosch   Bosch produces automotive equipment, household appliances (together with SIEMENS), communications technology and capital goods. World-wide sales amounted to DM36 billion in 1995.

In 1886 Robert Bosch opened his first workshop in Stuttgart. His system of low-voltage magneto ignition was introduced by Daimler in 1897 and was followed by arc ignition. Overseas production began in 1909 in the US and there was also a representation in Great Britain.

The internationalisation of sales, investment and purchasing have characterised recent developments. To keep abreast of the world market, activities were increased in Asia, South Korea and China by way of joint ventures. Involvement was also increased by means of acquisitions and further expansion in the US and South America.

Car manufacturers world-wide have placed considerable pressure on component suppliers such as Bosch to reduce their prices. This, combined with high German wage costs and the revaluation of the DM in the wake of reunification, have undermined Bosch's profitability. Its foremost goal is therefore to reduce costs and improve earnings. This has led (through-

out the industry) to downward pressure on wage rates, combined with a renewed emphasis on research and development. Overall rises in sales are expected, particularly in export markets.
(EOS/ROS)

Brandenburg Brandenburg is one of the constituent BUNDESLÄNDER of the Federal Republic and one of the NEUE BUNDESLÄNDER on the territory of the former GDR.

Its capital city is Potsdam. It is 29 060km² in size and has a population of 2.54m (1996). Like the other new *Bundesländer*, it has experienced considerable economic difficulties in adapting to the free market system of the Federal Republic since unification. Heavy and manufacturing industries as well as agriculture contracted radically, producing high unemployment (14.2 per cent) and a GDP per head of just 24 830DM in 1995. Proposals to merge Brandenburg with BERLIN were rejected in 1996.

Brandenburg has emerged as the only new *Bundesland* in which the SPD is the strongest party and provides the MINISTERPRÄSIDENT (since 1990 Manfred Stolpe). After a period of leading an AMPELKOALITION from 1990–94, the SPD won an absolute majority in the 1994 LANDTAG election, largely on the basis of Stolpe's personal popularity. The CDU only just emerged ahead of the PDS as the next largest party.
(CJ)

Brandt, Willy Willy Brandt (1913–92) was the first post-war SPD Chancellor, holding office from 1969–1974. The young Willy Brandt was active and prominent in the Socialist youth movement up to 1933, when, following the election of HITLER as German Chancellor, he emigrated to Norway and became a Norwegian citizen. After the German invasion of Norway, he moved to Sweden. He resumed his German citizenship in 1947, entered the BUNDESTAG in 1949 and also became Governing Mayor of West BERLIN in 1957. A strong advocate of the programmatic modernisation in the SPD, Brandt fought unsuccessfully as the SPD's candidate for the Chancellorship in 1961.

Brandt entered Federal Government as Vice-Chancellor and Foreign Minister in the Grand Coalition of of CDU/CSU and SPD from 1966–1969. The 1969 *Bundestag* election delivered a majority for a new SPD–FDP coalition under Brandt. Brandt's tenure as Chancellor was in many ways a success. He oversaw the blossoming of the Federal Republic's OSTPOLITIK and was at least partly responsible for the SPD's electoral high-point in 1972. However, he was ultimately forced to resign under a cloud in 1974, following the so-called 'Guillaume affair', a spy scandal centred around one of his closest aides in the Chancellor's office.

Despite his resignation, Brandt continued to be a talismanic figure within the SPD. He served as party chairman from 1974 until 1987. Following the fall of the Berlin Wall in 1989, Brandt surprised many

observers by an advocacy of unification at the earliest opportunity which was far more passionate than the official policy of the SPD.
See BUNDESKANZLER; SOZIALLIBERALE KOALITION; SCHMIDT, HELMUT.
(CL)

Bremen   One of the three city–states (*Stadtstaaten*, alongside HAMBURG and BERLIN) which form constituent BUNDESLÄNDER of the Federal Republic. In terms of size (404km^2) and population (0.68m in 1996) Bremen is the smallest *Bundesland* in Germany. It consists of the two cities of Bremen and Bremerhaven, separated by a 60-km stretch of NIEDERSACHSEN. Bremen remains one of Europe's major ports, but the contraction of its shipbuilding industry, with over 60 per cent of jobs in this sector lost since 1975, has brought considerable economic problems. Despite a high GDP of per head (58 510DM), unemployment here was at its highest level (14 per cent) among the West German *Bundesländer* (1995 figures), and Bremen has extraordinarily high levels of public debt.

Bremen's LANDESREGIERUNG has always been led by the SPD since 1946, with a remarkable 20-year period of SPD electoral majority between 1971–91. The SPD's strength in elections to the LANDTAG (*Bürgerschaft*) has, however, eroded rapidly since 1991, and, following a period of AMPELKOALITION from 1991–95, has now formed a coalition with the CDU under MINISTERPRÄSIDENT Henning Scherf. Recent elections have seen strong performances by the far-Right DVU (1991), the GRÜNE and the labour protest group, *Arbeit für Bremen* (1995).
(CJ)

Breschnew-Doktrin   The Brezhnev Doctrine underlined the limited sovereignty of individual communist countries, including the GDR. After the crushing of the Prague Spring in 1968, the Soviet leader Leonid Brezhnev declared that all members of the Soviet bloc had a responsibility to intervene in the internal affairs of another communist country in the event of a threat to the communist system. The sovereignty of individual socialist countries could not, it was insisted, be counterposed to the interests of world socialism. Brezhnev made it clear to Erich Honecker during a private meeting in July 1970 that this principle also applied to the GDR. In Brezhnev's view, the GDR was the result of the sacrifice of millions of Soviet lives during World War II and its continued existence was in the common interest of the socialist community. Moreover, according to Brezhnev, the GDR's survival was dependent on the power and the support of the Soviet Union.
See SINATRA-DOKTRIN.
(MD)

Bund   In a general sense a *Bund* is a federal state, but the word is used more typically in Germany as a collective term for federal-level institutions, in particular the Federal Government and the BUNDESTAG, in their role in German federalism.

The institutions of the *Bund* have the primary role in the making of legislation in Germany, with the exception of those areas which fall under the exclusive legislative powers of the BUNDESLÄNDER. They have the exclusive right to make laws in some areas, in particular foreign policy and defence, citizenship, immigration and customs, currency, railways and air transport, and post and telecommunications. In other areas not falling under exclusive *Bundesländer* powers, *Bund* institutions either set out framework conditions within which the *Bundesländer* have to work, or have legislative priority over the *Bundesländer*.

In a more colloquial sense, '*Bund*' is commonly used as a shorthand for BUNDESWEHR.

See BUNDESREGIERUNG; FÖDERALISMUS.

(CJ)

Bund der Vertriebenen   The League of Expellees is one of several associations created by refugees who fled to Germany from former German territories now in Poland and Russia, or from the Czech Sudetenland after World War II.

Expellee organisations initially helped in searches for lost refugees to bring families together and organise material support. They were dissolved as a result of an Allied decision, but in 1948 associations of refugees were given a new legal standing. The new associations were soon organised on a national level to pursue their members' economic and political interests. In the 1954 Charter of Refugees, their national body demanded equal social and economic opportunities, the integration of refugees, and the right to *Heimat* (i.e. of access to their original places of residence), while explicitly rejecting the idea of revenge and favouring reconciliation. It was only in 1957 that all associations of refugees managed to create one representative national body, the *Bund der Vertriebenen*.

While associations of refugees even secured parliamentary representation at federal and BUNDESLÄNDER level in the early years, their level of influence in politics gradually waned. Only in BAYERN, where the Sudetenland question is kept alive by geographical proximity and the relocation of most Sudeten Germans to Bayern after the war, is the issue still a live one.

(ECM)

Bund Freier Demokraten   The League of Free Democrats was a short-lived alliance of East German liberal parties during the unification process. While the LDPD (see BLOCKPARTEIEN) hesitated over a complete break with its past, new liberal parties emerged in the GDR. The German Forum Party, a breakaway faction of New Forum in Chemnitz, was founded in December 1989 and in February 1990 the Free Democratic Party held its founding conference. After Rainer Ortleb replaced Manfred Gerlach as the chairman of the LDPD in February, all three liberal parties joined together in the League of Free Democrats. This electoral alliance obtained 5.3 per cent of the vote in the March 1990 *Volkskammer* election. Soon afterwards, in August 1990, all three East German liberal parties merged with West Germany's FDP.

See FDP.

(MD)

Bundesanstalt für Arbeit   The Federal Labour Office in Nürnberg is the body responsible for most aspects of labour market policy (*Arbeitsmarktpolitik*) in the Federal Republic. It conducts research into labour market conditions, and takes measures to support those who become unemployed and to help their reintegration into the labour market. In the support role, it administers contributions to and payments from unemployment insurance (ARBEITS-LOSENVERSICHERUNG) and administers other social welfare payments such as *Kindergeld*, or child benefit. In the latter role of reintegration, it implements measures to create employment, as well as offering vocational (re-)training services, careers advice, and job centre services.

It is responsible to the Federal Ministry for Labour (*Bundesministerium für Arbeit*) and presides over a structure of eleven regional and 184 local labour offices (*Arbeitsämter*). Its budget has risen significantly since unification as it has sought to provide support for the East German unemployed and offer measures for the improvement of the labour market in the East. Its total expenditures in 1994 were DM100 billion as opposed to DM40 billion in 1990.

See FAMILIENPOLITIK.

(CJ)

Bundesbank   See DEUTSCHE BUNDESBANK.

Bundesgrenzschutz (BGS)   The Federal Border Police is a small force whose main duties consist in patrolling the German borders and also government buildings and installations. It has both policing and paramilitary functions and can be called upon by the government to support the federal police in measures concerning internal security. In emergencies such as war the BGS can be asked to fight alongside the BUNDESWEHR. The framework in which the BGS works is laid down in the GRUNDGESETZ.

(RW)

Bundeskanzler   The Federal Chancellor is the head of the Federal Government (BUNDESREGIERUNG) of the Federal Republic and is directly elected by, and responsible to, the BUNDESTAG.

The position of the Chancellor in the Federal Republic was deliberately strengthened in the GRUNDGESETZ in reaction to the weaknesses of the Chancellorship in the Weimar Republic (WEIMARER REPUBLIK). Two central problems of the Weimar era needed to be addressed: the overlap of powers in governmental leadership between Chancellor and President; and the frequency with which Chancellors were unseated in votes of no-confidence. Both problems contributed to the political instability which afflicted and weakened the Weimar political system. In view of these problems, the *Grundgesetz* reduced the role of Federal President (BUNDES-PRÄSIDENT) to that of a largely ceremonial head of state, while upgrading that of the Chancellor to become an unrivalled and stable source of governmental leadership.

The strength of the position arises from the following: Chancellors have the power to 'hire and fire' their ministerial teams, which are responsible to them rather than the *Bundestag*; they have the power to determine the guidelines of government policy (*Richtlinienkompetenz*), within which their ministers have to work. The introduction of a 'constructive' vote of no-confidence (KONSTRUKTIVES MIßTRAUENSVOTUM) has also made it more difficult for the *Bundestag* to dismiss a sitting Chancellor by imposing a requirement to elect a new Chancellor at the same time as rejecting the sitting Chancellor. In addition, Chancellors chair and co-ordinate the Federal Government and are assisted in doing so by the Federal Chancellery (BUNDESKANZLERAMT), a powerful office of advisors and civil servants.

The strength of the Chancellor's position led, in particular in the period of office of the Federal Republic's first Chancellor, Konrad ADENAUER (1949–63), to the Federal Republic being dubbed a 'Chancellor Democracy' ('KANZLERDEMOKRATIE').This designation, which implied a potentially over-strong role for the Chancellor, has, however, proved to be ill-suited to describe the position of subsequent Chancellors, who have faced considerable checks and balances to the exercise of their powers.

Bundeskanzler since 1949:

1949–1963	Konrad Adenauer (CDU)
1963–1966	Ludwig Erhard (CDU)
1966–1969	Kurt Georg Kiesinger (CDU)
1969–1974	Willy Brandt (SPD)
1974–1982	Helmut Schmidt (SPD)
Since 1982	Helmut Kohl (CDU)

(CJ)

Bundeskanzleramt The Federal Chancellery supports the Federal Chancellor in his role as head of the Federal Government. It consists of around 500 staff and is normally headed by a cabinet minister. It is organised as a Federal Government in miniature, with individual departments 'shadowing' the individual federal ministries. These departments monitor the work of the ministries, providing liaison between the Chancellor and his/her ministers and ensuring the Chancellor's policy guidelines and the decisions of the Federal Government are observed and carried out.

See BUNDESKANZLER; BUNDESMINISTERIUM; BUNDESREGIERUNG.

(CJ)

Bundeskartellamt The Federal Cartel Office, together with the courts and the Federal Minister of Economics, enforces legislation concerning cartels. The Act against Restraints on Competition, or anti-trust legislation, was introduced in 1957 by Ludwig Erhard, following seven years of controversy. It initially outlawed, subject to exceptions, the traditional German cartel (*Kartell*). Mergers (*Fusionen*), and therefore market dominance, were not tackled until amendments were enacted in 1965, 1973, 1980 and 1990. Retail price maintenance was also abolished in 1973. In addition, the Monopoly Commission advises on the development of market dominance. (EOS)

Bundesländer The 16 *Bundesländer* are the component sub-national units of the German federal system. Following German unification in 1990, the five NEUE BUNDESLÄNDER of East Germany joined the existing 11 *Bundesländer* (BADEN-WÜRTTEMBERG, BAYERN, BERLIN, BREMEN, HAMBURG, HESSEN, NIEDERSACHSEN, NORDRHEIN-WESTFALEN, RHEINLAND-PFALZ, SAARLAND, SCHLESWIG-HOLSTEIN). The *Bundesländer* differ considerably in area and population, and in economic and party-political structure.

Each *Bundesland* has its own constitution, which provides for a complete system of government with parliament (LANDTAG), government (LANDESREGIERUNG) and judicial system (GERICHTE). The *Bundesländer* exercise important powers in the German federal system. They possess autonomous, or exclusive, legislative powers in a limited number of fields, in particular cultural policy (education and broadcasting), policing and the organisation of local government (KOMMUNALE SELBSTVERWALTUNG). They also implement most federal-level legislation and, through the BUNDESRAT, a body of representatives of the *Landesregierungen*, also participate in the making of federal-level legislation.

The tendency towards POLITIKVERFLECHTUNG between the federal level and the *Bundesländer* in German federalism (FÖDERALISMUS) has had important implications for the *Bundesländer*. It has tended to increase the powers exercised by the *Landesregierungen* at the expense of the *Landtage*. This has raised concerns about the democratic accountability of decision-making within the *Bundesländer*. *Politikverflechtung* also places a strong onus on their ability to secure agreement among themselves on the political issues on which they co-operate with the federal level. Securing agreement has become more difficult since unification, given the different background and problems the *neue Bundesländer* have brought with them into the federal system.
(CJ)

Bundesministerium Each Federal Ministry is led by a Minister belonging to the Federal Government and is responsible for the development and execution of policy in particular policy fields. There are currently over 15 Federal Ministries, ranging from the traditional (and still most influential) ministries for foreign affairs, home affairs, finance, justice and defence to more recently established ones like the Ministry for the Environment, which reflect the broadening of the tasks of government during the twentieth century.

Ministers are appointed by the Federal Chancellor and are normally drawn from the membership of the BUNDESTAG. They are assisted in their work by Secretaries of State (*Staatssekretäre*) who are either senior civil servants or, in the case of *Parlamentarische Staatssekretäre*, members of the *Bundestag*, and by civil service staffs of varying size. Since the governments of the Bundesländer (LANDESREGIERUNGEN) are responsible for the implementation of most Federal Government policies, only two ministries – foreign affairs and defence – have a large civil service staff. The role of the civil servants is to provide advice to the minister in making decisions, and to carry them out (or, where the *Bundesländer* are responsible for implementation, to monitor how the *Bundesländer* carry them out).

See BUNDESKANZLER; BUNDESREGIERUNG.

(CJ)

Bundespräsident   The Federal President is the head of state of the Federal Republic. The President is elected for a period of five years by the Federal Assembly (BUNDESVERSAMMLUNG). The office may be held by an individual for a maximum of two five-year periods.

The main powers of the President are of a formal, ceremonial nature, and merely confirm decisions taken elsewhere. They include the summoning and dissolution of the BUNDESTAG, the nomination of a candidate for election as Federal Chancellor following each *Bundestag* election, the appointment of the Federal Chancellor thus elected, the appointment and dismissal of the ministers in the Federal Government, the signing of federal legislation, and the declaration of a state of emergency. The President also formally represents the Federal Republic in international law, for example signing international treaties on behalf of the Federal Republic.

This largely ceremonial role reflects the experience of the Weimar Republic, when a strong Presidency rivalled the Chancellorship in the role of governmental leadership and helped to undermine political stability. The role of the President was therefore downgraded in the GRUNDGESETZ, in order to establish the Federal Chancellor as the unrivalled head of government.

Despite its limited powers, the Presidency has evolved into a position of considerable political authority. Detached from party politics (Presidents traditionally let party membership lapse on entry into office) and day-to-day political problems, Presidents have been able to act as a source of critical moral leadership and political integration. This was a role performed most prominently hitherto by President Richard von WEIZSÄCKER (1984–94).

Bundespräsidenten since 1949:

1949–1959	Theodor Heuss (FDP)
1959–1969	Heinrich Lübke (CDU)
1969–1974	Gustav Heinemann (SPD)
1974–1979	Walter Scheel (FDP)
1979–1984	Karl Carstens (CDU)
1984–1994	Richard von Weizsäcker (CDU)
since 1994	Roman Herzog (CDU)

See BUNDESKANZLER; WEIMARER REPUBLIK.
(CJ)

Bundespressekonferenz The German press is organised in the Federal Press Conference, which meets several times a week for briefings by invited spokespersons of the Federal Government. The conference occasionally invites Federal Ministers or even the Chancellor to present their views.

The *Bundespressekonferenz* is seen as an important expression of open government and freedom of the press. The foreign press has its own conference, the *Verein der Auslandspresse*.
See PRESSEFREIHEIT.
(RW)

Bundesrat The *Bundesrat* is composed of representatives of the governments of the BUNDESLÄNDER (LANDESREGIERUNGEN) and acts as the second chamber, alongside the BUNDESTAG, in the federal-level legislative process. The number of votes each *Landesregierung* possesses in *Bundesrat* decision-making is loosely related to the population of the *Bundesland* concerned. Votes must be cast *en bloc*.

The *Bundesrat* has graded powers in federal legislation. Laws proposing constitutional changes (VERFASSUNGSÄNDERUNGEN) must secure a two-thirds majority in the *Bundesrat*. Over half of federal laws fall into a second category of 'consent laws' (*Zustimmungsgesetze*), which must secure a 51 per cent majority. These are laws which in some way affect the central interests of the *Bundesländer*. A final category are 'objection laws' (*Einspruchsgesezte*). Only in this category can a *Bundesrat* majority against the proposed law be overturned by an equivalent majority in the *Bundestag*. Although the *Bundesrat* may introduce legislation on its own initiative, it rarely does so. If *Bundesrat* and *Bundestag* fail to agree on proposed legislation, a compromise solution is sought in their joint Conciliation Committee (VERMITTLUNGSAUSSCHUß). The preparation of *Bundesrat* business is conducted in a range of committees (AUSSCHÜSSE), normally covering the same policy fields as Federal Ministries.

In addition, the *Bundesrat* elects half of the members of the Federal Constitutional Court and has powers of participation in decision-making under the Emergency Laws (NOTSTANDSGESETZE).

Decision-making in the *Bundesrat* has a party-political dimension. For most of the period since unification, SPD-led *Bundesländer* have held a majority of *Bundesrat* votes. The SPD has at times sought to use this majority to block legislation passed by the governing coalition of CDU/CSU and FDP in the *Bundestag*.

Fears that the *Bundesrat* would be transformed into an instrument of SPD opposition have, though, been overstated, since the SPD shares power with a number of other parties in the various *Landesregierungen*, and cannot necessarily guarantee their support for its priorities.

Bundesrat: voting weights and governmental composition by *Bundesländer* (December 1996):

Baden-Württemberg	6 votes CDU–FDP
Bavaria	6 votes CSU
Berlin	4 votes CDU–SPD
Brandenburg	4 votes SPD
Bremen	3 votes SPD–CDU
Hamburg	3 votes SPD–Stattpartei
Hessen	5 votes SPD–Green
Mecklenburg-Vorpommern	3 votes CDU–SPD
Niedersachsen	6 votes SPD
Nordrhein-Westfalen	6 votes SPD–Green
Rheinland-Pfalz	4 votes SPD–FDP
Saarland	3 votes SPD
Sachsen	4 votes CDU
Sachsen-Anhalt	4 votes SPD–Green
Schleswig-Holstein	4 votes SPD–Green
Thüringen	4 votes CDU–SPD

See BUNDESMINISTERIUM; BUNDESVERFASSUNGSGERICHT.
(CJ)

Bundesregierung The Federal Government is chaired and co-ordinated by the Federal Chancellor. The Chancellor leads a team of ministers who each head a Federal Ministry responsible for particular areas of policy which fall under the responsibility of the federal level of government in Germany, and who collectively form the cabinet. Cabinet ministers are usually, but not necessarily, members of the BUNDESTAG. Individual ministers are formally accountable only to the Chancellor and not the *Bundestag* and are appointed and dismissed by him. The Chancellor, however, is accountable to the *Bundestag* on behalf of the government, and can be dismissed by it in a constructive vote of no-confidence (KONSTRUKTIVES MIßTRAUENSVOTUM).

Federal Government business is conducted according to three principles. First, the Chancellor Principle empowers the Chancellor to set out the general guidelines of government policy (*Richtlinienkompetenz*). Second, the Departmental Principle empowers individual ministers to carry out government policy within the framework of the Chancellor's guidelines as matters of their own responsibility. Third, the Cabinet Principle provides for collective decision-making in matters where individual ministers disagree over policy.

The interplay between these principles depends on a number of factors. The Chancellor Principle and the Chancellor's power to 'hire and fire' ministers provide him with overall leadership powers. The Departmental Principle, however, gives ministers considerable authority, especially since they tend to enjoy long periods in office and thereby build up considerable and indispensable expertise in their policy field. A further factor is that all Federal Governments hitherto have been coalition governments, which imposes a need for compromise and strengthens the collective Cabinet Principle.

Federal Government coalitions have been led either by CDU (1949–69 and 1982 to the present day) or SPD (1969–1982) Chancellors. For almost the entire period since 1949, the smaller FDP has acted as the junior coalition partner.

See ABGEORDNETE; BUND; BUNDESKANZLER; BUNDESMINISTERIUM; KOALITION.

(CJ)

Bundesrepublik Deutschland – BRD   The Federal Republic of Germany, or FRG, was established in May 1949. It is by far the longest-lasting democratic state in German history. The foundations of the FRG were laid in the period of Allied occupation of Germany after World War II. As the tensions of the Cold War heightened, the Western Allies began to accelerate the reconstruction of their occupation zones on a Western model of democratic government and market economics (just as the Soviet Union began to shape its occupation zone in its own political and economic image). Close co-operation between the US and British occupation zones was extended to the French zone as well with the Western currency reform (WÄHRUNGSREFORM) of June 1948. This fundamental decision for the reconstruction of the Western German economy separate from that of the Soviet zone was followed, against the background of the Soviet blockade of the Western sectors of BERLIN, by an equivalent decision on political reconstruction: a Parliamentary Council (PARLAMENTARISCHER RAT) of German politicians was established in September 1948 with the task of drawing up a constitution for a West German state. This constitution, the Basic Law (GRUNDGESETZ), came into force on 23 May 1949, thus establishing the Federal Republic. An equivalent process was taking place in the Soviet zone of occupation, leading to the establishment of the German Democratic Republic, or GDR, in September 1949.

The first national elections were held in August 1949, returning a coalition government under the Chancellorship of Konrad ADENAUER. The

Adenauer Chancellorship was characterised by a period of sustained economic growth known as the 'economic miracle' (WIRTSCHAFTSWUNDER), a political stability unknown in the Weimar years, and a Western-oriented foreign policy firmly aligned to the interests of the wartime Western Allies in the new international situation of Cold War. While this loyal pro-Western stance made any positive relationship with the GDR impossible, it did secure remarkably quickly the international rehabilitation of the Federal Republic, as seen in its membership of NATO in 1955 and its founder member status of the institutions of European integration from 1951 onwards.

The combination of economic success, political stability and international rehabilitation reaped considerable electoral reward for Adenauer's Christian Democratic CDU and its Bavarian sister party, the CSU. Their combined share of the vote rose from 31 per cent in 1949 to 50.2 per cent in 1957 (the only absolute majority ever recorded in the Federal Republic). The electoral dominance of the CDU/CSU led to a policy rethink by the main opposition party, the SPD, which had hitherto opposed both the market economics and the Western-oriented foreign policy of the Christian Democrats. By the late 1950s, the SPD had taken on board the broad principles of CDU/CSU domestic and foreign policy and begun a process of electoral recovery which would take it into Federal Government by 1966.

The SPD's reorientation was one feature of a period of transition through the 1960s. Another was Adenauer's retirement as Chancellor in 1963, due in part to his age, but also to the feeling that his Western foreign policy was too one-dimensional, preventing constructive relations with the GDR and the other communist states in a period of thawing superpower relations. A new, although initially very cautious, opening to the East followed under the next two Chancellors, Erhard and Kiesinger. The final core feature of the transition was in the economy. The FRG faced its first economic downturn in 1965–66. Although this was extremely mild by contemporary standards, it had an impact made disproportionate by memories of the economic collapse of 1929–30 and the subsequent erosion of Weimar democracy, the latter exacerbated by the fleeting appearance of a far-Right party, the NPD, as a significant political force. The downturn led both to a new emphasis on government intervention in the economy, which endured through to the 1980s, and to the entry of the SPD into government in 1966 as part of the Grand Coalition with the CDU/CSU.

The latter provided a springboard for the SPD to take over leadership in government, in coalition with the FDP, after the 1969 elections. The Chancellorship of Willy BRANDT (1969–74) was marked by the failure to enact promised social reforms and the resounding success of a new OST-POLITIK, which put the FRG's relations with the GDR, the Soviet Union and the other communist states on as normal a footing as was then possible. Brandt's successor, Helmut SCHMIDT, governed through a difficult period dominated by the economic difficulties thrown up by the 1970s' oil crises, by a wave of terrorism, and by a new freeze in superpower relations from 1979–80. While Schmidt is generally regarded as having managed these problems well, he gradually lost the commitment of the left-wing of his own party, disappointed at the lack of progress in social reform, and of an increasingly free market-oriented FDP.

In 1982, the FDP left the coalition and joined forces with the CDU/CSU to establish a new coalition under Chancellor Helmut KOHL. Kohl's Chancellorship was initially rather colourless. The promised change (WENDE) to a policy of 'rolling back the state' role in economic life, like that pursued by Prime Minister Thatcher in Great Britain, was implemented only fitfully and the performance of the government was generally viewed critically by public opinion. The coalition lasted through the 1980s less due to its own achievements than to the weakness of an opposition fragmented between SPD and the new parliamentary force of the GRÜNE.

Kohl and his government met, though, with a momentous turning point with the collapse of communist rule in the GDR in 1989–90. The subsequent German unification process, culminating in the incorporation of the former GDR into the FRG, was managed with great speed and surefootedness by a Kohl government emphatically returned to office in the first all-German elections of December 1990. However, the domestic policy problems thrown up by unification have proved to be unexpectedly difficult, and have not been addressed with conspicuous success, with the Kohl government generally relapsing into the colourlessness of the 1980s. Only in European policy has a real sense of purpose been displayed, with the FRG spearheading the drive towards closer European integration in the Maastricht Treaty and beyond. Otherwise – and again like the 1980s – the weaknesses of an SPD and GRÜNE opposition, now further fragmented by the PDS, seem the main factor in maintaining the CDU/CSU-FDP coalition in power.

Such was certainly the case in the 1994 BUNDESTAG election and cannot be ruled out in the next election in 1998. More generally, as the earlier example of Adenauer showed, real change in politics and policy is unlikely to happen until as long-serving a Chancellor as Helmut Kohl (who overtook Adenauer's record as longest-serving Chancellor in 1996) retires.

See BERLINER BLOCKADE; BESATZUNG; BUNDESKANZLER; DDR; ENTSPANNUNG; EUROPAPOLITIK; GROßE KOALITION; HAUSHALTSPOLITIK; KALTER KRIEG; SOZIALLIBERALE KOALITION; TERRORISMUS; VEREINIGUNG; WIRTSCHAFTSPOLITIK.

(CJ)

Bundestag   The *Bundestag* is the directly elected first chamber of parliament in the Federal Republic. Following the 1994 *Bundestag* election, it consisted of 672 deputies (ABGEORDNETE), or MdBs (*Mitglieder des Bundestages*). The MdBs are organised in party-political groupings (FRAKTIONEN), either supportive of the government or forming the opposition.

The *Bundestag* performs four main functions. First, it establishes the Federal Government by electing the Federal Chancellor at the start of each parliamentary period. Second, it monitors and controls the activities of the Federal Government through mechanisms ranging from question hours (*aktuelle Stunden*), debates and committees of inquiry through to the ultimate sanction of dismissing the Federal Government by replacing the Federal Chancellor in a constructive vote of no-confidence (KONSTRUK-TIVES MIßTRAUENSVOTUM). Third, it helps to legitimise the political process by representing the views of the electorate through political parties. And finally and most importantly, it legislates in the policy fields which, according to the GRUNDGESETZ, fall under the responsibility of the federal level. Its powers in legislation (GESETZGEBUNG) are conducted in parallel with those of the second chamber of parliament at the federal level, the BUNDESRAT. In cases of disagreement between *Bundestag* and *Bundesrat*, the Mediation Committee (VERMITTLUNGSAUSSCHUß) is convened to find a solution.

The parliamentary timetable is set down by a Committee of Elders (*Ältestenrat*), and the plenary sessions are chaired by the *Bundestag* President, who is elected for a full parliamentary term. Most of the detailed work of the *Bundestag* is carried out in its various committees (AUSSCHÜSSE) rather than in the plenary sessions.

The normal parliamentary period between elections is four years, although this period can be shortened if the *Bundeskanzler* calls and loses a vote of confidence. This has happened on two occasions: in 1972, when Chancellor Willy BRANDT sought a new electoral mandate after losing his *Bundestag* majority due to defections to the opposition; and in 1983, when Chancellor Helmut KOHL engineered his own defeat in a vote of confidence. Kohl did this in order to bring about a new *Bundestag* election to secure electoral confirmation of his elevation to the Chancellorship following the successful constructive vote of no-confidence in Chancellor Helmut Schmidt a year earlier.

The 1994 *Bundestag* election confirmed in government the coalition of CDU, CSU and FDP which has governed since 1982, albeit with a reduced majority compared to the 1990 election result. The opposition parties returned were the SPD, the GRÜNE and the PDS. The next parliamentary election is scheduled to take place in the autumn of 1998.

See BUND; BUNDESKANZLER; BUNDESRAT.

(CJ)

Bundesverfassungsgericht The Federal Constitutional Court (FCC) is Germany's highest court. It acts as guardian and interpreter of the GRUNDGESETZ and is the highest judicial organ in the horizontal separation of powers (GEWALTENTEILUNG) in the Federal Republic between legislative, executive and judicial institutions.

The FCC has a number of functions. It adjudicates in disputes between the federal level (BUND) and BUNDESLÄNDER, and more widely between Germany's other political institutions, over the distribution of competences between them in the *Grundgesetz*. It examines the compatibility of laws with the *Grundgesetz* and can, in case of incompatibility, declare a law invalid. It can ban political parties with unconstitutional aims and withdraw basic rights (GRUNDRECHTE) from individuals in order to protect the constitutional order. And, in the major part of its workload, it ensures the operation of the rule of law (RECHTSSTAAT) by assessing the validity of constitutional complaints (VERFASSUNGSBESCHWERDEN) by individuals against alleged infringements of their *Grundrechte* by state institutions.

The FCC consists of two Senates, each with eight judges serving twelve-year periods of office. Half of the judges are elected by the BUNDESTAG and half by the BUNDESRAT. The FCC sits in Karlsruhe.

The criticism has been made in recent years that the *Bundesverfassungsgericht* has taken on the role of 'surrogate legislator' ('*Ersatzgesetzgeber*'). This reflects in part the Court's tendency to issue over-prescriptive judgements, but also and increasingly, the inability of the *Bundestag* to reach agreement on important, but politically controversial issues, on which the Court is then called on to provide guidance. Recent examples of the latter include asylum rights, abortion policy, and the deployment of the BUNDESWEHR outside NATO territory.

Despite its growing involvement in political controversies, however, the *Bundesverfassungsgericht* retains its position as Germany's most highly regarded institution.

See ABTREIBUNGSRECHT; ASYLRECHT; BLAUHELM-EINSÄTZE.

(CJ)

Bundesversammlung   The Federal Assembly is the body convened to elect the Federal President. It consists of all of the members of the BUNDESTAG and an equal number of representatives elected by the parliaments of the BUNDESLÄNDER. The number of representatives sent from each LANDTAG is weighted in proportion to the population of the *Bundesland* concerned, and their party-political affiliations reflect the relative strength of the parties represented in that *Landtag*. If none of the candidates standing for election to the Presidency secures an overall majority in the majority in the first or second ballot of the Federal Assembly, a third and decisive ballot is held in which the candidate who receives the most votes (not necessarily a majority) is elected.

See BUNDESPRÄSIDENT.

(CJ)

Bundeswehr   The German Armed Forces comprise three separate services – the army, navy and airforce. The *Bundeswehr* was founded in 1955, as the West insisted on Germany re-arming against possible Soviet aggression. From the outset the *Bundeswehr* was designed to be fully integrated within NATO and all *Bundeswehr* forces were to be assigned to NATO in times of alert. To calm French fears about a newly armed Germany the *Bundeswehr* did not have its own General Staff but relied on NATO for all main command and control functions. During the Cold War the *Bundeswehr* developed into the largest army in Western Europe, deploying the most modern weapon systems in NATO's Central Front. It did not, however, possess any nuclear weapons.

The collapse of the Soviet Union and the German unification drastically altered the *Bundeswehr*'s tasks and composition. Almost overnight it had to absorb the personnel and equipment of the former GDR army, the NATIONALE VOLKSARMEE, as well as reorient its rationale from participation in all-out nuclear war in central Europe to small, mobile peace-keeping operations outside the NATO area.

The unification treaties limit the new *Bundeswehr* to a size of 325 000 men. This was achieved by massive reductions in manpower and voluntary early retirements.

The Federal Constitutional Court ruling permitting the deployment of German forces overseas opened the way for the participation of *Bundeswehr* units in UN operations in Somalia and former Yugoslavia. The *Bundeswehr* has altered its combat structure and is now training many units in small-scale peace-keeping operations, as may be required from a possible permanent German seat in the UN Security Council.

Completion of its new structural plan, *Bundeswehr 2000*, would give German foreign-policy-makers a flexible military force capable of operating world-wide in peace-related missions.

See BLAUHELM-EINSÄTZE.

(SS)

Bündnis '90 Alliance '90 is an alliance of several civil rights and opposition groups. *Bündnis '90*, originally forged as an electoral pact for the March 1990 VOLKSKAMMER election, consisted of New Forum, Democracy Now and the Initiative on Peace and Human Rights. While the citizens' movements in the alliance accepted German unification as inevitable, they insisted on protection for GDR interests through a gradual drawing together of the two states. They also sought guarantees of the right to work, equal rights for men and women and a minimum standard of living for everyone. In addition, they advocated in their election programme various forms of basic democracy such as the holding of regional and national referendums. The low vote for the alliance in March 1990 (2.9 per cent), though by no means a surprise, was deeply disappointing to leading figures such as Bärbel Bohley and Jens Reich. Subsequently, the alliance entered into a closer relationship with the East German Greens. In the December 1990 *Bundestag* election, the electoral pact of *Bündnis '90/Grüne* (East) obtained 6 per cent of the vote in the five new *Bundesländer* and eight seats in the BUNDESTAG.

In order to improve their electoral chances and to cement their common interests on issues such as human rights and ecology, *Bündnis*

'90/Grüne (East) and the much larger Western German Greens (GRÜNE) formed into one national party with the title of *Bündnis '90/Grüne*. The strategy helped the party to obtain 7.3 per cent of the vote and 49 seats in the 1994 *Bundestag* election. However, the party is far from well integrated and support in the East is much weaker than in the old BUNDESLÄNDER.

See BÜRGERBEWEGUNGEN.

(MD)

Bürgerbewegungen   The citizens' movements of the former GDR were the most significant form of critical opposition during the HONECKER era. They took root in the late 1970s in an alternative political culture, in which a series of issues relating to peace, gender, ecology and human rights were articulated outside SED-controlled channels. These issues were propagated by small groups and were largely confined to the relatively protective space afforded by the Protestant Church.

During 1989, a crucial form of opposition to the SED emerged from the alternative political culture in the shape of small citizens' movements and embryonic political parties such as Democratic Awakening (DA), Democracy Now (DJ), the Social Democratic Party (SDP) and New Forum. Church ministers, artists and intellectuals were especially active in the early stages. The most important of these new groups was New Forum whose September 1989 Manifesto calling for a broad political platform for widespread discussion on reform attracted 200 000 signatures within two months. While its representatives were to the forefront in rallying East Germans against the regime, New Forum itself remained a loosely structured organisation.

As the new movements began to take shape, they sought to define a common set of principles in the Joint Declaration issued on 20 October 1989. This called for a democratic sovereign GDR with political pluralism, freedom of travel and association, an independent judiciary and the introduction of an ecologically responsible policy. Representatives of groups such as DA, DJ and the United Left favoured some form of socialism. On the other hand, the SDP was drawn to the West German social market economy.

While the citizens' movements can rightly claim to have made a vital contribution to the destruction of SED rule, their idealistic notions of grass-roots democracy and many aspects of their economic and ecological policies lacked popular resonance. As unification took over the agenda, most of the citizens' groups abandoned their goal of an independent GDR. Indeed, DA joined the Alliance for Germany and the SDP drew closer to West Germany's Social Democrats, as signified by its change of name to SPD at the national delegates' conference in January 1990. The March 1990 VOLKSKAMMER results were a great disappointment with BÜNDNIS '90, an alliance of some of the more prominent groups, scoring

2.9 per cent of the vote and others faring equally poorly. Local and regional elections held later in the year brought little change in fortune.
See ALLIANZ FÜR DEUTSCHLAND; BÜNDNIS '90; RUNDER TISCH.
(MD)

Bürgerinitiativen   Citizens' initiatives are loose and often short-lived organisations of citizens focused on particular issues of common concern, most typically in the field of environmental protection.

Citizens' initiatives evolved from the mid-1960s in an era in which people became less willing to conform to the decisions of a state apparatus which intervened increasingly in social and economic life, yet whose decision-making structures were seen to be remote and inaccessible. A further role was played by the Grand Coalition of CDU/CSU and SPD between 1966–69, which faced little genuine parliamentary opposition and provoked a strong and activist protest movement outside parliament. This – focused in particular in the student movement – contributed to the atmosphere of self-assertion which supported the citizens' initiatives and was ultimately to feed into the emergence of the GRÜNE ten years later.

Citizens' initiatives seek direct confrontation with public authorities through mobilising popular concern, often in direct action like information campaigns, petitions and demonstrations.

Citizens' initiatives are likely to continue to play a role in providing an autonomous, flexible, open and direct link between society and political institutions in a way traditional parties and interest group organisations find hard to match.

See AUßERPARLAMENTARISCHE OPPOSITION; GROßE KOALITION; STUDENTENBEWEGUNG.
(ECM)

C

CDU (Christlich-Demokratische Union)   The CDU is the main conservative party in Germany, and occupies the centre-right of the political spectrum. The party was founded in 1945 under the leadership of Konrad ADENAUER and was the first in German party history to bridge the denominational divide between Catholics and Protestants. The programme it has developed since the foundation of the Federal Republic in 1949 has been structured around the idea of the social market economy (SOZIALE MARKTWIRTSCHAFT), which combined a free market economy with comprehensive welfare provisions, and around Western integration in foreign policy. Together with the CSU, the CDU has dominated federal elections and governments, being returned as the largest party in all federal elections except 1972, and providing the Federal Chancellor (BUNDESKANZLER) until 1969 and again from 1982.

During the 1950s, the party developed into a so-called VOLKSPARTEI (catch-all party), integrating workers, Catholics, Protestants and millions of refugees from the GDR and elsewhere in Eastern Europe into its ranks. Since 1973 Helmut KOHL has been the party leader, and, since 1982, also the Chancellor. In recent years, the party, and especially Helmut Kohl, has pursued a European policy (EUROPAPOLITIK) focused strongly on securing closer European integration.

However, its traditional voter clientele, church-going Catholics, has been shrinking in size, and this, combined with a general decline in the strength of party loyalties, has resulted in CDU/CSU's federal election performance slipping consistently from 48.8 per cent in 1983 to 41.5 per cent in 1994.

The CDU stands in all the BUNDESLÄNDER except BAYERN, home of its sister party, the CSU. However, as both parties form a single parliamentary group (*Fraktion*) in the *Bundestag*, the two parties are usually treated as one.

Future problems for the CDU lie in renewing its membership, which is increasingly old and male, and shoring up its steady electoral decline. A crucial question which will face the party is that of selecting Kohl's successor on his retirement, although this seems to have been deferred for some

time given Kohl's apparent enthusiasm to stay on until after the 1998 *Bundestag* election.
(SG)

CDU/CSU   See CDU and CSU.

Commerzbank   The Commerzbank is the fourth largest German bank with 30 000 employees and a net income of DM980 million in 1995. Founded as the Commerz- und Disconto-Bank in Hamburg in 1870, it moved its focus of activities to Berlin on taking over the Berliner Bank in 1905. After further acquisitions of regional and private banks between the wars, it formally assumed its present title in 1940. Like other big German banks it was deconcentrated by the Allies after the end of World War II but reconstituted in 1958. In 1990 it moved its headquarters to Frankfurt am Main where it has occupied Europe's tallest office building since 1995. In the 1990s the bank has seen unprecedented profitability. Like the DEUTSCHE BANK and DRESDNER BANK it has commenced a process of introducing greater transparency to provide shareholders with ever deepening insights into the development of the bank's business and earnings – a corporate culture symbolised by the openness and transparency of the bank's new Frankfurt building.
See FINANZWESEN.
(EOS)

CSU (Christlich-Soziale Union)   The Christian Social Union is Bavaria's leading party and while closely allied to the CDU, is distinguished by its mix of social conservatism, economic liberalism and strong links to the Catholic Church.

Founded in 1946, the CSU quickly established itself as the dominant force in Bavarian politics, winning an absolute majority of the votes in all LANDTAG elections since 1970. Much of the party's success was due to the enduring popularity of Franz Josef STRAUß, who led the party for 27 years up to his death in 1988.

Following Strauß's death, however, the party has found it difficult to find a leader of similar stature to replace him. As a result, it has opted to split its two power bases, the party leader, who typically plays an important role in federal-level politics, and the post of Bavarian MINISTERPRÄSIDENT, between two individuals. This has not always been a harmonious arrangement, with considerable differences emerging over European Policy between the current party leader (and Federal Finance Minister), Theo Waigel, and *Ministerpräsident* Edmund Stoiber.

The CSU only stands for election in Bavaria, but forms a single parliamentary grouping with the CDU in the BUNDESTAG. This relationship has generally worn well, although the CSU did briefly break from the CDU to underline its political independence in 1976.

The CSU has been gradually losing support since 1974, though still dominates the Bavarian *Landtag*. Under Stoiber's influence, it has recently sought to emphasise its 'Euro-sceptic' credentials in order to mobilise support.

See BAYERN.

(SG)

D

DAAD (Deutscher Akademischer Austauschdienst) The German Academic Exchange Service is an agency of the Foreign Office of the Federal Republic and has the task of promoting international academic exchange. It was founded in 1925 and re-established in 1950 with its head office in Bonn and around a dozen further offices all over the world.

The organisation also acts as an intermediary in cultural matters between the Foreign Office and other countries It is the national agency for EU Programmes promoting academic exchange such as SOKRATES, LEONARDO and TEMPUS. It is best known for the teaching assistants (*Lektoren/Lektorinnen*) it provides all over the world, and for its academic scholarships for both German and non-German academics. In 1995 the total number of foreign and home academics funded exceeded 50 000.

See GOETHE-INSTITUT.

(RW)

Daimler-Benz Daimler-Benz is Germany's largest industrial group by turnover. It was transformed into a conglomerate during the 1980s through the acquisition of AEG and a number of aerospace companies.

It was founded in 1926 by the merger of the motor vehicle manufacturing companies Daimler and Benz, named after their respective founders. Their most prestigious and best-known product is the Mercedes but from World War I to the end of World War II they also manufactured aero and marine engines. Thereafter the company concentrated on commercial vehicles and the quality car market.

In 1995 the company attained total sales of over DM100 billion with more than 300 000 employees, three-quarters of whom work in Germany. The group also reported its first post-war loss and the biggest loss in German corporate history of DM6 billion.

Financial assistance was withdrawn from the loss-making Dutch aerospace company, Fokker, in which Daimler-Benz had taken a controlling stake a few years earlier. Similarly, unprofitable parts of AEG were to be sold off. Yet the car division continued to return high profits, and foreign sales have continued to account for 60 per cent of turnover.

Historically, there is a strong link between the DEUTSCHE BANK and Daimler-Benz. The chief executive of the bank is normally the chairperson of the group's non-executive board.
(EOS)

Datenschutz Data protection regulates the potential conflicts which arise between demands for access to information and demands for privacy in an increasingly computerised society.

The Federal Republic established relatively comprehensive data protection laws in the 1970s. These were motivated by a concern to protect the privacy of the individual and to empower him/her, wherever possible, to establish the conditions under which personal data could be made publicly accessible.

Such legislation is arguably now outdated. It was developed to deal with technical developments in computerisation in the 1970s (when computers were typically stand-alone units) and is less equipped to control access to personal information in today's world-wide network of linked computer systems.
(CJ)

Deutsche Bahn (DB) Deutsche Bahn is the reorganised railway industry, which has succeeded the former West German *Deutsche Bundesbahn* and the former GDR *Deutsche Reichsbahn*. In 1995 its turnover was DM30 billion, with 312 500 employees and a net income of DM264 million.

A formerly profitable railway sector began to decline following World War II as both private and commercial motor vehicles were gradually substituted for rail transport (and with, at one point, every sixth job in West Germany dependent on the motor-vehicle industry). But the Western rail network was not substantially pruned and a system which had run generally east to west was transformed in a north–south system. In the East the railway system had suffered from chronic under-investment.

In 1994, the Deutsche Bundesbahn and Deutsche Reichsbahn were amalgamated and became known as Deutsche Bahn. In one sense, this was regarded as a 'privatisation' since the railways lost their public authority status and became a publicly quoted company. The Federal Government is initially the only shareholder.

The Bundesbahn was in crisis before unification. There had been 14 official reports on revitalising the system in the post-war era, all of which were simply noted. Meanwhile, between 1950–90 the market share of freight transport fell from 60 to 29 per cent and the share of passenger transport fell from 36 to 6 per cent. The labour force of the Bundesbahn was more than halved from 512 000 to 222 000 between 1957–93 (a process extended to the East after unification, with Reichsbahn employment falling from 222 000 to 176 000 from 1991–93). Nevertheless, Bundesbahn debts rose inexorably – so much so that financial collapse was predicted by 1996.

As well as central services, there are four business divisions in the new company: passenger traffic, freight transport, permanent way and rolling stock. Income from passenger services seems more buoyant than freight revenue. DBKom, the only nationwide telecommunications network outside of DEUTSCHE TELEKOM, is to operate separately. Its facilities will be made available on a commercial basis for use by third parties. A telecoms joint venture with one or more of the many new entrants into this rapidly expanding industry was also envisaged. In mid-1996, it was announced that the partner would be a MANNESMANN-led consortium. See PRIVATISIERUNG.

(EOS)

Deutsche Bank   The Deutsche Bank is the largest German bank with 75 000 employees and a net income of DM2.1 billion in 1995. The Deutsche Bank was founded in Berlin in 1870 and steered into financing international and domestic industrialisation by Georg von Siemens. When he left the executive board in 1900, the bank was the leading financial institution of the German Reich. In the 1920s the Deutsche Bank took over the house banks of both Daimler and Benz and subsequently became the company's largest shareholder. It was deconcentrated into ten regional banks by the Allies after World War II and much of the bank's reconstitution into a single nationwide entity was masterminded by Hermann Josef Abs, who also played a crucial role in the wider post-war economic reconstruction process in the Federal Republic. The headquarters are now in Frankfurt am Main.

A change in direction was signalled in 1989 when the bank acquired Morgan Grenfell in the City of London for £1 billion. In 1995, the Deutsche Bank announced that it was concentrating its entire investment services division on its London base by forming Deutsche Morgan Grenfell. A series of financial disasters and poor corporate results in Germany (DAIMLER-BENZ and Klöckner-Humboldt-Deutz losses) probably hastened the process.

Another signal that the Deutsche Bank intended becoming a key global player was the publication in 1995 of accounts drawn up using International Accounting Standards. See FINANZWESEN.

(EOS)

Deutsche Bundesbank   The German Federal (or central) Bank was established in 1957. It succeeded the *Bank deutscher Länder* which was owned by the central banks of the BUNDESLÄNDER (*Landeszentralbanken*, or LZBs). Its governing council (appointed by the LZBs) elects the presidents of both the council (*Zentralbankrat*) and directorate (*Direktorium*). The *Bundesbank* is owned by the Federal Government, which also appoints the directorate. Members of its directorate have full voting rights along with the presidents of the LZBs. Unification led to the LZBs' governing council representation being reduced to nine members, together with a maximum directorate of eight.

The sole goal of the *Bundesbank* is to safeguard the currency and ensure price stability. It has developed its own monetary policy (*Geldpolitik*) instruments whose use is independent of other policy-makers. The strength of the DM means that the fortnightly meetings of the council are observed closely throughout the world.

The *Bundesbank* has been the victim of its own success. International demand for the DM rivals the demand for domestically produced tradable goods. Short-term capital inflows are attracted by the relatively high rate of return guaranteed by low inflation and a steady revaluation of the DM. This latter process reduces inflationary pressure by lowering import prices. By the same token it undermines the price competitiveness of exports.

The *Bundesbank* model is being adopted by the European Union for monetary union purposes.

See BUNDESREGIERUNG; EUROPAPOLITIK; FINANZWESEN; ZAHLUNGS-BILANZ.

(EOS)

Deutsche Demokratische Republik (DDR)   The German Democratic Republic, or GDR, existed from 1949–90. The foundations of the GDR were laid whilst it constituted the Soviet Zone of occupation (BESATZUNGSZONE) in Germany (1945–49). Under the ideological umbrella of an anti-fascist democratic revolution, the judiciary and police were restructured, large landowners expropriated and a thorough denazification implemented. With the intensification of the Cold War, the Soviet Zone began to draw closer to the Soviet model and the GDR was founded on 7 October 1949.

The early years of the GDR saw a comprehensive restructuring of East German society. The construction of socialism, as proclaimed at the SED's 1952 conference, involved the socialisation of small and medium-sized industrial enterprises, the start of collectivisation in agriculture and crafts, the introduction of new regional administrative units (*Bezirke*) and the tightening of SED control over the mass organisations and all other political parties. The regime's measures aroused much opposition among private farmers, the Churches and the middle classes. Hundreds of thousands emigrated to the West and in June 1953 the workers spearheaded a major revolt against SED rule.

Later in the decade, the SED regime received a boost from the announcement by Khrushchev in July 1955 that German unification would not take place to the detriment of the 'socialist achievements' of the GDR and ULBRICHT proved sufficiently skilful to control the outburst of revisionism after Khruschchev's denunciation of Stalin in 1956. However, the SED's acceleration of agricultural collectivisation and planning distortions precipitated a major economic crisis and fuelled the mass exodus in 1960 and 1961. Another setback was the failure of Khrushchev during the second Berlin crisis of 1958 to 1962 to improve the international standing of the GDR.

After the construction of the Berlin Wall, the SED sought to woo the population by economic reform and by an improvement in living standards. Although there were indications of a GDR state consciousness during the later 1960s, the reform programme had to be abandoned in 1970 and economic centralisation was reimposed.

The early years of the HONECKER era (1971–1989) witnessed several positive developments: higher living standards, a cultural thaw, improvements in housing and international recognition of the GDR in the wake of the 1972 GRUNDLAGENVERTRAG with the Federal Republic. Furthermore, Honecker received much credit in 1983/84 for his insistence on keeping contacts open with the West during the deep freeze in superpower relations. However, the SED responded feebly in the later 1980s to the international crisis of communism, as exemplified by declining growth rates and a widening technological gap with the West. The regime's problems were compounded by the failure to implant the notion of the GDR as a socialist nation and the rise of an alternative political culture.

During 1989 the situation in the GDR developed into a struggle for the survival of SED rule as tens of thousands of East Germans fled across the border after Hungary dismantled the Iron Curtain in September or escaped via the West German embassies in Prague, Budapest and Warsaw. Within the GDR, demonstrations against the SED mushroomed in the autumn of 1989 and new political groups questioned the SED power monopoly openly. The initial demands for a reformed GDR were overwhelmed soon after the fall of the Berlin Wall by a popular movement for the introduction of the D-Mark and unification with the Federal Republic.

See AUFSTAND (1953); BERLINER MAUER; BÜRGERBEWEGUNGEN; KRENZ, EGON; MODROW, HANS; NEUES ÖKONOMISCHES SYSTEM; PLAN-WIRTSCHAFT; SMAD; STALINISMUS; VEREINIGUNG.

(MD)

Deutsche Frage The 'German question' concerns the central role historically played by Germany in the maintenance – or disruption – of peace and stability in Europe. Three inter-related components make up the *Frage*: Germany's power potential; her geo-political position; and third, the domestic make-up of the state. Germany's proven status as an economic giant and her potential to translate this into military power have been and remain a pivotal factor in creating security in Europe. The geo-political aspect of the German question refers to the inherent problems of Germany's *Mittelage*, or central position, in Europe, which means that any change in her foreign policy is of immediate consequence for her numerous neighbours. Linked to this, the domestic character and distribution of power within Germany are of importance since, in the past, problems in the domestic sphere were 'exported' via aggressive foreign policies.

The German question became a wider European concern after the forging of national unity under Bismark in 1871. After World War II and with the onset of the Cold War the question was largely mitigated via national division and USA–Soviet Union preponderance in international relations.

The end of the Cold War and national unification in 1990 brought about renewed topicality to the German question. Today, as well as the traditional concerns over German power and intentions in East and Central Europe, the German question is closely bound up with questions over Germany's commitment to European integration and the impact of national unification upon German society and political culture.

(KL)

Deutsche Telekom (DT)   Deutsche Telekom was founded in 1989, having previously been one of the three services (postal, postal banking and telephone) of the Post Office (*Deutsche Bundespost*), as a first step in a privatisation process. It is still a public enterprise with nearly 220 000 employees and a turnover of DM66 billion in 1995. On 1 January of that year it was converted into a plc. Shares have been quoted on the stock market since November 1996 but the government is legally bound to keep a stake of at least 51 per cent for the next five years.

Deutsche Telekom has four main client groups: private clients (34 million), business clients (1.7 million), mobile telephone clients (3.5 million) and the biggest corporate clients (200) to whom DT offers seamless global services. At present the company is the most successful information technology network operator world-wide. It provides the biggest on-line service in Germany, T-Online, a wholly owned subsidiary of DT.

DT aims to be a global player and therefore has subsidiaries internationally, holds shares in other telecoms companies (Hungary and Indonesia, a number of states of the Russian Federation, and the Czech Republic), has strategic alliances (e.g. with the US-Carrier Sprint Corp.) and joint ventures. It is faced by increasingly tough competition with the electricity corporates RWE, VEBA, VIAG and VEW, as well as SIEMENS, MANNESMANN and a number of other companies which have sought to develop telecoms operations.

DT is also one of the partners in two European satellite channels and has a cooperation agreement with Intel and Microsoft in multimedia technology. Together with other major players in the media industry DT founded a media operating company in 1995 (MMBG) in order to standardise the decoding system for digital TV.

Competitiveness will further depend on the company shedding around 50 000 employees over the next few years. The management hopes that this will mainly be achieved by natural wastage.

See RUNDFUNK UND FERNSEHEN.

(RW)

Deutscher Städte- und Gemeindebund   The *Deutscher Städte- und Gemeindebund* is, alongside the *Deutscher Städtetag* and the *Deutscher Landkreistag*, one of the three local government associations in the Federal Republic. The *Deutscher Städtetag* represents the interests of towns in relation to those federal and BUNDESLÄNDER authorities. Similarly, the *Deutscher Landkreistag* represents the interests of the *Landkreise*, or districts (the administrative level between the *Bundesländer* and local councils, or *Gemeinden*.) The *Deutscher Städte- und Gemeindebund* acts as the umbrella organisation for these two associations, representing its members' interests in relation to legal and administrative bodies, providing members with advice and promoting the exchange of information and experience.

The membership of the *Deutscher Städte- und Gemeindebund* currently covers over 14 500 towns and districts in the Federal Republic.

See KOMMUNALE SELBSTVERWALTUNG.

(SRF)

Deutsches Reich   The German Empire was established in 1871, following a series of wars conducted by Prussia from 1866–71, which were directed at the establishment of a unified German state. The Empire united 25 separate German states in a monarchical federation. The first Emperor was William, the King of Prussia, and the first Chancellor was Otto von Bismarck. Given the size of the Prussian state, which extended from the eastern Baltic to the Rhineland, the Empire was (and was designed to be) Prussian-dominated. While allowing free elections by universal male suffrage to the REICHSTAG, the Empire's constitution did not equate to democratic government. The *Reichstag* had few powers, and the main source of political authority shifted between the Chancellor and the Emperor, together with the monarchs and other heads of state of the federation, whose governments formed the more significant legislative institution, the Imperial BUNDESRAT. Domestically, significant policies were the 'Cultural Struggle' (*Kulturkampf*) against the Catholics (or more precisely papal influence) in the 1870s, and a rather more protracted attempt to contain the influence of the growing labour movement and the SPD. The latter was reflected in a 'carrot and stick' strategy combining repression with incentives for conciliation in the form of the most extensive social welfare legislation of the time. The era of the Empire was also significant for the rapid industrialisation of Germany, which had come at least to match Great Britain as an industrial power by World War I.

In foreign policy, key features were the acquisition of an overseas empire in Africa and the Pacific, and a rapid expansion of the German armaments programme, including the building of a naval fleet capable of rivalling that of the major naval power of the time, Great Britain. The arms drive, together with an aggressive alliance-building strategy in eastern Europe contributed to the deterioration of international relations and to the slide into war in 1914. Germany's defeat four years later at the hands of an alliance whose main partners were Britain, France, Russia (until the revolution in 1917) and the USA (from 1917), led to the collapse of the Empire and the establishment of the Weimar Republic.

See FÖDERALISMUS; PREUßEN; WEIMARER REPUBLIK.

(CJ)

Deutsches Rotes Kreuz (DRK)   The German section of the international Red Cross follows the principles of the international organisation founded in 1863 by Henri Dunant. These are for a humane, non-partisan, independent, voluntary and united movement to provide medical support for war victims, and victims of other catastrophes. At the end of 1992 membership of the organisation stood at 4.6 million.

In Germany, the DRK focuses on ambulance services, caring for the sick, the old and the disabled, providing help to young people, help for asylum seekers and AUSSIEDLER (settlers from former German territories). It is part of the *Bundesarbeitsgemeinschaft der Freien Wohlfahrtspflege* (the Federal Association of Welfare Groups).

The DRK was strongly involved in providing medical support and humanitarian aid during the war in former Yugoslavia.

See ARBEITERWOHLFAHRT; EVANGELISCHE KIRCHE DEUTSCHLANDS.

(SRF)

Deutschlandvertrag   The German Treaty came into force on 5 May 1955 and regulated the relationship between the Federal Republic, the United States, Britain and France, having been agreed on 26 May 1952.

The Treaty was also known as the Relations Convention or the Bonn Convention. It was necessary because the Allies had not signed a peace treaty with Germany and retained a number of residual powers in the Federal Republic's affairs. The *Deutschlandvertrag* basically granted the Federal Republic full jurisdiction over its own internal and foreign affairs.

The 'Two-plus-Four Treaty' signed on 12 September 1990 superseded the *Deutschlandvertrag*, restoring full sovereignty to the united Federal Republic.

See AUßENPOLITIK; GRUNDLAGENVERTRAG; ZWEI-PLUS-VIER-VERTRAG.

(NM)

DG Bank (Deutsche Genossenschaftsbank)   The DG Bank occupies a place among the top ten banks in Germany, with 11 300 employees and profits of DM176 million in 1995. Its origin can be traced back to the formation in Berlin of the Preussische Central-Genossenschafts-Kasse in 1895 – four decades after the founding of the German co-operative banking movement. The basic purpose of this movement was to provide, at a time of rapid industrialisation, the small savers in both the agricultural and crafts (or urban) sectors of the economy with modest loans at reasonable cost.

The former Prussian bank was renamed Deutsche Genossenschaftskasse when it was re-established in Frankfurt am Main in 1949.

It was only in the early 1970s that the agricultural and urban branches of the movement were amalgamated. The local branches owned the regional banks, which in turn owned the national bank. In the 1980s the DG Bank took over a number of regional banks, and, after unification, re-assumed the functions of central bank for the East German co-operative banks.

Maintaining close links with members but achieving the economies of scale of a large banking institution remains a seemingly intractable problem for the movement. However, with nearly 2 600 local co-operatives, 20 000 branches and over 13 million members, the movement will clearly remain a considerable force in German banking and finance.

See FINANZWESEN.

(EOS)

Dolchstoßlegende   See VERSAILLER FRIEDENSVERTRAG; WEIMARER REPUBLIK.

Dresdner Bank   The Dresdner Bank is the second largest bank in Germany with 47 000 employees and a net income of DM1.2 billion in 1995. Today it still retains the name of the city in which it was founded, along with house colours (green and white), which are the same as the flag of the former Kingdom of Saxony. It moved headquarters to Berlin in 1884 and then to Frankfurt am Main after the war. Like the DEUTSCHE BANK and COMMERZBANK, it re-emerged from a deconcentrated organisation to become a single entity in 1957.

Also like the Deutsche Bank it purchased a London merchant bank (Kleinwort Benson) for £1 billion in 1995. Although the bank has not yet felt it appropriate to adopt the International Accounting Standards it has taken a further step towards greater transparency in the form of a higher level of disclosure.

Like the other leading German banks, the Dresdner started to offer comprehensive financial services (*Allfinanz*) from the late 1980s, incorporating insurance products into its range of services. The ALLIANZ has a 22 per cent holding of the Dresdner's capital.

See FINANZWESEN.

(EOS)

Drittes Reich   The Third Reich was the National Socialist dictatorship established under the leadership of Adolf HITLER in 1933, which lasted until the German defeat in World War II in 1945. The name 'Third Reich' was to imply a direct succession from the Empire of Charlemagne through Bismarck's Empire of 1871 to the 'Empire' of 1933. It was established on the basis of a series of decrees which dismantled the constitution of the Weimar Republic in 1933, the most important of which was the 'Enabling

Law' (ERMÄCHTIGUNGSGESETZ). These decrees abolished the democratic institutions of the Weimar state, together with all political parties other than the National Socialist Party (NSDAP). Independent organisations like trade unions and other interest groups were also either abolished, or nazified in a process of *'Gleichschaltung'* ('synchronisation'). All opposition was suppressed, including that within the National Socialist movement in the ranks of the paramilitary SA. Only very limited and sporadic resistance (WIDERSTAND) to the dictatorship was offered down to its collapse in 1945. The negligible level and effect of resistance were due in part to the scope and deterrent brutality of the Nazi security services, in particular the GESTAPO. It also reflected the fact that most Germans welcomed the regime, not least for its apparent success in stimulating economic recovery after the Great Depression and for restoring German prestige in foreign affairs.

The political organisation of the Third Reich was quite unique. It rested partly on the peculiar form of authority exercised by the *Führer* (supreme leader), Hitler. This combined a charismatic style of inspirational leadership with a relative detachment from day-to-day decision-making (except in foreign policy). Day-to-day decisions were taken by a wide and competing range of prominent individual Nazis such as Hermann Göring and Heinrich Himmler, state bureaucracies inherited from the Weimar Republic, and a new NSDAP bureaucracy with largely overlapping remits. No single body had the capacity to co-ordinate these various policy-making organs. The result was an often chaotic decision-making process in which different institutions competed – in part by developing ever more radical policies – to interpret and implement the *Führer's* will. A key example was in economic management which, despite radical improvement in the general economic situation, was not effectively harnessed to the needs of an aggressive foreign policy. A further example was the regime's anti-Jewish policy. Inspired by National Socialism's ideology of racial anti-semitism (ANTISEMITISMUS), anti-Jewish policy evolved through a series of ever more radical phases without any evidence of a clear direction and ultimate purpose. Anti-Jewish policy nevertheless remains the defining feature of the Nazi dictatorship, given the unprecedented barbarity and cynicism with which some 6 million European Jews were murdered.

Only in the field of foreign policy was there clear evidence of purposeful policy planning focused on the aim of securing 'living space' (*'Lebensraum'*) for the German racial community (*Volksgemeinschaft*) in Eastern Europe Here, clear evidence of Hitler's guiding and co-ordinating hand exists, from the early days of throwing off the restrictions imposed by the Versailles Peace Treaty (rearmament, the end of the occupation of the Rhineland, the incorporation of Austria and the Czech Sudetenland into the Reich), through the securing of the western front in campaigns in western Europe in 1940, to the near-successful eastern front campaign against the Soviet Union in 1941–42. Even in defeat, with the refusal to surrender in 1945 although most of German territory had been conquered, Hitler's leadership was clear.

The legacy of the Third Reich was an immense one, leading, unlike at the end of World War I, to the complete occupation of Germany, and then to its division. Both post-war German states were profoundly influenced by the National Socialist experience, the GDR in the official ideology of anti-fascism and the Federal Republic in the myriad ways in which its Constitution, the GRUNDGESETZ, was explicitly constructed in order to prevent both the abuse of state power characteristic of the Third Reich and the weaknesses of democratic government in the Weimar years which had made the Third Reich possible.

Even today the legacy of the Third Reich remains alive in the continuing impact of historical memory and the problem of coming to terms with the past (VERGANGENHEITSBEWÄLTIGUNG) have on politics and society in the present.

See BESATZUNG; HISTORIKERSTREIT; HOLOCAUST; KONZENTRATIONS-LAGER; NÜRNBERGER GESETZE; REICHSKRISTALLNACHT; VERSAILLER FRIED-ENSVERTRAG.

(CJ)

DSU (Deutsche Soziale Union) The German Social Union was one of the new political parties formed in the GDR after the fall of the Berlin Wall. Founded in Leipzig in January 1990, it brought together a variety of small liberal, conservative and Christian–social groups who articulated the ecological and socio-economic grievances of East Germans in SACHSEN and THÜRINGEN. The DSU and its first chairman, the Leipzig pastor Hans-Wilhelm Ebeling, were heavily supported by the Bavarian CSU and the party soon emerged as a proponent of rapid unification and a determined adversary of any kind of socialism. A partner in the ALLIANZ FÜR DEUTSCHLAND, it captured 63 per cent of the vote in March 1990. Thereafter, disagreements among its leaders and fierce disputes over its political orientation cost it most of its electoral support. In the December 1990 *Bundestag* election, it managed a mere 0.9 per cent of the East German vote.

(MD)

Duales System The dual system of German apprenticeships is unique in that it combines practical training with theoretical study. Apprentices work for three days a week in their training company and attend school *(Berufsschule)* for two days.

There are 377 recognised trades in which apprentices can train. The majority of training places are offered by medium-sized businesses. At the workplace a master craftsman is responsible for the training of the apprentice. In school, apprentices study core subjects such as mathematics and German as well as subjects related to their specific field of training. The certificate at the end of the three-year training period is the *Gesellenbrief.*

It enables the successful apprentice to apply for qualified jobs or go on to study for a master craftsman certificate or a higher school leaving certificate.

There is a severe shortage of training places compared to the number of school leavers with a leaving certificate. Students leaving school without a leaving certificate have only a poor chance of finding work or qualifying further.

See MITTELSTAND; VOLKSHOCHSCHULE.

(AW)

DVU (Deutsche Volksunion)   The German People's Union is a party of the far Right. Formed in 1971, the party is led by Gerhard Frey, a publisher who made his fortune with the xenophobic newspaper the *Deutsche National Zeitung*. Of all the right-wing parties, the DVU thus has by far the greatest financial resources. In 1987, Frey relaunched the party as an electoral alliance with the NPD, and achieved representation in the BREMEN election of 1987. The DVU was represented there between 1987 and 1995, and also in SCHLESWIG-HOLSTEIN between 1992 and 1996.

Apart from isolated successes mentioned above, election results have been so poor for the DVU that it decided not to contest a number of recent elections. The DVU has, moreover, not been able to supplant the REPUBLIKANER as the main party on the far Right. An attempt by Frey in 1994 to establish an alliance was largely unsuccessful.

As with other right-wing parties, the DVU has been losing members and the authorities estimate its current membership at around 20 000. The DVU relaunched its campaigning in 1995, targeting Bremen in particular, where the party has enjoyed its highest levels of support. However, its meagre result of 2.5 per cent of the vote in the 1995 Bremen election is indicative of its overall decline.

See AUSLÄNDERFEINDLICHKEIT.

(SG)

E

Einigungsvertrag   The Treaty on Unification of 31 August 1990 was, along-side the Treaty on Monetary, Economic and Social Union of 18 May 1990 and the 'Two-plus-Four' Treaty of 12 September 1990, one of the major staging posts on the road to German unification.

The Treaty on Unification came into force on 3 October 1990 with the accession of the five NEUE BUNDESLÄNDER to the Federal Republic. The various chapters of the treaty dealt successively with: immediate changes to the GRUNDGESETZ to facilitate unification; the requirement to consider whether other constitutional changes might be necessary in the light of unification; the adoption of the (West) German statute book in the East; the co-ordination of the international treaty obligations of the Federal Republic and the GDR; public administration; public assets and debts; a range of other issues of legal co-ordination in economic, social and environmental policy; and a number of transitional regulations pending the coming into force of the treaty. The net effect was to extend the constitutional and legal framework of the Federal Republic to the territory of the GDR.

This mechanism of legal unification dealt swiftly and neatly with what would otherwise have been a long and tortuous process of legal adaptation. It did, however, strengthen the perception of many Easterners that they had been 'annexed' by West Germany, contributing to a new sense of post-unification division between OSSIS and WESSIS. There was also a considerable problem in turning legal provisions into practice given the lack of qualified civil servants and administrators in the East. While the latter problem is no longer as significant, the indirect legacy of the Treaty of Unification in contributing to the 'wall in the head' between *Ossis* and *Wessis* remains strong.

See MAUER IM KOPF; VEREINIGUNG; VERFASSUNGSÄNDERUNG; WIRT-SCHAFTS-, WÄHRUNGS- UND SOZIALUNION; ZWEI-PLUS-VIER-VERTRAG.

(CJ)

Einwohnermeldeamt   The *Einwohnermeldeamt* is a local authority office where everyone, Germans as well as foreigners, have to carry out their

Meldepflicht, the duty of registering their address as soon as they take up residence.

Several documents are needed for registration, including passport, visa if necessary for entry to the Federal Republic, and proof of address (often a rental contract or MIETVERTRAG). It is important to check opening times and which documents are required before going to register.

(RW)

Engholm, Björn   Björn Engholm is a former Minister-President of Schleswig-Holstein, and was leader of the SPD from 1991 to 1993. Born on 9 November 1939 in Lübeck, Björn Engholm rose swiftly through the local SPD hierarchy in his home *Bundesland* of SCHLESWIG-HOLSTEIN. He was a member of the BUNDESTAG from 1969 to 1982 and Minister for Training (*Bundesbildungsminister*) in the Social-Liberal coalition from 1981 to 1982. He entered the Schleswig-Holstein *Landtag* in 1983 and became leader of the SPD *Fraktion* in 1988. He was elected Minister-President in the same year, overturning a long-standing CDU majority following the sudden collapse of CDU support amid a scandal involving alleged electoral irregularities at the previous *Landtag* election (the so-called 'Barschel-Affair').

Following Oskar LAFONTAINE's failure to unseat Helmut KOHL in the 1990 *Bundestag* elections, Engholm became SPD leader and provisional SPD candidate for Chancellor in 1991. However, following revelations that he had lied over aspects of the 'Barschel Affair' in Schleswig-Holstein, Engholm stood down from his post and was replaced by Rudolf SCHARPING.

Despite his meteoric rise to power, the whiff of scandal that surrounds him means that Engholm's career is now effectively at an end. He is no longer a major figure within the SPD.

(CL)

Entartete Kunst   'Degenerate art' was a term used by the Nazi regime to condemn all art which was not, according to their ideology, 'healthy' and '*völkisch*' (racially pure). Artists who did not produce works according to the (classicist) Nazi ideal were forbidden to work, appear in exhibitions or publish. They were persecuted and their work which had already been published was destroyed. They included painters (e.g. Beckmann, Kokoschka) as well as writers (e.g. Thomas Mann), musicians and composers (e.g. Schönberg). Many emigrated, partly to countries where the Nazi regime would later spread, partly to the USSR, the USA and Switzerland. In 1937 the regime hosted an exhibition called *Entartete Kunst* in München which then toured other German cities. During the same year Hitler opened the *Haus der Deutschen Kunst* (Museum of German Art) and hosted the *Große Deutsche Kunstausstellung* (Great German Art Exhibition), where officially sanctioned artists could exhibit their works.

Whereas the formerly despised works of *Entartete Kunst* which survived the Nazis are now exhibited world-wide, the products of the official art of the Third Reich are stored in the cellars of the *Haus der Kunst* in Munich. In 1992 the *Altes Museum* in Berlin showed the 1937 exhibition in order to remind people that repression extended even into art in the Third Reich. The exhibition *Kunst und Macht im Europa der Diktatoren 1930 bis 1945* hosted by the Deutsches Historisches Museum in Berlin in 1996 took a more European view of the role art had played in the dictatorial regimes of the time.

See BAUHAUS; DER BLAUE REITER; NATIONALSOZIALISMUS.

(RW)

Entnazifizierung Denazification was one of the major principles set out at the Potsdam Conference of 1945 to guide the occupation of Germany by the victorious wartime Allies, the USA, the Soviet Union, Great Britain and France.

Denazification policies comprised the dissolution of the National Socialist Party and all its related organisations and the revocation of all laws establishing the Nazi regime and its policies of racial, religious and political discrimination. In addition, all Nazi party members who had played an active role in the Third Reich were to be removed from any public offices they held, while senior members and officials were to be imprisoned and war criminals brought to trial.

While the abolition of Nazi organisations and laws was relatively straightforward, the calling to account of active participants in the regime was much more difficult to implement. On the one hand, around one-fifth of Germany's population had been members of Nazi organisations; to have removed all of these from public life would have paralysed public administration. On the other, the growing divergences of approach to occupation policies between the Western Allies and the Soviet Union (along with significant differences of emphasis even among the Western Allies) meant that a standard approach to implementing denazification was impossible. In fact the only area in which a common policy was attempted was in the prosecution of war criminals in the Nuremberg Trials (*Nürnberger Prozeß*), in which eleven Nazi leaders, including Hermann Göring, were condemned to death, seven others, including Rudolf Hess and Albert Speer, imprisoned, and three acquitted. Otherwise, denazification policies were inconsistently applied, with the Soviet Union probably the most scrupulous in removing Nazis from public life, but with all the Allies prepared to make unscrupulous exceptions wherever use could be made of individuals' expertise in public administration or scientific knowledge or of their economic clout.

See BESATZUNG.

(CJ)

Entspannung *Entspannung* is used to describe an easing of tension, or *détente*, in relations between states which have otherwise been hostile. The term is typically used to refer to the period in the late 1960s when tensions between the two superpowers, the USA and the Soviet Union, were reduced. The USA sought to 'de-escalate' the Cold War and move towards 'peaceful co-existence' with the Soviet Union in the late 1960s. Its clearest manifestations were the pursuit of arms control through until the late 1970s and the Federal Republic's new OSTPOLITIK of the early 1970s.

The Federal Republic had a pivotal role to play in the *Entspannung* process being the border between East and West. The hardline policy established by ADENAUER towards the GDR and the Soviet bloc was gradually modified during the 1960s as the SPD in particular committed itself to peaceful co-existence with the GDR. An improvement of relations between the two parts of Germany, which included easing of travel restrictions, trade and cultural exchanges was proposed during the CDU/CSU–SPD Grand Coalition of 1966 to 1969. However, the GDR's demand that the Federal Republic formally recognise it acted as a barrier to progress. The advent of an SPD–FDP government in 1969 led to the concept of *Entspannung* being a central part of governmental thinking, feeding in centrally to the *Ostpolitik* pursued by Chancellor Willy BRANDT.

See BERLINABKOMMEN; GROßE KOALITION; GRUNDLAGENVERTRAG; KALTER KRIEG; SOZIALLIBERALE KOALITION.

(NM)

Entwicklungspolitik   The political, economic and social Development Policy of the Federal Government is a component of Germany's wider foreign policy directed towards the countries of the Third World.

As a consequence of Germany's very brief phase as a colonial power (1894–1918), and its preoccupation with the East–West tensions during the Cold War, relations with the developing world have been of minimal importance in German foreign policy. A further factor is the relative financial insignificance for Germany of its economic relations with most developing countries.

In 1991 the Federal Government outlined new criteria to guide the content and direction of development co-operation. These criteria included the observance of human rights, the existence of a democratic government, and the reduction of high arms expenditure by recipients of aid.

There are problems (both financial and political) for the Federal Government as it attempts to balance Germany's interest in encouraging the political, economic and social transformation in Central and Eastern Europe and the aspiration to maintain an acceptable level of commitment to its broader development policy.

See AUßENPOLITIK.

(PH)

Erhard, Ludwig   See WIRTSCHAFTSWUNDER.

Ermächtigungsgesetz   The 'Enabling Law' of 23 March 1933 was the most important legal staging post in the transformation of the Weimar Republic into the Third Reich, awarding dictatorial powers to Chancellor Adolf HITLER.

Adolf Hitler's appointment as Chancellor in January 1933 was entirely legitimate under the terms and conventions of the Weimar constitution. His National Socialist Party (NSDAP) was by far the largest party represented in the REICHSTAG though it did not have an absolute majority. It was also committed to the abolition of the democratic constitution. A first step followed the *Reichstag* fire of 27 February 1933. This was portrayed as an attempt at a communist coup and led to the issuing of a presidential decree 'for the Protection of the People and the State' which removed constitutional rights against arbitrary arrest and to free speech. An election held on 5 March 1933 under conditions of extreme political intimidation delivered a *Reichstag* majority for the NSDAP and its nationalist allies, and preparations for the Enabling Law, which required a two-thirds majority in the *Reichstag*, commenced. The KPD was subsequently banned, making the task easier.

The Enabling Bill presented to the *Reichstag* on 23 March proposed giving Hitler's government unrestricted decree-making power for a five-year period. Only the SPD spoke and voted against it. After the Enabling Law was thus passed, the last vestiges of democratic government and freedoms were steadily abolished, establishing the dictatorial state which led Germany into World War II and the HOLOCAUST.

See DRITTES REICH; NATIONALSOZIALISMUS; WEIMARER REPUBLIC.

(CJ)

Erziehungsgeld/Erziehungsurlaub See FAMILIENPOLITIK; VORSCHULISCHE ERZIEHUNG.

Europahaus 'European Houses' collectively form an International Federation founded in 1962 under the auspices of the European Council. By 1992 the Federation had 100 centres spread all over the European Union. The aim of the *Europahäuser* is to provide Euro-political educational facilities in three areas: European education, education of the young generation and job-orientated education. Seminars and conferences have an international orientation and cover EU-related topics as diverse as the problems faced by the mentally handicapped or the older generation, Franco-German exchange, the social dimension of the EU and German unification.

See POLITISCHE BILDUNG.

(AW)

Europapolitik European policy refers to the Federal Republic's involvement in, and policies for, European integration. The Federal Republic is a founder member of the institutions of European integration, now brought together under the single heading of the European Union. It has typically had a positive commitment to closer European integration rooted in a number of factors: the desire for international rehabilitation through constructive international co-operation after World War II; the related concern to reassure its neighbours by tying itself into strong multilateral structures of policy-making; the strategic importance of West European integration to a divided country in the Cold War era; and the economic benefits of market integration to a traditionally export-oriented economy.

This positive commitment was strongly reaffirmed in the course of German unification under the leadership of Chancellor Helmut KOHL. Kohl was concerned in particular to reassure Germany's neighbours that unification would not change the Federal Republic's commitment to integration and co-operation and lead to an overt assertion of German power in European affairs. Kohl's Federal Government has accordingly committed strong German support to the establishment of European Economic and Monetary Union, as foreseen by the Maastricht Treaty of 1993, and to the speedy enlargement of the European Union to incorporate the new democracies to Germany's east, above all Poland, the Czech Republic and Hungary.

A number of obstacles, however, have emerged in achieving these aims. First, the wider atmosphere in the European Union has, in particular in Britain, become sceptical of closer European integration. Second, public opinion in Germany is suspicious of Economic and Monetary Union and enlargement. And third, a number of other domestic political institutions can impose constraints on the development of European policy, including the BUNDESRAT and BUNDESTAG, which won new European policy powers in constitutional changes passed in 1992, and the DEUTSCHE BUNDESBANK, which is reluctant to see the establishment of a common European Union currency in Economic and Monetary Union.

Kohl, however, remains committed to his vision of closer European integration and seems likely to continue to throw his considerable political weight as the European Union's longest-serving head of government behind that vision.

See VERFASSUNGSÄNDERUNG; WIRTSCHAFTS- UND WÄHRUNGSUNION.

(CJ)

Evangelische Kirche Deutschlands (EKD) The German Protestant Church is, alongside the Catholic Church, one of the two main Churches in Germany. Today, both have a roughly equal number of members but Protestants are predominant in the North and East of Germany, and in the South in the area around Nürnberg and München.

When the reformers Luther, Zwingli and Calvin were preaching in the early sixteenth century, they had a universal religious revival in mind. Instead, the church became divided, with the *Evangelische Kirche* splitting from the Catholic Church.

In Prussia and other mainly Protestant areas of what was to become the German Reich after 1871, the Protestant Church developed into a State church, administered and regulated by the monarch and later by the government of the day. In the Third Reich it split into the regime-supporting *Deutsche Christen* (German Christians) and the *Bekennende Kirche* (Confessing Church) which called for opposition against Hitler.

The EKD is organised into 24 *Landeskirchen*. These are represented in the synod (legislature) and the *Kirchenkonferenz* (Churches Conference) which in turn elect the executive, the *Rat* (Council) of the EKD. In the 1990s the EKD has just under 30 million members of whom around 5 per cent attend church. Its annual income from the *Kirchensteuer* (tax for the churches, deducted at source) and collections is around DM7.5 billion, with the majority coming from the old *Bundesländer*.

The EKD is also active in social affairs through its *Diakonisches Werk* (institutions caring for the elderly, the sick, the disabled, children, and other marginal groups of society) and *Brot für die Welt* ('Bread for the World', a fund-raising support organisation for projects in developing countries). It also maintains over 100 schools and a number of institutions of higher education.

The main problems the EKD – like its Catholic counterpart – faces today are providing answers to contemporary ethical questions, securing the interest of the young generation, and achieving progress in the dialogue between the Churches.

See KATHOLISCHE KIRCHE.

(RW)

F

Fachhochschule (FH)   These specialist colleges offer applied courses with direct relevance to professional careers such as architecture, electronics, engineering, economics etc. Successful students receive a *Diplom (FH)*, normally at the end of a four-year course.

Students applying for a place at a *Fachhochschule* need the *Abitur* or *Fachabitur*. Their studies are accompanied by intensive work placements, for many one of the main attractions of *Fachhochschule* study. Career prospects at the end of a course are often better than for graduates with a university degree.

Out of a total student population of 1.85 million students in 1995/96, around 398 000 were at a *Fachhochschule*.

See HOCHSCHULE; STUDIENABSCHLÜSSE; WEITERFÜHRENDE SCHULEN. (AW)

Familienpolitik   Family policy refers to the branch of social policy designed to ensure that the decision to have a family does not bring with it material disadvantages in comparison to those who do not take such a decision. This approach reflects the viewpoint that a traditional family structure and environment have benefits for parents and child, and for society more generally.

A large number of policy measures fall under the heading of family policy. The following are the most important. *Mutterschutz* (mother's protection) forbids pregnant women certain types of work which might be dangerous to the woman and her unborn child, and provides for periods off work, with full pay, both before (six weeks) and after (at least eight weeks) giving birth.

Erziehungsgeld (infant care payments) is available (and varies according to income levels) for up to two years after birth. In addition, *Erziehungsurlaub* (time off work for infant care) can be taken by a parent for up to three years after birth, with full rights to return to the previous job after the time-off period. *Kindergeld* (child benefit) is paid to all parents to help with the costs of child-raising, normally up to the child's 17th birthday. Payments vary according to the number of children and (beyond a flat-rate payment for the first child) income levels. A *Kinderfreibetrag* (child tax allowance) reduces parents' tax payments by a specific amount (currently DM4 104) per child per year, normally up to the child's 19th birthday. Low-income parents who do not benefit from the tax allowance receive a supplement to child benefit (*Kindergeldzuschlag*). Finally, in the field of housing policy the system of housing benefit provides an important means of financial support, especially for low-income parents with large families.

With the obvious exception of *Mutterschutz*, all the above are equally open to either a male or a female parent in a family, whether married or not. This commitment to equal entitlements has brought substantial change for East Germans, since entitlements were in part restricted to women only in the GDR.

Additional levels of support are frequently available for single parents, the number of whom has risen substantially to currently more than 2 million.

See FRAUENPOLITIK; GLEICHBERECHTIGUNG; SOZIALPOLITIK; WONUNGS-POLITIK.

(CJ)

FDP (Freie Demokratische Partei)   The Free Democratic Party was founded in 1948 as a fusion of centre–left, social liberal and centre–right, economic liberal traditions. Its electorate is based mainly in the self-employed middle classes and the small business sector. From 1961–83, when only three parties were represented in the BUNDESTAG, the FDP enjoyed a 'kingmaker' function, in which its support was typically needed by either of the two larger parties (CDU/CSU or SPD to form a majority government. It was thus able to form coalitions with both the CDU/CSU (1961–66, 1982 onwards) and with the SPD (1969–82), and was only excluded from government during the period of Grand Coalition from 1966–69.

Although the emergence of the GRÜNE has undermined the 'kingmaker' function of the FDP, it was able to maintain its position through the stature and popularity of Hans-Dietrich GENSCHER, Federal Foreign Minister and leading FDP politician from 1974–92. His role during the German reunification process reaped handsome rewards at the 1990 federal election, with the FDP scoring especially strongly in the new LÄNDER. However, the passing of the torch to a new generation, which began with Genscher's retirement in 1992, heralded a turn in the party's fortunes. The new leader, Klaus KINKEL lacked the charisma of his predecessor. Moreover, the gradual move to the centre by the CDU/CSU and SPD meant that the FDP has lost its distinct liberal profile and is being seen increasingly as an appendage to the CDU/CSU.

Between late 1993 and mid-1996, the FDP failed to pass the 5 per cent hurdle in 12 of 16 LANDTAG elections. Moreover, it only just managed to be returned to the BUNDESTAG in 1994. Although it recovered in

Landtag elections in 1996, its long-term problems of finding a stable electorate remain. Its weakness has put a great strain on the federal coalition, as well as accentuating the internal differences between the two traditional wings of the party.

Unless the FDP's current leader, Wolfgang Gerhardt, manages to build on recent electoral successes, the party's future seems bleak.

See FÜNFPROZENTKLAUSEL; GROßE KOALITION.

(SG)

Fernuniversität   The *Fernuniversität* (in Hagen) is an open university where study for university degrees is conducted by correspondence, or 'distance learning'. It was founded in the 1970s as a joint initiative of around 50 HOCHSCHULEN and had around 35 000 students in 1992/93.

Experience has shown that although the *Fernuniversität* caters well for those who are unable to study at a conventional university, students lack the opportunity to exchange ideas and can feel isolated. As a result, centres for distance learning (*Zentren für Fernstudien und universitäre Weiterbildung*) have been founded across the Federal Republic, where students can meet. Intensive courses and final exams are also held at these centres.

Course materials play a key role in enabling students to complete their course successfully. These are produced by the Ministries of Culture (*Kultusministerien*) of the BUNDESLÄNDER (which collectively act as the supervisory body for distance learning), along with the *Deutsches Institut für Fernstudien (DIFF)* in Tübingen, the *Bundesinstitut für Berufsbildungsforschung* in Berlin and the *Zentralstelle für Fernunterricht der Länder* in Köln.

See HOCHSCHULE; STUDIENABSCHLÜSSE; UNIVERSITÄT.

(AW)

Feste und Feiern   Festivals and holidays in Germany can be of two types: national or religious. National holidays commemorate certain historical events of national importance and help to promote a sense of national identity. In Germany these holidays are celebrated each year on the same date. 1 May is Labour Day and was first celebrated in 1889 as a result of the pressure by the trade unions and the SPD for recognition of the role and aims of the working class in society. In the GDR, as elsewhere in the communist bloc, it was the most important – and typically highly militarised – celebration of the existence and strength of the communist system. 1 May is also celebrated as a more traditional 'Mayday' in some areas. On 20 July the Germans commemorate the unsuccessful attempt by Count von Stauffenberg and others in 1944 to end the Third Reich and the war by killing Hitler. All those involved in the plot (along with many others not involved) were executed as a consequence. This day is a regular working day. 3 October is the *Tag der Einheit* (Day of Unity), commemorating the accession of the GDR to the Federal Republic on 3 October 1990. It is celebrated by a day off work and commemorative festivities around the country.

Religious holidays reflect the freedom of religious expression laid down in the GRUNDGESETZ. All the major (Christian) holy days are holidays, including Christmas, Easter and Pentecost (the ascension of the Holy Spirit). Other religious festivals may be celebrated as holidays, depending on traditions in particular *Bundesländer*. *Fastnacht* or *Karneval* is celebrated just before the beginning of Lent, 40 days before Easter. The strongest traditions are in predominantly Catholic areas (notably the Rhineland) where fancy dress is worn. With carnival processions (in major cities as well as towns and villages), celebrations reach their climax.

(AW)

Finanzausgleich Financial equalisation is a system of apportioning tax revenues between the federal level (BUND) and BUNDESLÄNDER to ensure that each has sufficient resources to fulfil its constitutional functions and thereby maintain a uniformity of living standards across the Federal Republic.

Financial equalisation was placed on a constitutional and statutory basis in the late 1960s. Vertical equalisation governs the respective shares in the total tax revenues allocated to the federal level and the *Bundesländer* (and below the latter, the local authorities). Horizontal equalisation seeks to ensure a fair distribution of tax revenue per head of population between *Bundesländer* with higher and lower tax revenues.

The new *Bundesländer* were only incorporated into the equalisation system in 1995. In the interim period, a temporary mechanism, the German Unity Fund (FONDS 'DEUTSCHE EINHEIT'), which was mainly funded by the federal level), provided them with necessary funds for the fulfilment of their constitutional responsibilities.

The horizontal equalisation formula is designed to ensure that each *Bundesland* receives a minimum of 95 per cent of the average tax revenues per head in all of the *Bundesländer* and determines whether any individual *Bundesland* is a net contributor or a net recipient of financial equalisation. The methods used in horizontal equalisation have been subject to criticism over the years by both contributor and recipient *Bundesländer*.

BREMEN, the SAARLAND and the five NEUE BUNDESLÄNDER will be net recipients for the forseeable future. BERLIN is another city state whose public finances are in perilous condition.

See HAUSHALTSPOLITIK; NEUE BUNDESLÄNDER.

(EOS)

Finanzwesen The financial system comprises the markets in which personal, corporate and government financial business is conducted through intermediaries. Insurance products are also marketed within the system.

In Germany, private-sector banks account for only 26 per cent of banking business, public-sector banks (*Sparkassen*) have a 36 per cent share and co-operative banks have 15 per cent. Specialised banks account for the remaining 23 per cent.

Public-sector banks consist of over 700 local savings banks which rely on their 11 centralised institutions for central support services (*Landesbanken*). Similarly, the 2 600 urban and agricultural co-operative banks (*Volks- und Raiffeisenbanken*) now largely rely on their national institution, the DG BANK for such services.

The stock exchange in Frankfurt am Main dominates domestic financial markets, but its attempts to become an internationally important financial centre (the so-called '*Finanzplatz Deutschland*') have been undermined by a number of factors, including the concentration of investment services, foreign-exchange and Euro markets in London.

Very generally, it can be said that the historical links between the banks and non-financial businesses are manifested by the 'Big Three's' influence (DEUTSCHE BANK, DRESDNER BANK, COMMERZBANK) in large industrial enterprises while the small business sector (*Mittelstand*)tends to rely on loans from their local savings and and the DG BANK.

(EOS)

Fischer, Joschka   Joshka Fischer has been the most prominent leader of the GRÜNE over the last ten years and is now one of the most high-profile politicians in the Federal Republic. Born on 12 April 1948 in Gerabronn, Fischer came to the Greens via the 1960s student movement (STUDENTENBEWEGUNG) and its associated new Left, alternative politics. He established himself firmly on the moderate ('*Realo*') wing of the party. Fischer came to national prominence as the first Green Minister for the Environment in HESSEN from 1985–87 and again from 1991–94, where he gained a reputation as an effective minister capable of securing the stringent implementation of existing environmental laws.

Following the Western German Greens' failure to pass the 5 per cent hurdle in the 1990 BUNDESTAG elections, Fischer was centrally involved in reorienting the party as more moderate and responsible party of the post-materialist Left. The 1994 *Bundestag* elections saw the (now unified, all-German) Greens re-enter parliament with Fischer at the helm.

Since then, Fischer has attempted to move his party further into the political mainstream, even hinting that co-operation with the CDU was not out of the question. Such a strategy has meant persuading the Greens' membership to accept contentious changes in the party's policy stance, most recently on support for the deployment of German troops in Bosnia.

See BÜNDNIS '90; NEUE SOZIALE BEWEGUNGEN.

(CL)

Flächenstaat   See BUNDESLÄNDER.

Föderalismus   Federalism is a form of state organisation in which powers are typically distributed vertically between two levels of government. The *Federal* Republic of Germany distributes its powers of government between the federal, or central level (the BUND) and the BUNDESLÄNDER. Federalism is one of the basic and unamendable principles of the GRUNDGESETZ. It was introduced as a means of vertical division of powers (GEWALTENTEILUNG) designed to prevent over-centralisation and abuse of power such as had occurred under the National Socialists. The form of federal system introduced drew on the examples provided in German constitutional history in the German Empire and the Weimar Republic and was also influenced by the post-war Western occupying powers.

The distribution of powers between the federal level and the *Bundesländer* has a number of features. Most legislation is passed at the *Bund* level, though the *Bundesländer* do have their own exclusive legislative powers in a small (and declining) number of policy fields. Most of the powers to implement legislation are, however, allocated to the *Bundesländer*. In addition, the governments of the *Bundesländer* (LANDESREGIERUNGEN) are represented in the BUNDESRAT, which acts as the second parliamentary chamber alongside the BUNDESTAG, and has important powers in shaping *Bund*-level legislation. A complex system of financial equalisation (FINANZAUSGLEICH) has been established in an attempt to ensure that each level of government has sufficient financial resources to fulfil its constitutional duties.

This form of distribution of powers has been termed 'cooperative federalism'. *Bund* and *Bundesländer* perform complementary roles in the wider legislative process, with the *Bundesrat* helping to shape laws passed at the *Bund* level and the *Bundesländer* then implementing most of those laws. In order for laws to be made and implemented effectively, the two levels of government must therefore co-operate closely. This has been termed POLITIKVERFLECHTUNG, an 'entanglement' of the two levels.

The federal system currently faces two serious challenges: the problem of integrating the five NEUE BUNDESLÄNDER of Eastern Germany alongside the original 11 Western *Bundesländer* following unification; and the problem in European policy of ensuring that the domestic relationship between the two levels of government is not unbalanced by the effects of the European integration process.

See BESATZUNG; EUROPAPOLITIK.

(CJ)

Fonds 'Deutsche Einheit'   The German Unity Fund was established to help finance the restructuring of the former GDR following German unification. The Treaty of Unification made provision for the creation of a German Unity Fund by the Federal Government and the Western BUNDESLÄNDER to support the unfunded deficit of the East German public authorities. The Fund had the status of a shadow budget and was intended as an interim measure until the five new *Bundesländer* were incorporated into the financial equalisation scheme (FINANZAUSGLEICH) in 1995. DM115 billion were to be provided for this purpose, with DM90 billion being raised by borrowing. This allowance proved to be too low: between 1990 and 1994, DM160.7 billion were transferred from the Fund.

See NEUE BUNDESLÄNDER; VEREINIGUNG.

(MD)

Fraktion A *Fraktion* is a parliamentary grouping, either in the BUNDESTAG or in a LANDTAG, equivalent to a parliamentary party in Britain.

To form a *Fraktion*, a political party must have at least 5 per cent of the seats of the legislature. The status is important because it confers parliamentary rights and privileges on the party, including state subsidies for the *Fraktion*'s activities. In the current *Bundestag*, only the PDS does not have the status of *Fraktion*.

As well as conferring important rights upon a party, the *Fraktion* also plays an important role in organising the party's MPs. Each *Fraktion* is headed by a committee (*Fraktionvorstand*) and has a number of working groups (*Arbeitsgruppen*) covering the various policy areas. It is also responsible for party discipline, for which the whips (*Parlamentarische Geschäftsführer*) are responsible. When the *Bundestag* is in session, the working groups and the *Fraktion* each meet once a week to co-ordinate policy positions.

The post of leader of a parliamentary party (*Fraktionsvorsitzender*) is a position of considerable political importance, and the holder often wields more influence on policy than even a senior minister. However, this position is not necessarily held by the leader of the party: in the governing party, moreover, the Federal Chancellor has never simultaneously been *Fraktionsvorsitzender*.

See CDU; FDP; GRÜNE; SPD.

(SG)

Frankfurter Schule The Frankfurt School was a group of sociologists and philosophers which formed around Max Horkheimer and Theodor Adorno in Frankfurt in 1929. Most members of the group spent the years between 1935 and 1950 in exile in the USA.

At the basis of what they called 'critical theory' is a broadly (though undogmatically) Marxist concern with describing how mankind is dominated by sets of power structures brought about through the economic order of the day. Members of the 'school' believed to varying degrees that their work might benefit people through the development of an enlightened way of talking about these mechanisms of domination and ultimately through the achievement of a more democratic society.

The ideas of the school were popularised by the students movement (STUDENTENBEWEGUNG) of the late 1960s. In its rejection of the supposed superficiality of West German society and bourgeois authoritarianism in the universities, the students used critical theory (if at times only superficially understood) as their intellectual weapon for justifying street riots and disturbances in the universities. Even the Institute where Adorno and his colleagues worked was occupied by rioting students and Adorno's lectures were interrupted.

A concrete outcome of critical theory which emerged from the students' movement was a change in school curricula in many of the BUNDESLÄNDER, with the emphasis placed not just on the acquisition of facts but also their critical discussion and evaluation.

See MARXISMUS-LENINISMUS.

(RW)

Frauenbewegung   The origins of the German women's movement for political, social and cultural equality lie in the 1848 revolution and industrialisation of Germany. Women first organised themselves in the General German Women's Club in 1865. Other associations were subsequently set up, leading to the founding of the Association of German Women's Clubs in 1894.

The central aims of the movement were improved education, opportunities for women to work outside the house, the protection of pregnant working women, equal career opportunities and equal pay for equal work. The need to integrate women into the labour market during World War I saw some progress in these areas, and 1918 finally also saw the franchise extended to women.

During the Nazi regime many of these advances were reversed, as the party stressed the role of women as mothers and wives in the home and dissolved independent associations. With continuing inequality in the Federal Republic, the women's movement increasingly became left-wing and feminist, focusing on the restructuring of (a male-dominated) society and developing a counter-culture based on autonomous women's groups and initiatives.

A significant step in the monitoring and promotion of women's equality has been the appointment of women's representatives (*Frauenbeauftrage*, or Officers for Women's Affairs) in the public sector. These representatives examine whether laws and procedures are discriminatory, draw up plans to promote women and provide advice to women working in this sector. A second important development has been the establishment of safe houses for women (*Frauenhäuser*) escaping domestic violence. Such houses now exist in most German towns and cities.

Women's equality in Germany (as elsewhere) still remains a distant reality, requiring increased participation of women in state and interest groups as well as the extension of autonomous women's networks to provide support and advice for women. It is a particular problem in the former GDR, where many working mothers have been forced out of the labour market or into poorly paid jobs in the restructured economy since unification.

See FAMILIENPOLITIK; FRAUENPOLITIK; NEUE SOZIALE BEWEGUNGEN.

(SRF)

Frauenpolitik   Women's policy is largely synonymous with policy on equal opportunities (GLEICHBERECHTIGUNG) in Germany. It is designed to ensure that opportunities for personal and professional development open to women are equivalent to those open to men. A core concern is that efforts should be made to ensure that women's roles in family life – as child-bearers and parents – should not undermine opportunities for career development and involvement in public life.

A core problem, however, is that the patriarchal traditions in European civilisation remain deeply engrained and difficult to overcome. So while equal rights for men and women are formally guaranteed in the GRUNDGESETZ, practice reveals that stereotypes about women's roles and 'duties' persist. Women still perform a disproportionate amount of family responsibilities, tend disproportionately to be employed in lower-skilled and lower-paid jobs, and relatively rarely rise to senior positions in professional life and politics. Awareness of these problems was raised by the Women's Movement (FRAUENBEWEGUNG) which rose to prominence amid the wider social protest movements in the Federal Republic in the late 1960s. As a result, a wide range of measures have since been instituted, including extending opportunities for career advancement and representation of women's issues in both public and private sector employment; anti-discrimination measures; measures against sexual harassment in the workplace; and measures in the field of family policy (FAMILIENPOLITIK) to ensure that women who need time off work for child-bearing and raising are not disadvantaged in their career development. The main political parties have also sought, with varying levels of commitment and success, to place women in prominent political positions. Nevertheless, progress has remained only fitful and partial.

Two issues are of particular concern in the 1990s. First, the application of (West) German women's policy in East Germany has been controversial since unification. Formal provisions for women in the former GDR were more extensive than those of the Federal Republic, especially in the fields of employment and state childcare provision (though opportunities for advancement to senior positions in professional and public life were just as, if not more, restricted than in the West). Many have found the process of adaptation difficult. Second, the issue of the right to abortion (ABTREIBUNGSRECHT), which straddles the fields of equal opportunities and wider ethical debates, has been an especially difficult question. The more extensive abortion law in the former GDR proved extremely difficult – at the cost of considerable dissatisfaction in the East – to reconcile with

the relatively more restrictive interpretation of the right to abortion which had emerged in the post-war Federal Republic.
See AUßERPARLAMENTARISCHE OPPOSITION; NEUE SOZIALE BEWEGUNGEN.

(CJ)

Friedensbewegung　The origins of the post-war Peace Movement in the Federal Republic can be traced back to unsuccessful opposition to the reforming of the *Bundeswehr* and the decision to join NATO in 1955.

Opposition was organised predominantly by the SPD, the Churches and the trade union movement. However, the movement expanded rapidly following the announcement by the SPD-FDP Federal Government in 1979 that nuclear weapons would be stationed in the Federal Republic as part of the NATO 'twin-track' decision to match Soviet nuclear deployment in eastern Europe. Again the focus of the movement was the churches and trade unions along with sections of the SPD and members of the new social movements (NEUE SOZIALE BEWEGUNGEN). The movement was loosely organised and concentrated on local action, although several hundred thousand people took part in a wave of demonstrations in 1981 and 1982. It was also estimated that close to 3 million citizens took part in the week of action prior to the final decision on the deployment in 1983, while over 2 million signatures were collected by the communist-organised Krefeld appeal. The failure of the peace movement to halt the deployment led to its waning with the dissolution of the movement's co-ordinating committee.

Further organisation and mobilisation did not occur until the Gulf War at the end of 1990. Here protesters focused against the decisions of Western governments to enter into a war which was perceived as securing economic interests (oil supplies) rather than protecting the Kuwaiti population.

A small peace movement also developed in the GDR prior to unification centred on the limited autonomy of the Protestant Church under the slogan of 'Swords into Ploughshares'.

With the recent re-interpretation of the GRUNDGESETZ allowing German troops to operate outside of German borders, it is possible that the movement may be galvanised again in protest against war, this time involving German troops. This did not however, transpire in the case of the German troops involved in the Bosnian conflict.
See BLAUHELM-EINSÄTZE; BUNDESWEHR; NATO-DOPPELBESCHLUß.

(SRF)

Fünfprozentklausel　The 5 per cent clause, or 'hurdle' is a central feature of the federal electoral system, which makes parliamentary representation dependent on gaining 5 per cent of votes cast.

The introduction of a 5 per cent barrier was introduced in the post-war Federal Republic as a means of preventing the kind of fragmentation of the party system as had occurred in the Weimar Republic. In its current form, the 5 per cent barrier dates from the Federal Election Law of 1956, which provides that parties must poll over 5 per cent nationally to gain representation to the BUNDESTAG. The 5 per cent hurdle had an important role in reducing the number of political parties represented in the *Bundestag* from 11 in 1949 to 3 in 1961.

The barrier was altered for the 1990 election to apply in separate West and East German electoral areas rather than nationwide in order to give fledgling Eastern parties a better chance of representation. However, it was reinstituted in its post-1956 form for the 1994 election.

The 5 per cent barrier also applies for all LANDTAG elections, although not for the parties representing the Danish and Sorbian minorities in SCHLESWIG-HOLSTEIN and SACHSEN respectively. At federal level, the 5 per cent barrier does not apply if a party wins 3 or more directly elected seats. Thus in 1994 the PDS was returned to the *Bundestag* by virtue of this feature, even though it polled only 4.4 per cent of the vote nationwide.

See WAHLRECHT.

(SG)

G

Gastarbeiter 'Guest workers' were non-German workers hired on a temporary basis to work in Germany from 1955–73. Germany's rapid economic growth during the 1950s and 1960s resulted in shortages in unskilled labour. To counter this, the Federal Government signed treaties with Italy (in 1955), Spain and Greece (1960), Turkey (1961), Portugal (1964), Tunisia and Morocco (1965) and Yugoslavia (1968) to hire workers to come to Germany as temporary, 'guest' workers on a rotational basis. However, the rotation principle proved to be contrary to industry's interests in a stable labour force. Moreover, the unions (GEWERKSCHAFTEN) quickly ensured the 'guest' workers' integration into industry collective agreements on pay and conditions.

In 1973, just before the first oil shock, a halt on recruitment (the so-called *Anwerbestopp*) was imposed. At that time there were almost 4 million *Gastarbeiter* in Germany. These stayed on and began to bring their families over to Germany from the late 1970s onwards. The slow realisation that these migrants were in Germany to stay forced the government to develop a 'foreigners' policy' (AUSLÄNDERPOLITIK) to deal with their residence. Initially, this focused on repatriation incentives, and only from the mid-1980s did integration measures move to the forefront of the policy.

The legal integration of the *Gastarbeiter* has been slow and few have taken out German citizenship. Today, there are over 2 million Turks in Germany. Without the benefits of EU citizenship, this group, two-thirds of whom have been in Germany for over ten years, is effectively treated as 'foreign' in both Germany and Turkey. Their full social and legal integration is one of the major challenges facing Germany in the years to come.

See STAATSANGEHÖRIGKEITSRECHT.

(SG)

Gemeinde See KOMMUNALE SELBSTVERWALTUNG.

Gemeinschaftswerk 'Aufschwung Ost' The 'Joint Action Upswing East' was a programme aimed at stimulating infrastructural investment at regional and municipal level in the five NEUE BUNDESLÄNDER.

Established in March 1991, the *Gemeinschaftswerk 'Aufschwung Ost'* programme authorised DM24 billion in 1991 and 1992 focused on investments in job creation schemes (DM5.2 billion), roads and railways (DM6.3 billion) and housing and urban development (DM2.2 billion). Other areas included in the programme were local authority investment projects, the replacement of run-down machinery and environmental protection.

Despite the considerable financial flows involved in this and other programmes, the outlays failed to meet the full needs of social and economic reconstruction.

See STEUERLÜGE.

(MD)

Genscher, Hans-Dietrich   Hans-Dietrich Genscher spent 18 years as Federal Foreign Minister and was Vice-Chancellor from 1974–92. His experience and stature on the international stage led to the term 'Genscherism' being associated with the style and content of German foreign policy during his tenure in office.

Born on 21 March 1927 in Reideburg, Genscher entered the national political arena as a senior member of the FDP at a very early age. From 1957–65 he worked for the FDP Whips office in the BUNDESTAG, then holding the post of Chief Whip from 1965 to 1969. Following this, he spent five years as Interior Minister in the SPD–FDP coalition elected in 1969, before becoming Foreign Minister and Vice-Chancellor in 1974. Genscher held this post for the next 18 years during both the SCHMIDT and KOHL Chancellorships, developing an understated but effective foreign policy style that helped to change perceptions of Germany around the world. Genscher's period in office was crowned by the collapse of the communist regimes in Eastern Europe and the unification of Germany in 1989–1990. His consensual foreign policy style contributed a great deal to securing a positive international view of German unification.

Since his retirement, Genscher has remained active as an elder statesman on the lecture circuit. His contribution to international politics has been recognised widely, not least in the award of an impressive number of honorary doctorates from universities as far afield as Seoul in South Korea, Salamanca in Spain, Georgetown in the United States and Essex in the United Kingdom.

See SOZIALLIBERALE KOALITION; VEREINIGUNG.

(CL)

Gerichte   Courts collectively constitute the judicial pillar of the separation of powers (GEWALTENTEILUNG) in the Federal Republic. Courts and their judges (*Richter*) are independent of the two other (legislative and executive) pillars.

There are five independent branches of the judicial system (*Gerichtswesen*), each with a federal court at their apex: criminal and civil law, headed by the *Bundesgerichtshof* (Federal Law Court); administrative law, dealing with the legal protection of the citizen in dealing with public institutions, and headed by the *Bundesverwaltungsgericht* (Federal Administrative Court); and labour, social and financial law, headed by Federal Labour, Social and Financial Courts and typically dealing with disputes over working conditions, social security entitlements and financial administration (especially taxation), respectively. In addition, constitutional law and constitutional complaints (VERFASSUNGSBESCHWERDEN) are dealt with by the Constitutional Courts (*Verfassungsgerichte*) of the *Länder* and, as the supreme judicial organ in the Federal Republic, the Federal Constitutional Court (BUNDESVERFASSUNGSGERICHT).

All the branches of the judicial system, including constitutional adjudication, are heavily called upon in a country with a much stronger tradition of litigation than Britain and a rising crime level. The courts are arguably over-burdened as a result, with large numbers of cases forming a substantial backlog in the system.
(CJ)

Gesamtschule   See WEITERFÜHRENDE SCHULEN.

Gesetzgebung   Legislation is passed either at the federal level (BUND), or in the BUNDESLÄNDER in accordance with the distribution of legislative powers in the GRUNDGESETZ.

The legislative process in the *Bundesländer* is relatively straightforward in that all but Bavaria have a single-chamber parliament, or LANDTAG, in which legislation must be accepted before it becomes law (the Bavarian second chamber, the *Senat*, has, however, only limited influence over the legislative process).

Federal-level legislation follows a more complex procedure. Most legislation is introduced on the initiative of the Federal Government (BUNDES-REGIERUNG). The Federal Government sends its bills first to the BUNDESRAT, which then presents an initial opinion before the Federal Government sends the bill on to the BUNDESTAG. Following the deliberation and, typically, the amendments of the *Bundestag*, the bill is presented again to the *Bundesrat*. In both *Bundestag* and *Bundesrat*, detailed consideration of bills is conducted in committees (AUSSCHÜSSE) responsible for particular policy areas. If the *Bundesrat* finally accepts a bill presented to it, the bill is passed on by the Federal Government to the Federal President (BUNDE-SPRÄSIDENT) for signature and becomes law. If the *Bundesrat* rejects the bill, the next stages depend on whether the bill is in a policy field in which the consent of the *Bundesrat* is required (*Zustimmungsgesetz*) or one in which it may only raise objections (*Einspruchsgesetz*). If the latter is the case, the bill can be passed if the size of a *Bundesrat* majority vote against the bill is exceeded by the size of a subsequent *Bundestag* majority vote for the bill. If the former is the case, the bill cannot become law unless it is amended in a way which can secure *Bundesrat* consent. In all cases where the *Bundesrat* rejects a bill sent to it by the *Bundestag*, the bill may be sent to the Mediation Committee (VERMITTLUNGSAUSSCHUß) of the *Bundestag* and the *Bundesrat*, which attempts to find a compromise suitable to both chambers.

A general feature of the legislative process is its compromise orientation. Unlike the situation in the UK, opposition input into drafting legislation is sought and facilitated by the emphasis on the committee stage. Legislative outcomes are therefore typically hard-fought compromises capable of accommodating party-political differences.

(CJ)

Gestapo (Geheime Staatspolizei)   The *Gestapo* was the German Secret State Police force made notorious by the Third Reich. Inherited from the Weimar Republic, the *Gestapo* was brought under the control of Heinrich Himmler's SS empire in the mid-1930s. It also massively extended its remit to cover not just individuals and activities considered politically harmful to the state (a category in any case much widened after 1933), but also to new categories of 'racial' criminality, including Jewish–non-Jewish relations and homosexuality. The *Gestapo*, though a relatively small force, was notorious for its efficiency in dealing with this remit, and the brutality it visited on those suspected of what was considered 'crime' in the Third Reich. The word *'Gestapo'* thus conjured up fear, giving the organisation a deterrent effect far out of proportion to the number of its officers.

See ANTISEMITISMUS; DRITTES REICH; NATIONALSOZIALISMUS; STASI.

(CJ)

Gesundheitswesen   The health care system in Germany is based on a number of competing principles: the right to health care when needed irrespective of income, social background or place of residence; the highest possible quality of health care provision; and the most cost-efficient use of health care resources possible.

While the record on the first two principles – comprehensive access to high quality care – has generally been good, the record on cost-efficiency has not. There has been a 'cost explosion' in health care over the last 20–30 years, as technological advances make new (and more expensive) treatments possible, and as the population has aged. A further cost pressure was added by unification and the need to improve provision in East Germany to reach the levels attained in the West. The cost of health care has risen, for example, from DM279 billion in pre-unification West Germany in 1989 to some DM 429 billion in 1992 (of which 369 billion was spent in the West). The cost explosion has placed considerable pressure on the financing mechanism for health care: Germany's comprehensive health insurance (KRANKENVERSICHERUNG) system. Unpopular rises in insurance contributions have resulted.

Attempts have been made to control the growth of costs by reducing levels of provision in some areas, for example, by reducing the minimum level of sick pay and limiting entitlement to the peculiarly German tradition of taking 'cures' (*Kuren*), by imposing price cuts on health care providers, for example chemists, by seeking private investment in health care, and by introducing market principles into the insurance system to encourage more efficient use of resources.

However, such methods have only been successful in part. They have also – like other attempts to reform the system of social welfare provision – been controversial and unpopular.

See SOZIALES NETZ; SOZIALSTAAT; SOZIALVERSICHERUNG.

(CJ)

Gewaltenteilung The separation of powers is an important principle of government in Western democracies and underlies the distribution of powers between different political institutions in the GRUNDGESETZ.

Powers of government are separated both vertically and horizontally in the Federal Republic. Vertical separation is that between the institutions of the federal level (BUND) and the BUNDESLÄNDER according to the federal principle enshrined in the *Grundgesetz*. Horizontal separation is that between legislative, executive and judicial institutions. In both *Bund* and *Bundesländer*, parliaments enact laws which are executed by governments, and whose legality is assessed by courts. The aim is that no one institution can act without being subject to controls, or 'checks and balances' by another.

Gewaltenteilung forms an important component of the rule of law. It was designed by the framers of the *Grundgesetz* to prevent a repetition of the arbitrary abuses of power conducted by institutions of the state in the Third Reich.

See FÖDERALISMUS; RECHTSSTAAT.

(CJ)

Gewerkschaften Trade unions were re-constituted after World War II on the principles of the *Einheitsgewerkschaft* (unified trade union) and the *Industriegewerkschaft* (industrial trade union). Trade unions were no longer divided along political or religious lines, a weakness of the movement in the Weimar Republic, but organise both white-collar and blue-collar workers in a plant. Although other trade unions were formed, the vast majority of employees are organised in industrial unions under the umbrella organisation of the *Deutscher Gewerkschaftsbund* or DGB (the German Trade Union Federation). Both the right to be a member of a trade union and the right of trade unions to bargain with employers' associations are recognised in the GRUNDGESETZ. Figures for the end of 1995 show membership of DGB unions at 9.4 million.

After successfully negotiating increases in real income during the post-war period, the 1980s saw unions faced by rising unemployment, the introduction of new technologies and new forms of work organisation. The need for the unions to adapt was highlighted by membership weaknesses amongst women, white-collar workers and young people in particular. Although the DGB initiated a reform process, this was largely overtaken by unification and the extension of Western trade unions and collective bargaining in the new BUNDESLÄNDER.

With unemployment topping 4 million in March 1996 and the need for Germany to remain competitive, trade unions are under increasing pressure to allow reduced labour costs and more flexibility at plant level. Economic collapse in the East has also led to difficulties in establishing the bargaining procedures which had proved so successful in the West.

Reform of both collective bargaining structures and unions themselves (there have already been mergers) appears necessary if the existing system of industrial relations and employee representation is to survive.

See ARBEITSLOSIGKEIT; AUSSPERRUNG; BETRIEBSRAT; STREIK; TARIF-AUTONOMIE; UNTERNEHMERVERBÄNDE.

(SRF)

Gleichberechtigung   Equal entitlement or equal opportunities refers in the Federal Republic to the removal of gender inequalities and seeks to ensure opportunities in politics, economy and society for women equivalent to those enjoyed by men. It does not normally have the wider connotations of equal opportunities which exist in Britain, which also refer to racial issues, the rights of the disabled, those of different sexual orientation, and so on. Policies on equal opportunities are therefore more or less synonymous with the field of women's policy, or FRAUENPOLITIK.

See AUSLÄNDERPOLITIK; FAMILIENPOLITIK.

(CJ)

Goethe-Institut   The Goethe-Institut was founded in 1951 and its role is that of cultural ambassador of Germany, representing its language and culture abroad. There are at present 17 institutes in Germany and 152 in 76 countries, offering courses, seminars and workshops for language learners, teachers and lecturers of German. The central office is in München.

Given the present austerity in public spending, the mission of the Goethe-Institut is also being questioned.

See DAAD.

(RW)

Golf-Krieg   In January 1991 a US-led coalition, comprising several European and Arab forces, attacked and expelled Iraqi forces occupying Kuwait in what became known as the Gulf War. On 2 August 1990 Iraqi forces invaded and occupied the small, oil-rich Gulf state of Kuwait. The UN Security Council called for an international trade embargo on Iraq, while the US and several European countries concentrated military forces in Saudi

Arabia. Following the failure of the embargo, the coalition forces launched air and ground attacks against the Iraqis, destroying the Iraqi forces and liberating Kuwait. German forces did not participate in the Gulf War coalition due to constitutional limitations. The Federal Government did, however, participate in financing the military actions and sent *Bundeswehr* aircraft to Turkey against a possible Iraqi invasion.

Germany's non-participation in the Gulf War coalition was heavily criticised both abroad and within the CDU/CSU-FDP coalition. A general expectation emerged that Germany should contribute more fully to the international order following unification and the ending of the constraints of Cold War and national division. These expectations were in part addressed in a new constitutional interpretation by the Federal Constitutional Court, under which German forces may now participate in multinational peace-keeping missions.

See BLAUHELM-EINSÄTZE; BUNDESVERFASSUNGSGERICHT; BUNDES-WEHR.

(SS)

Gotik   See STILE.

Grass, Günter   Günter Grass (born in 1927 in Danzig) is western Germany's leading writer. His first novel, *Die Blechtrommel* (1959), which with the novella *Katz und Maus* (1961) and the novel *Hundejahre* (1963) forms the so-called 'Danziger Trilogie', brought him instant fame and marks West German literature's breakthrough to European significance. A stream of major novels, dramas and poetry have established Grass as one of the most potent innovative forces of twentieth-century German literature. His most recent novel, *Ein weites Feld* (1995), brings together his characteristic narrative gifts: the book is a vast study of German history from unification under Bismarck in 1871 to the collapse of the Berlin Wall and the helter-skelter unification of the two Germanies in 1990. It is marked by a language of extraordinary vitality and a protean imagination few of his contemporaries have been able to match.

Grass's creative work has also included drawing and sculpture, which he studied in the 1950s under Karl Hartung in Berlin. Above all, he has made a significant contribution to German politics in many speeches, essays and electoral campaigns. His public support for the SPD in 1961, however, was not initially welcomed by the Party due to the notoriety of *Die Blechtrommel*, but by the end of the decade Grass's personal friendship with Willy BRANDT led to a combined campaign which propelled Brandt into the Chancellorship. This creative conjunction of writer and politician marks a unique moment in German political history.

Grass's commitment to democracy, his insistence on tolerance and the inviolability of the individual have led him into many political controversies over the last 30 years – no more so than in his denunciation of what he saw as the ruthless 'colonisation' of the former GDR by the Federal Republic after the euphoric reunification of the two Germanies in 1989. The desire of Germany's political leaders to relinquish their country's tragic nationalist past in favour of a co-operative future in a wider European context is underpinned by the combative energies of writers such as Günter Grass.

See BÖLL, HEINRICH.

(MGB)

Greenpeace International – Deutschland   The German branch of the international environmental organisation Greenpeace is organised into local groups based in 80 towns. The organisation employs 120 people centrally with almost 500 000 members.

Greenpeace was founded in Canada in 1971. It organises direct non-violent action on a wide range of environmental issues, notably opposing whaling and the destruction of the rainforest. Previous activities within Germany included the 1984 campaign to highlight acid rain.

Greenpeace was instrumental in protesting against the sinking of the Brent Spar oil platform in the North Sea in 1995. Protests and a boycott of Shell petrol stations organised by Greenpeace were particularly effective in raising awareness in Germany, pressuring the Federal Government to urge its British counterpart to halt the sinking. Greenpeace in Germany is currently emphasising the need to train its members to become technical and scientific experts to support the campaigning work as well as the development of 'Green Teams' focusing on environmental issues particularly in the new *Bundesländer*.

Greenpeace in Germany can be contacted at the following World Wide Web site: http://www.greenpeace.de

See UMWELTBEWEGUNG.

(SRF)

Große Koalition   The Grand Coalition refers to the period 1966–69, in which the Federal Republic's two largest parties – the CDU/CSU and the SPD – formed a coalition together under the Chancellorship of Kurt Georg Kiesinger.

The Grand Coalition was formed after the resignation of the FDP from the previous coalition with the CDU/CSU because of disagreements over the budget and questions of economic management. The resignation of CDU Chancellor Ludwig Erhard soon followed and the CDU/CSU invited the SPD into a government now led by Kiesinger. The main task of the new coalition was to tackle West Germany's first post-war economic recession. The coalition was largely successful by 1968, with unemployment falling and inflation at a historic low.

However, the coalition was always subject to mutual suspicion, especially within each party's rank-and-file. SPD activists objected to what they regarded as the SPD bailing out an unpopular government, whilst many in the CDU/CSU worried that the SPD intended to eventually take over the government from within the coalition. Moreover, the coalition was less successful in addressing the pressing political problems of the day, especially the growth of the so-called extra-parliamentary opposition on the Left and – more worryingly – the far-Right NPD. Indeed, many observers began to worry that the co-operation of the country's two largest parties in the Grand Coalition was actually aggravating the problem by failing to allow for an effective source of opposition within the BUNDESTAG. The Grand Coalition was replaced by an SPD–FDP coalition in 1969, with Willy BRANDT as Chancellor.

Although mentioned occasionally as a possible route for the SPD to return to government, Grand Coalitions are generally regarded as undesirable in anything other than exceptional circumstances, as they are held to force often legitimate opposition to the edges of the political spectrum and thus foster extremism.

See AUßERPARLAMENTARISCHE OPPOSITION; SOZIALLIBERALE KOALITION.

(CL)

Grundgesetz The Basic Law is the Constitution of the Federal Republic of Germany. It came into force on 23 May 1949 on the territory of West Germany. It was intended to be valid only on a provisional basis, until such time as the two German states were unified. On 3 October 1990 this provisional character effectively ended with the accession of the GDR to the Federal Republic within the framework of the *Grundgesetz*.

The *Grundgesetz* was drawn up in 1948–49 by a Parliamentary Council of West German politicians working under the supervision of the Western occupying powers. It was set up in such a way as to avoid the constitutional weaknesses which had contributed to the collapse of democracy in the Weimar Republic and to offer protection against the abuses of state power in the Third Reich. The Basic Law established a republic shaped by a number of unamendable constitutional principles: democracy, the rule of law, federalism, the welfare state, and the guarantee of basic rights. It also established a separation of powers among the major political institutions. Outside the areas covered by the unamendable constitutional principles, constitutional changes may be made. The Federal Constitutional Court acts as guardian and interpreter of the *Grundgesetz*.

Although some had argued for the adoption of a new constitution upon German unification in 1990, the legal scope of the *Grundgesetz* was in the end simply extended to the territory of the former GDR. Some temporary exceptions were made to allow time for the co-ordination of the previously different legal principles of the Federal Republic and the GDR, e.g. in the field of abortion law (ABTREIBUNGSRECHT). In addition, a Joint Constitutional Commission (*Gemeinsame Verfassungskommission*) of the

BUNDESTAG and BUNDESRAT was set up in 1991 to consider any constitutional changes made necessary by unification, leading to the adoption of a series of constitutional changes in 1992–93.

See BESATZUNG; BUNDESVERFASSUNGSGERICHT; DRITTES REICH; FÖDERALISMUS; GEWALTENTEILUNG; GRUNDRECHTE; PARLAMENTARISCHER RAT; RECHTSSTAAT; SOZIALSTAAT; VERFASSUNGSÄNDERUNG; WEIMARER REPUBLIK.

(CJ)

Grundlagenvertrag The Basic Treaty, signed on 21 December 1972 between the Federal Republic and the GDR, governed their relationship from that point through to 1990. It was a key element of the OSTPOLITIK of the SPD–FDP coalition which took over government in 1969.

The Treaty defined the basis of relations between the two German states. It secured the transition from the Federal Republic's claim to sole representation of the German people to the principle and status of equality between the two German states, and the related aim of developing normalised, good neighbourly relations. The Federal Republic recognised the separate existence of the GDR and guaranteed the inviolability of its borders. The Treaty allowed for the membership of both German states in the United Nations. It also provided for the establishment of diplomatic relations between the two German states through representatives known as High Commissioners rather than Ambassadors. The CSU government in Bavaria disputed the constitutionality of the Basic Treaty, arguing unsuccessfully that the Treaty contravened the mission set out in the GRUNDGESETZ of striving for German unification.

The objectives behind the signing of the Treaty differed considerably for the two Germanies. The Federal Republic hoped to improve communications between the GDR and the Federal Republic and in some way contribute to a better quality of life for the citizens of the GDR. Conversely, the aim of the GDR was the procurement of international recognition.

See BUNDESVERFASSUNGSGERICHT; ENTSPANNUNG.

(NM)

Grundrechte Basic rights are one of the fundamental and unamendable constitutional principles of the GRUNDGESETZ, and are set out comprehensively in its first chapter. This prominence accorded to basic rights in the *Grundgesetz* was a direct reaction to the atrocities committed by the National Socialists in abuse of basic human rights during the Third Reich. The catalogue of *Grundrechte* commences with a declaration that 'the dignity of man is inviolable', and continues with guarantees of the rights to self-fulfilment, life and physical integrity, equality of rights, freedom of faith, expression, assembly and movement, rights of privacy and asylum. Guarantees of *Grundrechte* can only be limited or qualified in cases where one basic right conflicts with another, or where the *Grundgesetz* explicitly makes the extent of the guarantee dependent on supplementary legislation, e.g. with regard to the right to asylum (ASYLRECHT).

Grundrechte are an important component of the rule of law (RECHTSSTAAT). The rights they confer must thus always be observed by the institutions of the German state. Individuals have the right to register a constitutional complaint (VERFASSUNGSBESCHWERDE) to the Federal Constitutional Court about alleged infringements of their rights by the state.

See BUNDESVERFASSUNGSGERICHT; DRITTES REICH.

(CJ)

Grundschule   The German primary school system is for all children from 6 to 10 years of age. The current primary school system originated in the Weimar Republic Law on Primary Schools of 1920. This determined that children of all backgrounds and abilities were to attend one common type of school. The new primary school therefore had to provide a basic social education and develop skills and abilities across the curriculum.

By the 1960s, the demands facing the primary school had changed. New curricula, schoolbooks and methods were introduced with the aim of supporting the gifted while ensuring equal educational opportunities in a more rigorous academic approach. In the 1980s a better balance was struck between academic demands and the need to provide education in a form appropriate for young children. It also gave equal importance to qualifications, on the one hand, and the child's personal development, on the other. Primary school teachers are required to study for six semesters at a university.

Contemporary problems facing the primary school have been created both by changing conditions (new media, limited living space as a result of high population density, diverse family patterns) and an increasing number of foreign children. These new conditions require a school which is not only a place of learning but which also complements family life. Financial cutbacks in recent years and the demands on staff and equipment which go with the school's new role have often proved incompatible. Challenges currently facing the primary school include the integration of disabled children into normal school life, and an extension of the daily timetable from 8 a.m. till 1 p.m. to cover the whole day.

See ORIENTIERUNGSSTUFE; SCHULPFLICHT; WEITERFÜHRENDE SCHULEN.

(AW)

Grund- und Hauptstudium   Today most university departments have divided their courses into two phases, the *Grundstudium* (foundation studies, usually to be completed within the first four semesters) and the *Hauptstudium* (main studies).

Streaming courses into phases has allowed better control of student numbers and has to some extent improved success rates. The *Grundstudium* offers courses in the basics of the subject including an introduction to academic working methods (researching bibliographies, critical reading and interpretation, discussion, writing and presenting papers). The *Hauptstudium* deepens and broadens the first phase by offering specialisation and contextualisation in the subject.

Some departments stream even more by providing a one-year introductory phase with written exams at the end, an intermediate phase and then the *Hauptstudium*.

Many *Bundesländer* have made qualifying exams (*Zwischenprüfung* or *Vordiplom*) at the end of the *Grundstudium* compulsory for students before they can take courses in the *Hauptstudium*.

See LEHRVERANSTALTUNGEN; SCHEIN; STUDIENABSCHLÜSSE; STUDIEN-DAUER.

(AW)

Grüne   The Greens have become one of the Federal Republic's leading political parties in the last fifteen years. The term '*grün*', or 'green' is also used more generally to describe political ideas based upon a commitment to environmental values.

The Greens in Germany arose out of the 'new social movements' (NEUE SOZIALE BEWEGUNGEN) of the late 1970s. In its early years the party was described by one of its leaders, the late Petra KELLY, as the 'anti-party party': a phrase that accurately described its rejection of the traditional forms of party politics at the time. However, by the mid-1980s, the Greens were embarking on tentative political co-operation with the SPD in many BUNDESLÄNDER, with the first 'Red–Green' coalition being established in HESSEN in 1985 and lasting until 1987.

Following their poor performance in the 1990 BUNDESTAG election, the West German Greens merged with their eastern counterpart, *Bündnis '90/Grüne (Ost)*, itself an amalgam of citizens' movements which emerged in protest at the former GDR regime and the smaller eastern Greens. The formal title of the new party is *Bündnis '90/Grüne*.

In recent years, the Greens have become increasingly moderate under the pragmatic leadership of Joshka FISCHER and are now established as the third largest party in the *Bundestag*. They are, or have been, in government with the SPD in a number of *Bundesländer*, including Hessen again (1990–), Niedersachsen (1990–94) and Nordrhein-Westfalen (since 1995), and are increasingly seen as potential coalition partners at the federal level by the SPD.

'Green' ideology in a broader sense is a description for a set of values that reflect a high commitment to environmental protection. In Germany these values are generally – but not exclusively – associated with post-materialism. They comprise an implicit rejection of the values of mass production and consumption and support policies which aim to protect or enhance environmental conditions. In recent years, the popularity of green ideas has led to parties of all political colours attempting to incorporate

the 'green' label into their policy proposals. The *Grüne* have termed this '*Themenklau*', the 'stealing' of their political themes.
See BÜNDNIS '90; POSTMATERIALISMUS.
(CL)

Grüner Punkt A 'green dot' can be found on all German packaging, from drinks cans to milk cartons. It means that such packaging can be recycled. This is guaranteed through the *Duales System Deutschland*, a business which, under the pressure of government legislation on packaging, was set up in 1991 to tackle the growing waste problem in Germany.

The *Duales System Deutschland* is responsible for licensing agreements with firms wanting or, rather, having to purchase the *Grüne Punkt* licence. At the same time they also have agreements with recycling firms and local communities regarding waste collection and recycling responsibilities. The cost of the *Grüne Punkt* is passed on to the consumer. This meant a price increase of 3–4 per cent per item.

For the unsuspecting foreigner, the waste system is complicated, not the least because each community can decide which items they collect separately (in separate bins) and whether they collect them at all. In some communities, the consumer has to take recyclable refuse to central waste units. If the refuse has not been sorted properly by the consumer it can be rejected. All packaging material needs to be cleaned before going into the waste bin.

Ever since the *Grüne Punkt* was put onto packaging, the Germans have over-achieved collection targets. There have been fierce debates about the cost of recycling itself and complaints were made, particularly in the early years, that there were containers full of recyclable waste but no capacity to process it. Recycling firms were accused of making excessive profits out of the legal requirement to recycle an increasing percentage of waste whilst consumers were paying for it. This has partially been remedied by tighter audit controls and legislation.
See UMWELTBEWEGUNG.
(RW)

Gymnasium See WEITERFÜHRENDE SCHULEN.

Gysi, Gregor Gregor Gysi is a leading figure in the PDS and has been a member of the BUNDESTAG since 1990. Born on 16 January 1948 in East Berlin, Gysi made a career as a lawyer in the GDR. Although he defended dissidents on occasion, his career path brought him into close contact with the GDR regime, as seen in his membership of the ruling party (the SED). This fact has dogged him in recent years.

After the fall of the Berlin wall, Gysi rose to national prominence as leader of the successor party to the SED, the PDS. His quick wit and charm provided a 'user-friendly' face for the party that served to divert the gaze of the electorate from the more unsavoury unreconstructed communist elements within his party.

Under Gysi's leadership, the PDS has consolidated its position as a regional party of protest in the former GDR, but has not made significant progress in the West. Moreover, accusations that Gysi had informed on colleagues and clients as a STASI informant during his years as a lawyer have dented his image.

(CL)

H

Habilitation The *Habilitation* is a post-doctoral qualification in the form of an extended dissertation (*Habilitationsschrift*) which is a prerequisite in all subjects (except art and music) to become a professor at a German university.

It is possible to be awarded a 'cumulative' *Habilitation* in which case an examination panel considers all published work by a candidate to see whether it is equivalent to a *Habilitationsschrift*. After gaining the *Habilitation*, appointment to a professorial chair does not necessarily follow. Without a chair a person is called *Privatdozent* and carries the title *Dr. habil.* He or she cannot normally be appointed to a chair at his/her own university. Once appointed to a chair, he or she will usually present an inaugural lecture (*Antrittsvorlesung*).

See HOCHSCHULE; HOCHSCHULLEHRER; PROMOTION.

(AW)

Hamburg Hamburg is one of the three city-states (*Stadtstaaten*), alongside BREMEN and BERLIN, which form constituent BUNDESLÄNDER of the Federal Republic.

Hamburg covers an area of 755km² and has a population of 1.7m (1994). It is the biggest port in Germany and the fourth biggest in Europe. Already an economically successful trading city, German unification and the opening up of the former communist bloc in Eastern Europe restored to Hamburg its traditional economic hinterland. As a result, Hamburg has emerged as a boom city since 1990, with the highest GDP per head in Europe (78 830DM in 1995), although unemployment remained relatively high at 10.7 per cent.

Hamburg has been a stronghold of the SPD during the Federal Republic. The SPD has held the office of MINISTERPRÄSIDENT (in Hamburg, *Bürgermeister*) since 1957 and has won an absolute majority of seats in the LANDTAG (*Bürgerschaft*) on nine occasions. Recent elections have seen the SPD and its main rival, the CDU, weaken, to the benefit of the GRÜNE and, in 1993, the protest group *Stattpartei*, with which the SPD currently forms the LANDESREGIERUNG under *Bürgermeister* Henning Voscherau.

(CJ)

Handwerk   See DUALES SYSTEM; MITTELSTAND.

Hauptschule   See WEITERFÜHRENDE SCHULEN.

Hauptstadtfrage   The 'capital city question' refers to the controversy over the location of the capital and seat of government of unified Germany. Article 2 of the Unification Treaty (EINIGUNGSVERTRAG) stated that Berlin is the capital of Germany but left undecided the seat of government. In June 1991, the BUNDESTAG decided by 337 to 320 votes for the government to be located in Berlin but left the timetable for the move open. The year 2000 was eventually identified as the date by which the transfer of the *Bundestag* and the government would be complete.

Until the final resolution of the question of the capital and seat of government in 1991, the choice of Berlin had been debated with great passion. The advocates of Berlin argued that it would stimulate economic recovery in the NEUE BUNDESLÄNDER, signal united Germany's new orientation and opening towards central and Eastern Europe and restore the city to its former status. Berlin's critics favoured the low-key city of Bonn as a symbol of German federalism over the megalopolis Berlin, objected to the heavy cost of the move and – given Berlin's role as the centre of government and aggressive foreign policy in the German Empire and the Third Reich – were concerned that it might raise fears of renewed German assertiveness in European affairs.

(MD)

Hauptstudium   See GRUND-UND HAUPTSTUDIUM.

Haushaltspolitik   Budgetary policy concerns the formulation of fiscal policies to influence the revenue and expenditure accounts of the three levels of government – federal, BUNDESLÄNDER and local – and of the social insurance (SOZIALVERSICHERUNG) funds.

During the 1950s surpluses were achieved because revenue was under-estimated while expenditure was over-estimated. In the 1960s, there was a gradual shift to formulating budgetary policy in order to affect employment levels, culminating in the Growth and Stability Act (1967). As the 1970s evolved, significant deficits emerged, due basically to successive oil price rises and international demands for West German reflation. Between 1982 and 1989 emphasis was placed on the reduction of taxation and government expenditure, and on privatisation programmes and deregulation. During the 1990s, budgetary policy has aimed at covering the costs of incorporating the former GDR, while simultaneously meeting the European policy goal of achieving the Maastricht criteria for a European currency (low inflation and long-term interest rates, and a budget deficit (*Staatsdefizit*) and national debt (*Staatsverschuldung*) respectively not exceeding 3 and 60 per cent of GDP).

After recording a minor budgetary surplus and introducing major tax reductions at the end of the 1980s, significant increases in tax, expenditure and deficits have characterised the 1990s.

Revenue from income taxes is shared by federal, *Bundesländer* and local governments, while corporation tax (*Körperschaftsteuer*) and VAT (*Mehrwertsteuer*, or *MWS*) receipts are jointly shared by the federal and *Bundesländer* governments. In addition, each level of government exclusively levies its own taxes. The Federal Government, for example, receives all excise duties (*Verbrauchssteuern*) – with the exception of beer duty which goes to the *Bundesländer*. The *Bundesländer* additionally receive all proceeds from inheritance and wealth taxes (*Erbschafts- und Vermögenssteuern*). Property taxes (*Grundsteuern*) as well as trade taxes (*Gewerbesteuern*) and fees (*Gebühren*) for public services accrue to the local authorities.

Total public sector debt will exceed DM2 trillion in the second half of the 1990s, and has created considerable difficulties for the Federal Government in meeting the Maastricht criteria.

See EUROPAPOLITIK; FINANZAUSGLEICH; WIRTSCHAFTSPOLITIK.

(EOS)

Herzog, Roman   Roman Herzog has been Federal President (BUNDESPRÄSI-DENT) since 1994. Born in 1934, Herzog was a CDU minister in BADEN-WÜRTTEMBERG from 1978 to 1983, when he was appointed to the Federal Constitutional Court. He served on the Court until 1994 and was appointed its President in 1987. On 23 May 1994, Roman Herzog became the 7th President of the Federal Republic.

Herzog's election in 1994 was subject to some controversy. Originally, Helmut KOHL, Chancellor and Leader of the CDU had favoured Saxony's Justice Minister Steffen Heitmann as the CDU's candidate. However, Heitmann turned out to be a highly unpopular choice, both within the party and the population at large and was dropped in late 1993 in favour of Herzog. Even then, Herzog lacked the popular support of his SPD rival, Johannes Rau. However, Herzog was eventually elected by the Federal Assembly (BUNDESVERSAMMLUNG) once the FDP had dropped its own candidate, Hildegard Hamm-Brücher, in favour of Herzog.

Despite this inauspicious start, Herzog has quickly gained the respect of the population by acknowledging Germany's moral debt for the Holocaust and promoting reconciliation, in particular with the Czech Republic.

Herzog has indicated that he will not stand for re-election when his term expires in 1999.

(SG)

Hessen   Hessen (Hesse) is one of the constituent BUNDESLÄNDER of the Federal Republic. It is a medium-sized *Bundesland* with an area of

21 114km² and a population of 5.98m (1994). Its capital city is Wiesbaden and its largest city is Frankfurt-am-Main. Formerly a strongly agricultural *Bundesland*, Hessen now has a dynamic economy which is strong in both manufacturing (chemicals, engineering, cars, electronics) and services. Frankfurt is Germany's main financial centre and site of the DEUTSCHE BUNDESBANK. Hessen has a high GDP per head (56 910DM in 1995) and an unemployment rate below the national average.

Hessen's LANDESREGIERUNG has always been led by the SPD, except for a short period of government when it was led by the CDU from 1987–91. The last two elections to the LANDTAG have returned 'red–green' coalitions of SPD and the GRÜNE under MINISTERPRÄSIDENT Hans Eichel.

(CJ)

Historikerstreit   The so-called Historian's Dispute of the mid- to late-1980s provided a fascinating and high-profile example of the continuing process of VERGANGENHEITSBEWÄLTIGUNG (coming to terms with the past) in the Federal Republic.

A group of conservative historians, most notably Ernst Nolte, Andreas Hillgruber and Michael Stürmer, variously argued, largely in the mass media, that: (a) it was time to stop focusing so much historical energy on the mere twelve years of the Third Reich to the detriment of more positive episodes in German history; (b) Nazi crimes, however appalling, were not unique in a roll-call of twentieth-century inhumanity extending from Turkish massacres of Armenians in World War I to Saddam Hussein's genocide of the Iraqi Kurds; and (c) at least some elements of Nazi policies were understandable given the threat to German and western civilisation posed by Stalin's (equally inhumane) Soviet Union.

A counter-attack by liberal and left-wing historians and social scientists, including Jürgen Habermas and Eberhard Jäckel, argued that the industrialised methods and sheer comprehensiveness of mass murder in the Nazi concentration camps stood without parallel in history and had constantly to be remembered as such, and that the Federal Republic had drawn its unprecedented stability as a democratic German state from its open confrontation with, and recognition of the horrors of, the Third Reich. As the then Federal President, Richard von WEIZSÄCKER, summarised the counter-argument in 1987 in a characteristically forthright and moral intervention into political debate: 'those who shut their eyes to the past will be blind to the future'.

There was no clear outcome of the *Historikerstreit*, save that the problems of historical experience were hauled forcefully back to contemporary debate and that the process of VERGANGENHEITSBEWÄLTIGUNG is not and cannot be complete. A more recent example of this was the high level of public interest shown in 1996 in the controversial book by the

American social scientist Daniel Goldhagen, *Hitler's Willing Executioners*, which argued that there was a high degree of public involvement in the execution of Nazi racial crimes.

See ANTISEMITISMUS; DRITTES REICH; NATIONALSOZIALISMUS.

(CJ)

Hitler, Adolf Adolf Hitler (1889–1945) was the leader of the National Socialist Party (NSDAP) from 1921 and Chancellor and subsequently *Führer* (supreme leader) of the Third Reich from 1933. Born in Braunau-am-Inn in Austria, his early adulthood was spent as a failed artist and drifter in Vienna, in which period he developed a crude anti-Marxist, anti-democratic and racialist *Weltanschauung*. He served in the German army in World War I, emerging at the end of the war embittered by what he saw as the betrayal of the German nation, in particular in the Versailles Peace Treaty, by the new democratic politicians of the Weimar Republic. He joined in 1919, and subsequently took control of, an extreme nationalist party in Munich, which became the NSDAP. His rhetorical and presentational talents saw the expansion of the party into one capable of launching an abortive coup against the Republic in Munich in 1923. A short jail sentence followed in which he wrote *Mein Kampf*, a garbled but potent attempt to lay down an ideology characterised by contempt for democracy, extreme anti-Marxism and racial anti-Semitism.

The NSDAP became a national political force during the Great Depression, when Hitler's oratory and energy helped to mobilise popular resentment against the weak Weimar system. As leader of, by 1932, the largest German party, Hitler's influence increased and he was invited to become Chancellor in January 1933. Within months, the remnants of Weimar democracy had been abolished, all opposition suppressed – including that within the National Socialist movement in the SA – and a dictatorship established. This, the Third Reich, was defined throughout by Hitler's unique form of charismatic leadership, in which propagandistic inspiration outweighed concrete decision-making wherever possible. Decisions were normally taken in competition between rival institutions and individual power bases each trying to claim the legitimacy of the *Führer's* will. With the exception of a few fields, most notably foreign policy, Hitler thus remained distanced from, but irretrievably responsible for, the political decision-making of the Third Reich.

In foreign policy, Hitler proved initially to be a skilled tactician, exploiting the weaknesses and prevarications of the other European states to rearm Germany, bring 'home to the Reich' ('*heim ins Reich*') German-speaking territories in Austria and Czechoslovakia, and conduct with great speed and skill the initial campaigns of World War II. The invasion of the Soviet Union in 1941, conducted in the name of securing extra 'living space' (*Lebensraum*) for the German race, however, overstretched German resources, with German forces eventually being pushed back in

1943, and commenced a chain of military defeats which culminated in German defeat in 1945.

From 1941–42, however, the genocide of European Jews was launched in the conquered territories in eastern Europe, culminating in the mass murders in the extermination camps. Although no documentary evidence of Hitler ordering mass murder exists, there is no doubt that he fully approved of the mass murder programme, which reflected in unprecedented form the extreme anti-Semitic prejudice he had first revealed in *Mein Kampf*. This was confirmed in his last public document for the German nation, the 'last testament' of 29 April 1945, issued one day before he committed suicide amid the wreckage of a Berlin, Germany and Europe devastated by the barbarity undertaken in the name of his National Socialist ideology.

See ANTISEMITISMUS; DRITTES REICH; ERMÄCHTIGUNGSGESETZ; HOLO-CAUST; NATIONALSOZIALISMUS; VERSAILLER FRIEDENSVERTRAG; WEIMARER REPUBLIK.

(CJ)

Hochschule   This is an umbrella term for a number of institutions of higher education conducting teaching and research which confer recognised academic degrees. It includes universities, *Technische Universitäten und Hochschulen*, FACHHOCHSCHULEN, *Gesamthochschulen, Kunst- und Musikhochschulen, Sporthochschulen, Pädagogische Hochschulen, Verwaltungshochschulen* and other specialist *Hochschulen*. *Gesamthochschulen* were first founded in the 1970s and incorporate several types of *Hochschulen* into one.

Hochschulen are run under the auspices of the BUNDESLAND concerned and no fees are payable by students. Some *Hochschulen* were founded and run by the church. Others – the *Bundesverwaltungshochschule* and *Bundeswehruniversitäten* – are run by federal authorities. More recently, a few private institutions have gained the status of *Hochschulen* and these may charge fees, e.g. *Private Wissenschaftliche Hochschule für Unternehmungsführung in Vallendar* near Koblenz or the *Private Hochschule Witten-Herdecke*.

The various types of *Hochschulen* have different entry requirements, either ABITUR or *Fachabitur* and possibly work placements.

Altogether there are currently just under 2 million students in Germany and three out of ten school leavers of any one year apply for a place at a *Hochschule*.

See STUDIENABSCHLÜSSE; TECHNISCHE HOCHSCHULE; UNIVERSITÄT.

(RW)

Hochschulgemeinde (HG)   The Catholic and Protestant Churches finance and staff Catholic and Protestant chaplaincies at each university. These chaplaincies are a major university resource in the field of pastoral care and also hold regular services and prayer meetings, together with other events of a religious or ethical nature. Some *Hochschulgemeinden* offer accommodation as well. The *HG* may also be active outside the university by providing social work involving students, e.g. in providing services for foreign children.

See EVANGELISCHE KIRCHE DEUTSCHLANDS; KATHOLISCHE KIRCHE.

(AW)

Hochschullehrer   The teaching staff of a HOCHSCHULE consists of two main groups of academically qualified personnel: professors and *Wissenschaftliche Mitarbeiter* (academic non-professorial staff).

Professors are appointed (*berufen*) to a chair (*Lehrstuhl*) by the minister responsible for education in the BUNDESLAND concerned and are chosen by a university appointment board on the strength of their publications and teaching. They have to have the HABILITATION. Professors are also obliged to take on administrative responsibilities within the *Hochschule*. *Wissenschaftliche Mitarbeiter* (also called *Mittelbau*) need to have a doctorate. They cannot normally give lectures but otherwise offer courses and can act as examiners like the professors. The *Studienrat im Hochschuldienst* (secondary school teacher working in a *Hochschule* for a fixed period) may be allocated certain courses, and can choose to teach others in accordance with course regulations. In areas where there is particular pressure on academic staff *Lehraufträge* (teaching contracts) can be offered to suitably qualified graduates to teach certain courses.

See LEHRVERANSTALTUNGEN; STUDIENABSCHLÜSSE.

(AW)

Hochschulrahmengesetz (HRG)   Framework legislation for higher education can be passed by the federal level (BUND) even though the BUNDES-LÄNDER have the main responsibility for the areas of culture and education. However, the consent of the BUNDESRAT is needed.

The HRG was passed in 1976 as a first step in higher education reform (HOCHSCHULREFORM). The BUNDESLÄNDER then adapted their legislation to be compatible with the framework law in the following years. The HRG sought to counter widespread criticism levelled against a university system which was still largely based on the educational ideals of the nineteenth century and was deemed to be inappropriate for the needs of a modern, participatory democratic society.

The HRG deals with the following areas: responsibilities of the HOCHSCHULEN (e.g. internal organisation, curricula and research coordination); entrance requirements; the participation of all levels of personnel in university administration; the recognition of qualifications and degrees; and the adaptation of laws passed by the *Bundesländer* and amendments to federal laws in these areas.

The HRG was first reviewed in 1985. The Unification Treaty of 1990 made further changes to the *HRG* necessary and all the *Bundesländer* have had to adapt their laws accordingly.

See AKADEMISCHE FREIHEIT; AKADEMISCHE SELBSTVERWALTUNG; EINIGUNGSVERTRAG; HOCHSCHULREFORM.

(AW)

Hochschulreform   Higher education reform concerns changes in policy taken to meet the needs of students, academic advance and the wider interests of the nation.

The Higher Education Framework Law (HOCHSCHULRAHMENGESETZ) is the legal basis for the reforms German higher education has undergone since 1976. These reforms have had two directions: (a) the re-organisation of higher education through the foundation of *Gesamthochschulen*, the integration of teacher training colleges into universities, and changes in staff structure; (b) coping with continuously growing student numbers and making their courses more relevant for today's economic needs through new course and exam regulations, effective student counselling, and reviews of the quality of teaching.

Current discussions focus on overcoming the NUMERUS CLAUSUS and shortening time spent at university, with the aim of making studying cheaper for the state and decreasing class sizes.

Examples of reform efforts include the *Fiebiger-Programme*, introduced in the 1980s by the Federal Government and introducing fixed term new-blood professorships. The BUNDESLÄNDER have also financed programmes for buying in qualified teachers to help reduce class sizes where courses are vastly oversubscribed.

After unification, universities in both East and West were faced with huge tasks. Partially with the help of Western *Gründungsdekanen* (foundation deans), teaching staff at East German universities were reviewed and renewed through new appointments, with a particular concern for the 'winding up' (ABWICKLUNG) of the employment of those closely associated with the former GDR regime. The new *Bundesländer* have now all passed their own higher education laws (*Landeshochschulgesetze*).

See HOCHSCHULLEHRER; HOCHSCHULRAHMENGESETZ.

(AW)

Hoechst   Hoechst was the sixth largest industrial company in Germany in 1995 with a turnover of DM52.2 billion, employing 165 928 people and a net income of DM2.25 billion. Founded in Höchst am Main (now part of Frankfurt) in 1863, the company eventually became known as Hoechst. Like BASF and BAYER, Hoechst was formed to exploit the British invention of synthetic coal dyes. Also like BASF and Bayer, Hoechst prided itself on the provision of 'exemplary' social benefits for its employees. In

1925, Hoechst formed IG Farben with five other companies, including BASF and Bayer. IG Farben used forced labour during World War II.

Today the company is represented in 120 countries, with production sites in 64 of them and laboratory sites in 15. A significant acquisition in 1995 was Marion in the USA. Hoechst's share in the world's largest pharmaceutical market consequently rose from 1 to 4 per cent. Along with the holding in the French Roussel Uclaf group, the new global, multicultural pharmaceutical company of Hoechst Marion Roussel was formed during 1996. The goal is to become 'the number one health care company worldwide in the next few years'.

The slump in chemicals caused profits to fall to DM756 million in 1993 compared to a previous peak of DM2.13 billion in 1989. In fact, German chemical production had lagged markedly behind growth in the USA and Japan. Profitability at Hoechst was below average in 1995 when measured against international competitors. Improving efficiency, particularly in Western Europe, is therefore a central goal. Core activities are to be expanded into a global business, either by internal expansion or by a process of mergers with 'strong partners'. This means concentrating on innovative, profitable activities, especially in the less cyclical health-care sector – where excellent world-wide growth prospects are perceived. Along with most other large German companies, enhancing 'shareholder value' is being accorded high priority.

(EOS)

Holocaust   The Holocaust – literally the mass destruction of life by fire – is the term often used to describe the final stages of the genocidal anti-Jewish policies of the Third Reich. Although Jews were murdered on a vast scale as a result of slave labour in concentration camps and during the invasion of the Soviet Union in 1941–42, the Holocaust refers in particular to the industrialised mass murder, mainly by gassing, of Jews in the extermination camps of occupied Eastern Europe from 1942–45. In total some 6 million Jews, well over half the Jewish population in Europe, were murdered.

It is argued by many that the term Holocaust should not be applied merely to the mass murder of Jews. Millions of others considered racially unfit – Russians, Poles, gypsies, homosexuals – were also gassed, worked to death in concentration camps or starved to death in prisoner-of-war camps.

Whatever the precise definition adopted, the scale of mass murder, literally incalculable amid the upheavals which preceded and succeeded it, is one unprecedented in history, and marks out the Third Reich as a regime of unique barbarity and criminality.

See ANTISEMITISMUS; DRITTES REICH; KONZENTRATIONSLAGER; NATIONAL-SOZIALISMUS.

(CJ)

Honecker, Erich   Erich Honecker (1912–94) was the long-serving General Secretary of the SED and Chairman of the Council of State (STAATSRAT) of the GDR. Born into a socialist mining family in the Saarland, he joined the German Communist Party in 1929 and became a full-time official of the Communist Youth Movement in the following year. After Hitler came to power, Honecker was active in the communist opposition in the Ruhr and Berlin. Imprisoned in 1935, he was sentenced to ten years penal servitude and remained in the Brandenburg-Görden jail until the end of the war.

After the defeat of the Third Reich, he was prominent in the establishment of a Soviet-type system in the Soviet zone of Germany. A loyal supporter of Walter ULBRICHT, he headed the Free German Youth (FDJ) movement between 1946 and 1955 and entered the SED *Politbüro* in 1950. In 1958, he was promoted to Central Committeee Secretary for Security, in which position he directed the building of the Berlin Wall. His dislike of deviations from the traditional Soviet-style system eventually brought him into conflict with Ulbricht over the latter's 'New Economic System' (NEUES ÖKONOMISCHES SYSTEM). In alliance with other traditionalists on the *Politbüro* and with Brezhnev's backing, he engineered the ousting of Ulbricht in 1971.

After his appointment as First Secretary (retitled General Secretary in 1976), he rapidly secured his power base by promoting some of his earlier FDJ associates and by adding to his own portfolio the chairmanship of the National Defence Council and of the Council of State. At home, Honecker sought to mobilise popular support through the 'unity of economic and social policy' which held out the promise of higher living standards, including better housing, on the basis of economic growth and labour productivity increases. In addition, a policy of *Abgrenzung* (demarcation) was pursued in order to shield the GDR from the potentially destabilising effects of closer relations with the Federal Republic following the signing of the GRUNDLAGENVERTRAG (Basic Treaty) in 1972. This included the propagation of the notion of a socialist nation in the GDR. However, Honecker came to appreciate the benefits of the closer links with West Germany, especially when the GDR's hard currency indebtedness reached crisis proportions in the early 1980s. He had, however, to postpone a visit to the Federal Republic as the Soviet Union took objection to the intra-German *détente* at a time when superpower relations were in deep freeze. Only when East–West relations improved after Gorbachev's accession to power were conditions suitable for Honecker to visit Chancellor Helmut KOHL in Bonn and his former home in the Saarland in September 1987. Disaster soon followed for the ailing SED leader, who did not possess the political and intellectual flexibility and capacity to cope with the general crisis of communism and the GDR's growing systemic problems in the later 1980s. In October 1989, Honecker was removed from power in a coup headed by Egon KRENZ and was later ejected from the SED. Unable to remain in Moscow after Yeltsin succeeded Gorbachev, Honecker returned to Germany in 1992 where he had to face a charge of manslaughter. After the abandonment of the trial because of his ill-health, he emigrated to Chile, still proclaiming the superiority of his brand of socialism over the capitalist system.

See DDR.

(MD)

I

Immatrikulation The first step of matriculation, or registration at a HOCHSCHULE, is the application either to the ZVS (*Zentralstelle für die Vergabe von Studienplätzen*, the central office administering university places), or the university directly – depending on the NUMERUS CLAUSUS situation. Once a student has been accepted by a *Hochschule*, matriculation itself can take place. The student receives a student identity card (valid for one semester) and *Studienbuch* (in which all the courses to be taken are noted and course certificates need to be filed).

Each semester students need to pay their *Sozialbeitrag* (contribution for accident insurance and other university-wide services) and provide proof that they have health insurance cover. The whole process is called *Rückmeldung* (re-registration) and means that the student intends to carry on with his/her studies. Following this re-registration students receive a new student card for the semester.

Deregistration is automatic after a PhD or when a student has failed exams such as the ZWISCHENPRÜFUNG, *Vordiplom* or *Abschlußprüfung* several times or has committed serious disciplinary offences. Students leaving a *Hochschule* because they have finished their degree or do not want to continue their studies have to deregister.

European Union students wanting to study at a German university need to write to the AKADEMISCHES AUSLANDSAMT (academic office for foreign students) of the university in question.

See LEHRVERANSTALTUNGEN; SCHEIN; STUDENTENAUSWEIS; STUDIEN-ABSCHLÜSSE.

(AW)

Industrie Dating from about 1870, Germany's impressive industrial growth was based on three industries: chemical, electrical (plus, later, electronic) and mechanical engineering, including motor vehicles. New products and techniques were introduced or developed and seats of learning and training systems in these new fields founded. Basic industries were also essential. Although now in decline, steel and coal mining (the *Montanindustrien*), along with the still-expanding energy enterprises, are examples still important in terms of their relative size.

One of the main problems facing Germany's industries today is that of competitive viability in terms of the continual rise in the DM exchange rate and relatively high labour costs. However, potential domestic productivity gains could continue to emerge from traditional (or post-war) economic and social strengths: high quality research and development and education and training, employee involvement through co-determination (MITBESTIMMUNG), social cohesion, and a generally sound infrastructure.

See VEREINIGUNG; WIRTSCHAFTSPOLITIK; WIRTSCHAFTS-, WÄHRUNGS-UND SOZIALUNION.

(EOS)

Internatsschulen Boarding schools are run privately or by the Churches and most have very distinctive educational features. They are fee-paying non-profit-making organisations. Many were founded in the nineteenth century in order to provide secondary education for children who were, for a number of reasons, unable to visit a day school. These schools typically have a distinctive approach to living together as a school community. Boarding schools integrate all three types of secondary schools (WEITER-FÜHRENDE SCHULEN).

Today there are two main reasons for sending a child to a boarding school: (a) when he or she is not doing well in the local day school and/or has behavioural difficulties; (b) when the parents' career commitments prevent the provision of the usual family support structure for education (e.g. in the case of diplomats).

(AW)

J

Jugendherberge The first youth hostels were founded at the beginning of the nineteenth century in order to provide simple accommodation for long-distance hikers at an affordable price. The more than 600 youth hostels established by 1995 are open not only to young people but also to families and senior citizens. They now offer comfortable accommodation, as well as organising activity weeks in crafts, mountaineering, etc. The national youth hostel organisation in Germany, the *Deutsches Jugendherbergswerk* (DJH), also organises world-wide trips.

Youth hostels are managed by *Herbergseltern*, who are responsible for the running of the hostel as well as the well-being of the individual group or guest. The price for an overnight stay varies according to facilities offered. The DJH is a charitable organisation and one needs to be a member to be able to make use of the facilities.

(AW)

Jugendstil Art nouveau was a European and American artistic movement at around the turn of the century. The German term was coined relatively late, taking as its inspiration the magazine *Jugend*, which was published in München from 1896.

Art nouveau's main characteristics are ornamental, often floral designs, expensive materials and a combination of ideas from arts and crafts. The style influenced many areas of life including painting, architecture, literature, philosophy and dress design.

A number of German cities still have houses built in this style (e.g. Leipzig, München), although cities elsewhere, most notably Paris and Brussels, which did not suffer so much war damage, probably have the largest collection of art nouveau buildings.

See BAUHAUS.

(RW)

Jugoslawien-Krise The crisis which developed in former Yugoslavia in 1990 continues to provoke international concern, with most major powers as well as NATO, the United Nations and the European Union playing a role. Armed conflict in the region began in June 1991, first in Slovenia and Croatia and then spreading to Bosnia-Herzegovina.

Yugoslavia was made up of six republics with Belgrade (situated in Serbia) as the capital of the state. As the Cold War came to an end, forces of disintegration, based largely around ethnic differences, came to the fore. The problem was exacerbated by the fact that each republic was not ethnically homogenous, for example more than 30 per cent of ethnic Serbs were living outside the Serbian Republic. Hence, when Slovenia made official her desire for independence in December 1990 Serbia became anxious about the fate of Serbs living under what would be foreign rule. Problems of this nature were then replicated throughout the region, intensifying between Croatia and Serbia after moves were made towards the former's independence (there were around 600 000 Serbs living in Croatia). Problems of mixed ethnicities became particularly problematic when fighting spread to Bosnia-Herzegovina, the most ethnically diverse of the republics.

On the issue of Croatian and Slovenian independence from Yugoslavia, Germany was particularly vociferous within European Union debates on the Yugoslav crisis. Germany announced that she would recognise the independence of the two states before Christmas 1991, thus forcing its EU partners to follow suit even before recognition conditions had been met. Croatia and Slovenia were recognised as independent states in January 1992 whilst Bosnia had first to hold a referendum in February. Despite being boycotted by Bosnian Serbs the independence of Bosnia-Herzegovena was subsequently asserted. By May 1992 Croatia, Slovenia and Bosnia all had UN membership.

The crisis in Bosnia has since stabilised. Bosnia Herzegovina now comprises three cantons; Muslim, Croat and Serb. NATO forces are present on the ground to enforce the peace agreement, and these include German forces on one of their first peace-keeping missions.

See BLAUHELM-EINSÄTZE.

(KL)

17 Juni

See AUFSTAND.

K

Kalter Krieg The Cold War refers to the period of East–West conflict that ensued after World War II. 'Cold' War implies a lack of actual fighting, or 'hot war'. The Cold War was a period of polarity in international relations symbolised in Europe by the Berlin Wall and the Iron Curtain dividing Europe into two opposing ideological, economic and political camps under the leadership of the United States in the West and the Soviet Union in the East.

The Cold War emerged as the wartime alliance crumbled. It became clear that the US and Soviet Union had very different visions of how the post-war world should be constructed. This could be seen in their disputes over what was to be done with Germany after the war which culminated in the division of Germany into a Western-oriented Federal Republic and the Soviet-sponsored GDR. A stalemate in Europe was reached by the 1960s as both superpowers had consolidated their positions, with the Federal Republic and the GDR becoming ideological flagships for the opposing camps. Outside Europe the superpower conflict extended also to arenas in Africa, the Middle East and Central America.

The Cold War was punctuated by periods of *détente* or 'relaxation of tensions' (ENTSPANNUNG), during which US–Soviet dialogue and arms control negotiations took place. In Europe *détente* allowed intra-German dialogue to proceed as well as a number of agreements between the Federal Republic and Eastern European countries under Chancellor BRANDT'S OSTPOLITIK.

The origins of the end of the Cold War can be traced to Gorbachev's assumption of power in 1985 and the internal reforms and policies of openness which loosened the Soviet grip on East and Central Europe. The end of the Cold War made it possible for German unification to take place. The legitimacy of the ruling SED was challenged from both within and outside the GDR. As the Cold War system came to an end German unification took place with the agreement of all World War II Allies and the two Germanies through the 'Two-plus-Four' formula.

See ZWEI-PLUS-VIER-VERTRAG.

(KL)

Kanzlerdemokratie 'Chancellor democracy' is a term used to describe the potential the office of Federal Chancellor is sometimes said to have for dominating decision-making in the Federal Republic. It reflects the enhanced constitutional position awarded to the Chancellor in the GRUNDGESETZ in comparison to the constitution of the Weimar Republic.

'Chancellor democracy' is associated in particular with the Chancellorship of Konrad ADENAUER (1949–63). In this formative phase of the Federal Republic, Adenauer was able to exploit the constitutional powers of the Chancellor to attain an unusually predominant role in West German politics. This reflected a number of factors: Adenauer's prominent personal role in dealing externally with the former Western occupying powers who at the time retained extensive control over the Federal Republic's foreign policy; the relative immaturity of those other political institutions designed to play important roles in the division of powers (GEWALTENTEILUNG) in the Federal Republic; Adenauer's own authoritarian style of leadership; and the exceptional popularity he enjoyed among the electorate for most of his period of office, which served to legitimate and support the predominant role he was playing.

Adenauer's successors have not been able to replicate his role. They have faced constraints from within the Federal Government, with individual ministers developing their own power bases and the compromises inherent in coalition government restricting the Chancellor's freedom of manoeuvre. The wider checks and balances of the Federal Republic's horizontal and vertical division of powers have also had a restrictive effect on the Chancellor. As a result, only in unusual and temporary circumstances, such as Chancellor Helmut SCHMIDT's economic 'crisis management' in the mid-1970s, or Chancellor Helmut KOHL's stewardship of the German unification process in 1990, have post-Adenauer Chancellors come close to emulating Adenauer's example.

See BESATZUNG; BUNDESKANZLER; BUNDESREGIERUNG; KOALITION; WEIMARER REPUBLIK.

(CJ)

Karneval See FESTE UND FEIERN.

Katholische Kirche There are two main Churches in Germany, Catholic and Protestant. Today both have a roughly equal number of members but Catholics are predominant in large parts of BAYERN, in the Pfalz (Palatinate) and the Rhineland.

Germanic tribes first became Christians when Boniface and a group of Anglo-Saxon missionaries sent by the Pope came to preach and convert what is now Germany. Boniface founded monasteries and in the Middle Ages these were the centres of religious and cultural life as well as of the arts and sciences. In the sixteenth century what was the 'Catholic', i.e. 'general' church split into the Catholic and Protestant Churches over the teachings of Luther, Zwingli and Calvin.

Catholicism suffered under Napoleon's secularisation in 1803 (dissolution of all monasteries and confiscation of all church property). The German Empire proclaimed in 1871 was basically Protestant. In terms of social status and job prospects, Catholics were second-class citizens. In his *Kulturkampf* (cultural battle, 1871–93) against the Catholics, Bismarck unsuccessfully tried to turn the Catholic Church into a state-controlled church. In the Weimar Republic the Catholic *Zentrumspartei* (Centre Party) tried, together with Social Democrats and Liberals, to stabilise democracy against anti-democratic movements, especially the National Socialists

The GRUNDGESETZ is strongly influenced by the Catholic values of human rights and solidarity. In the Federal Republic the relationship between the Church and the State is one of partnership.

The Catholic Church is organised into 27 dioceses and has just under 30 million members of which around 5 per cent attend church. Its annual income from the *Kirchensteuer* (church tax) and collections is around DM8.5 billion. Through the initiative of its lay members the church is active in charitable work and social work, in education and in the media, and also supports overseas aid projects. This work is organised through church-sponsored associations, including the *Katholischer Deutscher Frauenbund*, KOLPINGWERK, and the *Bund katholischer Unternehmer*.

The main problems both Churches currently face are providing answers to the ethical questions of today, securing the interest of the young generation and improving inter-Church dialogue.

See EVANGELISCHE KIRCHE DEUTSCHLANDS; WEIMARER REPUBLIK.

(RW)

Kelly, Petra   Petra Kelly (1947–1992) was the most vocal and high-profile of the leaders of the GRÜNE. She died in unusual circumstances in 1992. Born in Günzburg on 29 November 1947, Kelly went to the United States in 1960 where she also received her secondary and university education. In 1970, she returned to Europe, first studying in Amsterdam and then taking a post in the European Commission. During Kelly's sojourn in Brussels, she became active in the Women's Working Circle of the SPD.

However, in 1979, Kelly left the SPD and helped form the *Grüne*. Kelly's career in the *Grüne* was high-profile and idiosyncratic. She entered the BUNDESTAG in 1983 where she was part of the fundamentalist wing of her party, advocating e.g. the rotation of Green MPs. Over the next decade, her combative approach alienated much of the Greens' membership and, with the rise of the more moderate elements, associated with figures like Joschka FISCHER in the late 1980s, she became a peripheral figure within the party.

Despite the decline in her political fortunes, Petra Kelly remained a much respected figure and her death – apparently at the hands of her part-

ner, the former *Bundeswehr* General Gert Bastian – was greeted with genuine grief from political friends and foes alike.
(CL)

Kindergarten See VORSCHULISCHE ERZIEHUNG.
(AW)

Kinkel, Klaus Klaus Kinkel has been Federal Foreign Minister since 1992 and is a former leader of the FDP. Born on 17 December 1936 in Metzlingen, Kinkel did not take the conventional route into politics, instead joining the civil service. In a brilliant career, Kinkel's appointments included Head of Planning in the German Foreign Office from 1974–78 and President of the Federal Intelligence Service from 1983–87. From 1987–91 he was State Secretary in the Justice Ministry and then Minister for Justice from 1991–92, before succeeding Hans-Dietrich GENSCHER as Foreign Minister.

Kinkel's political career has been meteoric. He joined the FDP only in 1991, became its leader in 1993, and was elected to the *Bundestag* in 1994 before resigning as leader in 1995 in the face of growing criticism of his performance, in particular in the light of a succession of poor results by the FDP in LANDTAG elections from 1994–96. He remains in his post as Foreign Minister but he and his party's long-term future remain in the balance.
(CL)

Klassizismus See STILE.

Koalition Coalitions are alliances of political parties in government. Coalition government is the norm at the federal level in Germany and is widespread in the BUNDESLÄNDER. This is primarily a result of the electoral laws (WAHLRECHT) used in federal and LANDTAG elections. They establish forms of proportional representation which usually (at federal level) or often (in the *Bundesländer*) ensure that no one party wins a majority of parliamentary seats and therefore that a coalition of parties is needed to form a government with majority support in parliament.

Coalition governments at the federal level have always been either formations of the Centre–Right, led by the CDU/CSU, and normally including the FDP (1949–66, 1982–), or of the Centre–Left, comprising SPD and FDP in the period 1969–1982. The exception was the period of Grand Coalition between CDU/CSU and SPD from 1966–69. A range of coalition alignments may exist at any point in time in the *Bundesländer*, including those noted above, but also, and more recently, 'red–green' coalitions of SPD and GRÜNE and 'Traffic-Light' Coalitions of SPD, *Grüne* and FDP.

See GROßE KOALITION; SOZIALLIBERALE KOALITION.
(CJ)

Kohl, Helmut   Helmut Kohl has been party leader of the CDU since 1973 and Federal Chancellor since 1982. Born in 1930 in Ludwigshafen, Helmut Kohl was already an important figure in the RHEINLAND-PFALZ CDU by his mid-twenties. By the age of 29 he had been elected to the LANDTAG and served as Minister-President from 1969–76. He led the CDU in the 1976 federal election campaign, narrowly missing an absolute majority, yet still failing to lead the CDU into government. From 1976–82 he was leader of the CDU/CSU FRAKTION (parliamentary grouping). In October 1982 the FDP defected from its coalition with the SPD to join forces with the CDU/CSU, thereby installing Kohl as sixth Chancellor of the Federal Republic.

For most of the 1980s, Kohl was perceived as a gaffe-prone politician lacking in credibility. However, since 1990 he has been recognised as a political leader of remarkable skill and now enjoys world-wide recognition as an international statesman.

Kohl's greatest achievement as Chancellor was the management of German unification, which he orchestrated at breathtaking speed. Since then, his primary ideological goal has been European integration, a vision he pursued in tandem with France's former President, François Mitterrand. His goal now is to see Germany locked into an irrevocable economic and monetary union, which he sees as crucial to guarantee lasting peace in Europe.

Following the retirement of Mitterrand in 1995, Kohl's European project has faced growing difficulties amid growing opposition both at home and abroad. A central question given his advancing age is that of his successor. It is unclear whether Kohl will step down after the next election in 1998. A potential successor is currently not in sight.

See BUNDESKANZLER; EUROPAPOLITIK; MINISTERPRÄSIDENT; VEREINI-GUNG.

(SG)

Kollektivierung   Collectivisation was an intrinsic element of the GDR's command economy and the basic structural element of GDR agriculture. The artisan trades were also affected by the collectivisation process. During the 1950s, independent artisans were subjected to heavy pressure to join production collectives (*Produktionsgenossenschaften des Handwerks*, or PGHs). The latter increased in number from 85 in 1955 to 4 458 in 1970.

In 1972, the government restructured many PGHs into state enterprises and thereby nationalised them. Four years later, however, pragmatic considerations – bottlenecks in services and repairs and shortages of meat and bread – caused the government to change its policy and to promote both the PGHs and independent artisan trades by the extension of credits. In the mid-1980s, private enterprises accounted for 58.9 per cent of the output of artisan trades as against 41.1 per cent by PGHs, an indicator of the value of the small independent plumber, electrician, joiner, mechanic and builder in a system bedevilled by frequent shortages and bureaucratic procedures.

See LPG.

(MD)

Kolpingwerk The Kolpingwerk is a Catholic organisation founded by Adolf Kolping (1813–65) in order to help young men and families in their personal and social development as Christians, as masters in a trade, as fathers and as citizens. It is the oldest Catholic social organisation in Germany.

Today the Kolpingwerk is organised into dioceses with the central office in Cologne. The programme is open to men and women, Germans and non-Germans. The programmes offered focus on personal advancement (on questions of religion, ethics, psychology, health, art, culture), and basic and advanced training qualifications (school-leaving certificates, apprenticeships, computing). There are special programmes for senior citizens and the young.

The Kolpingwerk now has a world-wide training network, which supports programmes in basic and advanced training in the trades in 40 countries in all five continents.

(AW)

Kombinat Combines were the large-scale economic units which formed the organisational backbone of the GDR economy from the late 1970s. Combines were formed by the amalgamation of several nationalised enterprises (*Volkseigene Betriebe*) with similar production lines. Supplier enterprises and research centres were often located within a combine. A parent enterprise (*Stammbetrieb*), presided over by a general director, acted as the key structural link between the various enterprises. The average size of a combine ranged from 20 to 40 enterprises and the workforce between 800 at the *Konsum-, Druck- und Papierverarbeitung* combine and about 70 000 at Robotron.

The first significant wave of combine formation occurred during the era of the 'New Economic System' and the second one in the later 1970s to early 1980s. The number of combines increased from 45 in 1975 to 316 ten years later and many of the small ones were placed under the direction of the regional economic councils. The larger central combines were taken out of the control of the *Vereinigungen volkseigener Betriebe* (Associations of Nationalised Industries) and transferred to the appropriate ministry. By 1982, the combines' share of total industrial goods production and exports was over 90 per cent.

The SED leadership, in particular Günter MITTAG, hoped to reap a series of benefits from combine formation: economies of scale, a more rational division of labour between enterprises and ministries and the more rapid diffusion of scientific and technological research. Although the combines made progress in areas such as R&D and a more rational use of raw materials, their monopolistic position inhibited creativity and risk-taking, The whole combine structure was dismantled after unification by the TREUHANDANSTALT.

See NEUES ÖKONOMISCHES SYSTEM; PLANWIRTSCHAFT.

(MD)

Kommunale Selbstverwaltung   Local self-government provides the third level in the structure of the German state below those of the federal level (BUND) and the BUNDESLÄNDER. Local self-government is constitutionally guaranteed in the GRUNDGESETZ.

The particular structure of local government varies between the *Bundesländer* and is regulated by the respective *Bundesländer* constitutions. Units of local government are *Gemeinden* (municipalities), ranging in size from villages to major cities, and *Kreise* (districts). *Gemeinden* elect councils (*Gemeinderäte* or *Stadträte*) and in some *Bundesländer* they have directly elected mayors. *Kreise* also elect councils and normally appoint an official (a *Landrat*) to supervise local administration. Elections are typically contested by the same parties who are active at higher levels of government, though there is still a tradition of local, independent community groups standing for and succeeding in elections. More broadly, party politics at local level tends to be less partisan than in LANDTAG and BUNDESTAG elections.

In some *Bundesländer* (Baden-Württemberg, Bayern, Hessen, Niedersachsen, Nordrhein-Westfalen, Rheinland-Pfalz and Sachsen-Anhalt), intermediate and non-elected authorities between *Kreis* and *Bundesland*, called *Regierungsbezirke*, also exist, whose function is to supervise local administration on behalf of the *Bundesland* authorities.

Local governments carry out a number of compulsory responsibilities in such fields as schools, the fire service, road maintenance and sanitation along with so-called transferred responsibilities in such fields as tax collection, health care and housing, which are carried out on behalf of either federal or *Bundesland* authorities or both.

(CJ)

Konstruktives Mißtrauensvotum   The constructive vote of no-confidence is a procedure which can be used to replace a Federal Chancellor and initiate a change in Federal Government. It was introduced into the GRUNDGESETZ as a way of remedying the problems of the simple vote of no-confidence which was used in the Weimar Republic. This allowed parliament to unseat the sitting Chancellor without necessarily being agreed on a successor, and contributed to the governmental instability which helped to undermine Weimar democracy. The constructive vote of no-confidence only allows the unseating of a Chancellor if the BUNDESTAG simultaneously elects a successor. Such a successor would therefore have majority support and be capable of ensuring the stable government which the Weimar Republic lacked.

The constructive vote of no-confidence has been used successfully only once, when Helmut KOHL replaced Helmut SCHMIDT as Chancellor in 1982. This was made possible by the defection of the FDP from its coalition with Schmidt's SPD to join forces with the CDU/CSU, and thereby construct a new *Bundestag* majority in support of Kohl.

See BUNDESKANZLER; BUNDESREGIERUNG, WEIMARER REPUBLIK.

(CJ)

Konzentrationslager Concentration camps served a number of roles in the Third Reich: as penal institutions outside the normal bounds of the judicial process; as forced labour camps harnessed to the German rearmament and then war effort; and, in the form of extermination camps, as the sites of mass murder in the final phase of Nazi anti-Jewish policies during World War II.

Concentration camps came, from 1934, under the authority of the SS. The first camp to be set up was in Dachau near München, and was intended initially to house political prisoners interned following the National Socialist accession to power in 1933. New camps established during the 1930s, such as Sachsenhausen near Berlin and Buchenwald near Weimar in 1937, were set up to imprison 'asocials' deemed to be harmful for the development of the German 'racial community' (*Volksgemeinschaft*), including habitual criminals, beggars, pimps, tramps, gypsies, Jehovah's Witnesses and Jews with a criminal record. Additional camps, such as Mauthausen in Austria, were attached to quarries, brickworks and arms plants in order to exploit inmates as slave labour for the Nazi state's economic needs. Jews were increasingly sent to camps in large numbers following the REICHSKRISTALLNACHT (Night of the Broken Glass) of November 1938. During World War II the emphasis on slave labour ('extermination through work') increased, with over half a million inmates killed through exhaustion, starvation or disease by the end of the war.

A new form of camp, the extermination camp (*Vernichtungslager*) was established in occupied eastern Europe from 1941. These were geared to the mass murder of 'racial enemies', mainly the Jews. The most notorious was the camp at Auschwitz in present-day Poland, in which around 2.5 million inmates were killed. Auschwitz, where the use of gas chambers for conveyor belt-like mass murder was perfected, has become synonymous for many with the sheer scale and inhumanity of the HOLOCAUST.

See ANTISEMITISMUS; DRITTES REICH.

(CJ)

Konzertierte Aktion Concerted action was an attempt at reaching consensus over wages, price stability, employment and economic growth between government, employers and trade unions. Concerted action was proposed in 1964 by the committee of experts on economic development and was established by the Law to Promote Economic Stability and Growth, passed by the Grand Coalition in 1967. Although concerted action only set guidelines for collective bargaining negotiations, it was deeply mistrusted by many trade union members. In 1977 the unions withdrew from Concerted Action following the employers' decision to challenge the 1976 Codetermination Law before the Federal Constitutional Court.

Although there has been no return to concerted action, the so-called *Kanzlerrunden* (Chancellor Rounds), meetings between government, business and unions, continue to discuss economic and social problems. It is unusual for binding agreements to arise from such meetings. The government did, however, conclude a Solidarity Pact (SOLIDARPAKT) with business and unions in 1992 to promote growth in the NEUE BUNDESLÄNDER following unification. More recently discussions over an employment pact were initiated by the metalworkers' union IG Metall in an attempt to create employment and stop welfare cuts in return for wage concessions from the unions.

Although tripartite agreements can be reached over important economic and employment issues, these remain at best guidelines since they cannot intervene in the TARIFAUTONOMIE (freedom of collective bargaining) guaranteed by law.

See BUNDESVERFASSUNGSGERICHT; GEWERKSCHAFTEN; GROßE KOALITION; KORPORATISMUS; MITBESTIMMUNG; SOZIALPARTNERSCHAFT.

(SRF)

Korporatismus   Corporatism refers to a form of close involvement of interest groups, in particular trade unions and business, in the formulation and implementation of state policy. It was used frequently from the late 1960s onwards to describe the institutionalised 'tripartite' forms of co-operation between the Federal Government, unions and employers associations which grew out of the 1966–69 Grand Coalition and the Social-Liberal Coalition of SPD and FDP which followed. Its strongest expression was in the institutional framework of Concerted Action (KONZERTIERTE AKTION) in the period 1967–77.

Although institutionalised corporatist arrangements have not been revived, the Federal Republic's tradition of consensus and social partnership still secures extensive input for unions and business in policy-making, not least in the regular *Kanzlerrunden* (Chancellor Rounds) of consultation in economic policy.

See GEWERKSCHAFTEN; GROßE KOALITION; SOZIALLIBERALE KOALITION; SOZIALPARTNERSCHAFT; UNTERNEHMERVERBÄNDE.

(ECM)

KPD (Kommunistische Partei Deutschlands)   The Communist Party of Germany was founded in December 1918 as a radical offshoot of the SPD.

It aspired to the establishment of a communist state on the model of the Soviet Union. It regularly won over 10 per cent of the vote during the Weimar Republic, to whose overthrow it was committed. Such strong support for a party with such clear anti-system aims represented one of the weaknesses of Weimar democracy. Following the collapse of the Weimar Republic in 1933, the KPD was the first party banned by the National Socialists, one of whose central dogmas was anti-communism. The KPD nevertheless co-ordinated the most consistent and strongest opposition to the Third Reich from 1933–45.

The KPD re-emerged, with strong Soviet support, throughout Germany after the end of World War II. In the Western occupation zones it failed to compete effectively with its rival left-wing force, the reconstituted SPD, and came to contest the first two elections of the Federal Republic as a dwindling splinter party. The KPD was subsequently banned by the Federal Constitutional Court in 1956 for professing anti-constitutional aims. A successor party, the DKP, was established in 1968. Widely and correctly regarded as a GDR stooge, the DKP never made a significant electoral impact.

The KPD in the post-war Soviet occupation zone benefited from the patronage of the Soviet authorities. Although relatively weak in terms of popular support, the breakdown in relations between the Soviet Union and the Western Allies and the subsequent consolidation of Soviet-style communist rule in the GDR, combined to establish the KPD as a major political player. It was merged with the SPD in a 'shotgun marriage' to the detriment of the latter, to form the SED in 1946. The SED was then the ruling party of the GDR from 1949 through to 1989–90.

See BESATZUNG; BUNDESVERFASSUNGSGERICHT; DRITTES REICH; NATIONAL-SOZIALISMUS; POLITISCHE PARTEIEN; WEIMARER REPUBLIK.

(CJ)

Krankenversicherung Health insurance finances the costs of health care in the German health care system (GESUNDHEITSWESEN). Around 90 per cent of the population is insured in a range of different types of health insurance fund (*Krankenkasse*). These may have a regional base, or offer health care cover for particular professions or firms. The general local insurance funds (*Allgemeine Ortskrankenkassen*, or AOK) are, however, open to all and have the greatest number of members.

Health insurance is organised on similar lines to the other main branches of social insurance (SOZIALVERSICHERUNG): costs of care are covered by contributions paid into the funds, and not out of general taxation. Half the contributions are paid by the insured and half by their employers. Pensioners' contributions are covered by their pension insurance funds. Additional private insurance can be taken out, means permitting. All the insured have an automatic claim to care in case of ill-health, with insurance covering the costs of care in hospitals and general practices, as well as dental care, prescriptions, rehabilitative care, pregnancy care and sick pay (initially at a rate of at least 80 per cent of normal wages, after six weeks falling to 65 per cent).

Contributions are varied regularly in line with the principle that current health care expenditures should be covered as far as possible by current income from contributions. Wide variations in contribution rates may thus exist in different parts of the country.

The cost of the health care system – and the level of insurance contributions – have risen rapidly since the 1970s due mainly to technological advances in health care and an ageing population, and in part to inefficiencies in administration and provision. Only qualified successes have been recorded in the effort to reduce costs and streamline the system, in part by introducing market mechanisms such as a greater freedom for the insured to move between different insurance funds.

Further burdens have been imposed by unification, in particular the modernisation of the health care system in the East. It therefore remains a major priority to boost efficiency in administration and provision. Considerable pressure also exists in some fields to reduce the level of provision, for example in the level of sick pay awarded.

See ARBEITSLOSENVERSICHERUNG; PFLEGEVERSICHERUNG; RENTEN-VERSICHERUNG; SOZIALES NETZ.

(CJ)

Kreis   See KOMMUNALE SELBSTVERWALTUNG.

Krenz, Egon   Egon Krenz (1937–) was General Secretary of the SED and Chairman of the GDR Council of State (STAATSRAT) in 1989. Krenz, the son of a tailor and a teacher, belonged to the second generation of SED politicians. He earned his political spurs as Chairman of the Thälmann Pioneers (1971–74) and as First Secretary of the Free German Youth (1974–83). A protégé of Erich HONECKER, he entered the *Politbüro* in 1976 and held the important office of Central Committee Secretary for Security and Youth Affairs from 1983–89. Widely tipped to succeed Honecker, his prospects faded in the late 1980s when Günter MITTAG formed a closer relationship with the General Secretary. Krenz, growing increasingly dissatisfied with the obduracy of Honecker and Mittag, decided, after much hesitancy, to conspire with Günter Schabowski and other *Politbüro* colleagues to depose the SED primate. In October 1989, Krenz stepped into Honecker's shoes as General Secretary of the SED and as Chairman of the Council of State and head of the National Defence Council.

Krenz's campaign to reassert SED authority and influence soon foundered, partly because he was too closely associated in people's minds with the old regime and memories were still fresh of his expression of support on an official visit to Beijing for the Chinese leadership's violent suppression of the Tiananmen Square demonstrations. Even such dramatic concessions as the abandonment of the SED's leadership role in society and his authorisation of the opening of the Berlin Wall failed to boost his popularity. He resigned from all his offices in December 1989 and was expelled from the now renamed SED-PDS the following month.

Krenz's efforts to defend his reputation in newspaper articles and in his hastily written account of his role in the WENDE are continually undermined by his SED past. In March 1995, he was charged, along with several other *Politbüro* colleagues, for his part in the manslaughter of people attempting to escape from the GDR.

See BERLINER MAUER; SCHIEßBEFEHL.

(MD)

Krupp-Hoesch   Since the highly significant acquisition of Hoesch by Krupp, Krupp-Hoesch is the seventeenth largest company in Germany with external sales of DM 23.5 billion in 1995, 66 000 employees and a net income of DM 505 million.

The Krupps were probably Europe's richest family for many years. A 400-year dynasty, they began to make history by manufacturing gun barrels during the Thirty Years War. Over time vast holdings in armaments, iron and steel, coal and shipbuilding were added. Alfred Krupp was released early from imprisonment for war crimes by the Americans after World War II. His property was returned so that he could assist in the rebuilding of the West German economy. Shipbuilding disappeared from the product range, followed by coal when Ruhrkohle was formed in 1968.

In late 1991 Krupp, with the assistance of WESTLB, acquired first a quarter, then a majority stake in Hoesch. This rapid and decisive move made the take-over both big and hostile by German standards – not least because it outwitted the DEUTSCHE BANK which advised Hoesch. The merger was completed a year later when the new group was registered as Fried. Krupp AG Hoesch-Krupp. Given over-capacity and the relatively large number of former family-owned steel companies, however, rationalisation was inevitable but dramatic for the Ruhr district. In 1997, Krupp Hoesch (crude steel output 4.9 million tonnes in 1996) launched a hostile takeover bid for Thyssen (9.3 million tonnes). Stiff resistance from the Thyssen boards and employees caused the substitution of more amicable merger talks. A full merger would have produced the third largest European manufacturer.

The Hoesch take-over represents another stage in the vicissitudes of Krupp's corporate governance, as well as a case study in German capitalism. Although the firm was converted to a joint stock company in 1903, the Krupp family retained all but four of the shares, and Krupp remained unquoted on the stock exchange. Under Alfred Krupp (1907–67) it was reconverted to a sole proprietorship, but his son Arndt waived his inheritance so that his father's plans for founding a charitable foundation could be realised. In any case, the company had encountered a serious liquidity crisis and the rescue operation mounted by the banks was conditional upon the restoration of joint-stock status and stricter managerial controls. In 1974, the state of Iran acquired a quarter of Krupp, but the largest shareholder in the new Krupp-Hoesch group remains the Foundation.

From January 1993 Krupp shares have been traded on the German and Swiss stock exchanges. The aim is to highlight the company's strategy and value. This inevitably focuses more attention on profitability, yet following its flotation Krupp-Hoesch was not able to pay a dividend until 1995.

See FINANZWESEN; INDUSTRIE.

(EOS)

L

Lafontaine, Oskar Oskar Lafontaine has been SPD Minister-President of the SAARLAND since 1985, became leader of the SPD in 1995 and was earlier the SPD Candidate for Chancellor in the 1990 *Bundestag* election. On the left of the SPD, Lafontaine has been called 'the Napoleon of the Saar' because of his demeanour and combative political style.

Born on 16 September 1943 in Saarlouis, Lafontaine climbed the hierarchy of the local SPD in his native Saarland. He was a member of the LANDTAG from 1970 to 1975 and Mayor of Saarbrücken from 1976 to 1985. He has been a member of the BUNDESRAT since 1985.

Oskar Lafontaine's most significant role at the national level to date was as the SPD's Chancellor-Candidate in 1990. Along with the majority of his party, Lafontaine misread the popular mood over German unification and lost badly to Helmut KOHL and the governing coalition of CDU/CSU and FDP. In the following years, Lafontaine consolidated his power base in the SPD and played a supporting role in Chancellor-Candidate Rudolf SCHARPING's unsuccessful campaign for the 1994 *Bundestag* elections. However, with Scharping's position as leader of the SPD under increasing pressure in the summer and autumn of 1995, Lafontaine seized his moment and replaced Scharping at the party's annual conference in November 1995.

With Lafontaine firmly back at the helm, he and the SPD have two dilemmas to address. First, will he be tempted to run again as Chancellor-Candidate in the 1998 *Bundestag* elections or step aside and allow someone more electorate-friendly – such as Gerhard SCHRÖDER, the Minister-President of NIEDERSACHSEN – to run instead? Second, will the SPD run on a more explicitly left-oriented programme, in order to address electoral competition from the Greens, or will it continue to try and fight the CDU for the mainstream voters?

(CL)

Landesregierung The governments of the BUNDESLÄNDER (called *Senate* in Berlin, Bremen and Hamburg) are led by a MINISTERPRÄSIDENT (*regierender Bürgermeister* in Berlin, *Bürgermeister* in Bremen and Hamburg). The *Ministerpräsident* leads a team of ministers who are responsible for particular policy areas in the *Bundesland* concerned. The rules used in some *Bundesländer* allow *Ministerpräsident* and ministers to be drawn from outside the LANDTAG, though most are *Landtag* members.

Landesregierungen each send representatives to the BUNDESRAT, which is involved in the making of federal-level legislation. They are also responsible for the implementation of most federal laws within the *Bundesländer*. These functions involve the *Landesregierungen* in extensive policy co-ordination, or POLITIKVERFLECHTUNG, with the Federal Government. This co-ordination is conducted through two forms of committee. First, there is co-ordination between the *Landesregierungen* in committees bringing together ministers from different *Bundesländer* responsible for the same policy areas, for example the Cultural Ministers' Conference and at *Ministerpräsident* level, the *Ministerpräsidentenkonferenz*. Second, there are equivalent committees which bring together ministers responsible for the same policy areas in the *Bundesländer* and the Federal Government.

Landesregierungen are in principle accountable to and controlled by their *Landtage*. In practice, however, their involvement in federal-level legislation and *Politikverflechtung* co-ordination processes makes effective control difficult. The *Landesregierungen* have as a result become clearly the most powerful political institutions in the *Bundesländer*.

See BUNDESREGIERUNG; FÖDERALISMUS; STÄNDIGE KONFERENZ DER KULTUSMINISTER.

(CJ)

Landtag   *Landtage* are the directly elected parliaments of the 16 BUNDESLÄNDER (and are termed *Bürgerschaft* in Bremen and Hamburg and *Abgeordnetenhaus* in Berlin). The *Landtage* have four main functions: to legislate in those policy fields where the *Bundesländer* have exclusive legislative powers; to select the MINISTERPRÄSIDENT of the *Bundesland* concerned and, depending on the arrangements used in that *Bundesland*, to elect or endorse the other members of the LANDESREGIERUNG; to scrutinise and control the activities of the *Landesregierung*; and, through political parties, to represent the views of the electorates of the *Bundesländer*. In addition, the *Landtage* also elect representatives from among their membership to sit on the Federal Assembly, the body periodically convened to elect the Federal President.

The status of the *Landtage* has declined significantly since the foundation of the Federal Republic. The emergence of 'co-operative federalism' and the associated phenomomenon of POLITIKVERFLECHTUNG (political 'entanglement') have embedded the *Landesregierungen* in decision-making processes alongside federal level institutions, over which the *Landtage* have little effective control, and at the same time have eroded the scope of the legislative powers exercised in the *Landtage*.

See BUNDESPRÄSIDENT; BUNDESVERSAMMLUNG; FÖDERALISMUS.

(CJ)

Lehrveranstaltungen   Courses at university are taught in a variety of ways, according to the choice of the tutors concerned under the principle of academic freedom (AKADEMISCHE FREIHEIT).

The *Vorlesung*, or lecture, is the most traditional method of teaching, normally delivered only by professors. Lectures typically have the highest numbers of participants, often running into hundreds. The tradition of lectures is frequently criticised for not allowing two-way exchange between the professor and the students. *Übungen* and *Proseminare* (preparatory seminars) act as preparation for the more advanced *(Haupt)seminare* (main subject seminars). They provide an introduction to the basics of the subject and also to wider academic skills (researching bibliographies, critical reading and interpretation, discussion, writing and presenting papers). An *Arbeitsgemeinschaft* (workgroup) runs parallel to a *Vorlesung, Übung,* or *Proseminar* to allow work in small groups, and is normally taught by more advanced students (*Hilfswissenschaftler* or *Hiwis*).

In a *(Haupt)seminar*, students are expected to work more independently, sometimes in groups, looking at problems in a wider context. Advanced seminars (*Oberseminare* or *Kolloquien*) are for very advanced students who are normally invited to participate by the professor. Both students and professors present and discuss their research findings.

A *Praktikum* (work practice) offers students insights into what might be their later career. Common forms of *Praktika* are in schools (for those studying to become teachers) or in a lab (for scientists).

Completion of a *Lehrveranstaltung* is normally recognised by a SCHEIN.

See GRUND- UND HAUPTSTUDIUM.

(AW)

LPG (Landwirtschaftliche Produktionsgenossenschaft)   The agricultural co-operative was the basic model of co-operative ownership in GDR agriculture. Although the collectivisation of agriculture commenced in 1952, it was not until 1960 that the process was accelerated with a view to its completion. The proportion of agricultural land farmed by the LPGs increased from 45.1 per cent at the start of 1960 to 84.2 per cent by its close. The expropriation of their land aroused considerable opposition among farmers and induced many to leave for the West.

Three types of agricultural co-operatives were established according to the degree of socialisation of the means of production. Type III, in which all the agricultural means of production (land, livestock, machinery, buildings) were collectivised, was the dominant form. By the mid-1970s, about 98 per cent of agricultural land farmed by co-operatives was worked in this type of unit, with an average size of 1 180 hectares.

After the introduction of German monetary union and the incorporation into the Common Agricultural Policy of the EU in 1990, East German agriculture experienced a dramatic collapse as it struggled to adapt to the new economic conditions, i.e. privatisation, obligatory cutbacks in production and a change in the pattern of subsidies.

See KOLLEKTIVIERUNG.

(MD)

M

Maizière, Lothar de Lothar de Maizière (1940–) was GDR Prime Minister from April to October 1990. Born the son of a lawyer, de Maizière trained first as a musician and then as a lawyer at the Humboldt University, Berlin. He was a vice-president of the GDR synod of the Protestant Churches, a deputy vice-chairman of the Council of Lawyers' Associations (1987) and acted on behalf of peace activists. A member of the GDR-CDU since 1956, he was elected acting Chairman of the party on 11 November 1989. Unlike his predecessor, Gerald Götting, he was not closely associated with the GDR-CDU's past as a block party (BLOCKPARTEI). He entered MODROW's cabinet in the same month with responsibility for church affairs. In February 1990, he took the GDR-CDU into the Alliance for Germany (ALLIANZ FÜR DEUTSCHLAND). After the Alliance's success in the March 1990 VOLKSKAMMER election, he assumed, somewhat reluctantly, the position of Minister-President of the GDR. Whilst committed to representing and defending East German interests in the unification negotiations, he was very much overshadowed by the West German Chancellor, Helmut KOHL. With union complete, de Maizière entered Kohl's government as Minister without Portfolio and in December 1990 was elected to the BUNDESTAG.

His political career was damaged irreparably by charges of having been a STASI collaborator under the code-name 'Czerny'. Although denying the charge, he was obliged to resign from the government in December 1990 and to surrender his CDU party offices in September 1991. He continues to practise as a lawyer.

See CDU.

(MD)

Mannesmann Mannesmann was the thirteenth largest industrial company in Germany in 1995 with a turnover of DM32 billion, 122 700 employees and net profits of DM700 million.

The company's origins were in steel tubes and pipes. It developed into a vertically integrated steel producer, also mining its own coal to use for smelting. Financial assistance and encouragement came from the SIEMENS family and DEUTSCHE BANK. One of Germany's 'top ten' joint-stock companies was as a result formed in 1890 but the Mannesmann family possessed little business sense and was forced to resign in 1900.

When the company's 75th anniversary was celebrated in 1965, Mannesmann was still a vertically integrated steel producer. In 1969, however, coal mining was surrendered to RUHRKOHLE and, in a 'division of labour' agreement with THYSSEN, Mannesmann relinquished its rolling mill activities but doubled its pipe production. The four product divisions are now: machinery and engineering, automotive engineering, telecommunications and tubulars and trading. Telecommunications consists of Mobilfunk and Eurokom, where the former involves a network covering 1.45 million subscribers and the latter is a holding company with, for example, a 10 per cent stake in the French Cegetel consortium.

Although not quite as dependent on domestic and EU sales as KRUPP-HOESCH and Thyssen, the expansion in telecommunications will by its very nature be concentrated in these geographical areas. Moreover, investment in telecoms accounted for 35 per cent of total capital outlay in 1995, yet this division returned only 8 per cent of total sales. Machinery and engineering, on the other hand, had a sales share of 43 per cent, compared to 33 per cent of total investment. However, in 1996 a Mannesmann-led consortium secured a 49.8 per cent stake in DBKom – DEUTSCHE BAHN's extensive telecoms network.

There is little doubt that the group's 30-year transformation has been fundamental. However, telecoms may well be a highly competitive sector, at least as far as corporate business is concerned. Automotive components also face fairly stiff competition.

See BUNDESKARTELLAMT.

(EOS)

Marshall-Plan   The US Marshall Plan or Economic Recovery Programme (ERP) was first announced In June 1947 by General G.C. Marshall in order to provide a jump start for the war-torn economies of the whole of Europe.

Part of the overall US commitment to Western Europe, the Marshall Plan is best understood as the financial arm of the US policies directed against the spread of communism in Europe. The plan greatly contributed to the division of Europe and the emerging Cold War since the ERP's conditions made it impossible for the Soviets to participate. The Americans required access to recipients' economic intelligence as well as a commitment to free trade. The plan was also instrumental in the forging of Western European integration.

Together with the other Soviet satellite states the Soviet occupation zone of Germany was not allowed to join the plan. The Western Zones of Germany were full participants in the programme, thus signifying the first steps in West Germany's absorption into the Western camp. West Germany's so-called 'economic miracle' was in part fuelled by the ERP.

See WIRTSCHAFTSWUNDER.

(KL)

Marxismus-Leninismus The teachings of Marx (1818–83) and Lenin (1870–1924) together formed the basis of socialist doctrine first in the Soviet Union and then in the other states of the post-World War II communist bloc in Eastern Europe.

Marx's teachings make three basic assumptions: (a) all history is a history of the struggle of classes and classes are separated by the possession or lack of possession of capital; (b) in the era of capitalism (from industrialisation in the nineteenth century) the classes confronting each other are the oppressed workers (proletariat) and the dominant capitalists; (c) a revolution brought about by the proletariat is ultimately inevitable and will lead to a classless society.

Lenin based his political ideology on these assumptions. Despite the fact that Russia was mainly an agrarian state at the end of the nineteenth century, Lenin wanted it to become the first nation to have a successful revolution of the proletariat which was then to be exported to the other European states. He precariously defined the proletariat as the poor peasants, industrial workers and intellectuals, poised against the aristocracy, land owners and the bourgeoisie. He formed the Soviet Communist Party in 1918. It was to work as the vanguard of this revolution, mobilising the oppressed classes and forging an alliance between them. Marx's idea of the rule of the proletariat during a transition period was interpreted as a blank cheque for the domination of the Party in all areas of life. This gave the Party total power whilst making it virtually unassailable right up to the demise of the Eastern bloc.

The teaching of the Party as the supreme power and the politicisation of every aspect of human life were adopted in all the other Eastern bloc states, including the GDR. National school curricula prescribed *Marxismus-Leninismus* as a subject.

See SED; STALINISMUS.

(RW)

Massenorganisationen The mass organisations such as the Free German Youth functioned as so-called 'transmission belts' (i.e. routes for mass input) for the SED in the former GDR.

The most significant mass organisations – FDGB (*Freier Deutscher Gewerkschaftsbund*), FDJ (*Freie Deutsche Jugend*), DFD (*Demokratischer Frauenbund Deutschlands*), DKB (*Deutscher Kulturbund*) and the VdgB (*Vereinigung der gegenseitigen Bauernhilfe*) were incorporated into the Democratic Block of Parties and Mass Organisations and were also represented in the VOLKSKAMMER. Like other mass organisations such as the Ernst Thälmann Pioneers and the German Sports and Gymnastics Association, they catered for the specific interests of their own members alongside their transmission belt function. The SED's leadership role was accepted by all mass organisations. In addition, they provided a source of information about people's attitudes, acted as a training ground for cadres in the SED, state and economy, and the larger ones such as the FDJ (the socialist youth organisation) and FDGB (the integrated trade union organisation) performed useful advisory and consultative functions within a complex political network. Membership of the organisations was voluntary, but SED members always formed the nucleus of the leadership.

The mass organisations fell apart during the implosion of the GDR. Some, like the FDGB, were dissolved and their members incorporated into corresponding West German functional units, whereas the members of other bodies found no equivalent.

See DDR.

(MD)

Mauer See Berliner Mauer.

Mauer im Kopf The 'wall in the head' refers to the post-unification psychological differences which divide East and West Germans. The euphoria which swept through the GDR after the crumbling of the Berlin Wall and the introduction of monetary union in July 1990 was soon superseded by well-founded anxieties over the general economic situation and job security. In addition to this widespread anxiety and resentment against the ABWICKLUNG ('winding up') of the GDR, public opinion surveys began to pick up a nostalgia for aspects of the authoritarian paternalism of the former GDR. A survey conducted in late 1992 among 2 000 West and 1 000 East Germans by the Emnid Institute found that not only did 13 per cent of Easterners mourn the passing of the GDR but that 64 per cent of Westerners and 74 per cent of Easteners agreed with the statement that 'The Wall has gone but the wall in people's heads grows.'

In another Emnid poll of mid-April to mid-June 1995 two-thirds of the 1 000 East Germans polled were of the opinion that the wall in the head was growing and 15 per cent that it would have been better if unification had not taken place.

Although growing together is proving more difficult than was at first expected, convergence, though not homogenisation, between East and West Germans will be promoted by a shared language and territory, similarities between young people in their personal values and growing East–West social mobility.

See BERLINER MAUER; OSSI; TRANSFORMATION; WESSI.

(MD)

Mecklenburg-Vorpommern Mecklenburg-West Pomerania is one of the constituent BUNDESLÄNDER of the Federal Republic and one of the NEUE BUNDESLÄNDER on the territory of the former GDR.

Its capital city is Schwerin and its biggest city is Rostock. It is 23 415km² in size and with a population of 1.83m (1994) is the least densely populated German *Bundesland*. Its main industries during the period of the GDR were shipbuilding and agriculture, but both have experienced steep decline in the adaptation to the free market system of the Federal Republic since unification. Unemployment is high at 16.1 per cent, yet GDP per head has risen quickly to reach 22 540DM (1995).

The largest political party since 1990 has been the CDU, which has led the LANDESREGIERUNG in a coalition with the SPD which was renewed after the 1994 LANDTAG election under MINISTERPRÄSIDENT Bernd Seite. The only other party represented after the 1994 election was the PDS.

See FÖDERALISMUS.

(CJ)

Mietvertrag Renting a flat or a room in a flat is extremely common in Germany. The *Mietvertrag* is a standard contract regulating terms and conditions of the tenancy. This is a form which can be obtained from stationery shops. It is often the responsibility of the prospective tenant to buy this form. Some terms are flexible and can be changed by consent of the tenant and the landlord, other terms are legally binding as they are set out in the contract. It is important to read all the terms before signing. No solicitor is necessary. The German tenancy laws (*Mietrecht*) are, most would say, biased towards the tenant.

By signing the tenancy agreement the tenant is legally liable to register his/her new address at the residency registration office (EINWOHNER-MELDEAMT).

(RW)

Ministerpräsident Minister-Presidents are the Heads of Government of the BUNDESLÄNDER and are elected directly or indirectly by their respective LANDTAGE.

In most of the *Bundesländer*, Minister-Presidents, like the Chancellor at federal level, have the power to set out the general guidlines of policy pursued by their LANDESREGIERUNGEN. Minister-Presidents in most cases select their own ministerial team (subject to the endorsement of their *Landtage*). They chair and co-ordinate the *Landesregierung* and in doing so are assisted by an office of advisers and civil servants (*Kanzlei* or *Staatsministerium*) analogous to the Chancellor's Office (BUNDESKANZLER-AMT) at federal level.

Minister-Presidents play an important co-ordination role in German federalism in their *Ministerpräsidentenkonferenz* and in periodic collective meetings with the Federal Chancellor.

The office of Minister-President has become an important recruiting ground for office at the federal level. Helmut KOHL, Willy BRANDT and Kurt-Georg Kiesinger all became Federal Chancellor after spells as Minister-President, and most opposition candidates for the Chancellorship in BUNDESTAG elections in recent years have also simultaneously been Minister-Presidents (e.g. Rudolf SCHARPING in 1994, Oskar LAFONTAINE in 1990, Franz-Josef STRAUß in 1980 and Helmut Kohl in 1976).

See BUNDESKANZLER; FÖDERALISMUS.

(CJ)

Ministerrat der DDR   The Council of Ministers constituted the government of the GDR from 1949–90. In October 1949, the provisional VOLKS-KAMMER elected a provisional government of the GDR as the main organ of state. Its title was changed three years later to the Council of Ministers. The first Minister-President was the ex-SPD functionary Otto Grotewohl; Walter Ulbricht was selected as one of his deputies. The creation of the Council of State (STAATSRAT) in 1960 led to the transfer of several important governmental functions to the new body. This trend was quickly reversed after the fall of Ulbricht and the Council of Ministers' status was restored by new legislation in 1972 and constitutional amendments in 1974. According to the 1972 law on the Council of Ministers, the Council formulated the broad lines of governmental domestic and foreign policy on behalf of the *Volkskammer* and supervised the implementation of government policy in the political, economic, cultural and social welfare spheres in addition to those defence functions which were allocated to it. The primacy of the SED was, however, made clear by the law's reference to the Council carrying out its work 'under the leadership of the party of the working class'. The Council's main area of activity concerned the planning and supervision of the economy with the assistance of bodies such as the State Planning Commission and the Office for Prices. The Presidium acted as the 'inner cabinet' and most of its members were from the SED. The co-ordination of Council business was undertaken by the Secretariat.

Council members were elected by the *Volkskammer* for a five-year term (before 1971 for four years) and the Chairman was nominated by the largest political group in parliament. Willi Stoph, an experienced SED administrator, held this position for most of the period after 1964. In the late 1980s, Council membership was virtually monopolised by the SED, with all but five members recruited from the ruling party. Technical and professional skills, in addition to the customary political loyalty, were an essential requirement of office. Most of the constituent ministries and offices were responsible for a specific sphere of the economy such as light industry, finance, foreign trade, the State Planning Commission and the Office for Prices. Although most members were involved in an economic function, other spheres were also represented, among them justice, education and foreign affairs.

During the WENDE, the Council was opened up to representatives of opposition parties and groups. Under Hans MODROW, the SED-PDS Minister-President, the Council briefly occupied a strategic position in the attempts to resuscitate the GDR. The government of Lothar DE MAIZIÈRE, Modrow's successor, negotiated the terms of the GDR's union with the Federal Republic.

See DDR; PDS; VEREINIGUNG.

(MD)

Mitbestimmung   Co-determination refers to the participation of employees or their representatives in the management of business or economy. After World War II, the Western Allies introduced parity co-determination (i.e. with equal representation for unions and management) in the iron and steel industry under strong trade union pressure. The principle of co-determination was developed and extended by laws in 1952, 1972 and 1989 to apply to all sectors.

Co-determination applies at two levels: that of the plant; and that of the company. On plant level, the legally guaranteed key institution is the BETRIEBSRAT (works council) which gives employee representatives a role in shaping working conditions and obliges management to provide necessary information and allow regular meetings. At the enterprise level, employee representatives take direct part in the *Aufsichtsrat* (supervisory board) where they have five of 11 seats. This body elects the executive management board and influences the strategic decisions of the company.

See GEWERKSCHAFTEN; KONZERTIERTE AKTION.

(ECM)

Mittag, Günter   Born near Stettin, Günter Mittag (1926–94), the son of an agricultural labourer, joined the KPD in 1945 and the SED one year later. He carved out a career during the late 1940s and early 1950s as an official with the GDR railways and as a full-time trade union functionary. He was appointed candidate member of the SED Central Committee in 1958 and then a full member in 1962. He entered the *Politbüro* in 1962 and achieved full membership status three years later.

The main function through which he exercised his influence over economic policy-making was that of Central Committee Secretary for Economic Affairs. This office, which he occupied from 1962-73 and from 1976 until his political demise in 1989, gave him a high degree of control over many areas of the economy, notably public finance, planning, basic materials, construction, light industry, metallurgy and machine building. Along with Erich Apel, he was one of the leading proponents of the GDR's modest economic reform programme, launched in 1963 as the New Economic System of Planning and Management (NEUES ÖKONOMISCHES SYSTEM, or NES). The termination of NES and the ousting in 1971 of its progenitor, ULBRICHT, led to Mittag's temporary political demise; he lost his Central Committee Secretaryship and was moved into the position of First Deputy Chairman of the Council of Ministers. However, his experience and skills proved to be urgently required as the GDR's economy began to flag in the late 1970s and he was restored to his Central Committee Secretaryship. In contrast to his reformist views in the 1960s, the politically ambitious Mittag pushed through with great determination a programme of tight economic centralisation, characterised by the formation of large combines and a proliferation of central planning indicators, as well as an over-ambitious attempt to modernise the GDR economy on the basis of new technologies. Regarded by many Western observers as an efficient technocrat, his reputation waned rapidly after the WENDE when his dictatorial methods of running the economy and his centralising zeal were widely regarded as the reasons for the chronic condition of the economy. A close ally of HONECKER, who relied heavily on Mittag's advice and experience for the running of the economy, he shared his patron's political fate in October 1989 and was ejected from the SED in the following month. Imprisoned in December, he was released on account of ill-health in the summer of 1990.

See SED.

(MD)

Mitteldeutschland 'Central Germany' was a term initially used to describe the territory of the GDR by those who did not want to recognise (divided) Germany's post-World War II eastern border with Poland (on the Oder and Neisse rivers).

Its current use is restricted to the media sphere, where the name *Mitteldeutscher Rundfunk*, which covers SACHSEN-ANHALT, SACHSEN and THÜRINGEN, refers rather to the centre of Germany on a north–south axis.

See ODER-NEISSE-LINIE; RUNDFUNK UND FERNSEHEN.

(RW)

Mittelstand *Mittelstand* may be translated as 'middle class', but normally refers to the small and medium-sized business sector of the economy. The *Mittelstand* has played an important role in German economic success. The term refers to companies, partnerships, family and single-owner businesses in industry, services, the professions (*freie Berufe*) and an amorphous group of bakers, tailors, plumbers, and so on (collectively known as '*Handwerker*', or artisans). In order to own a *Handwerker* enterprise, and therefore undertake responsibility for training apprentices (*Lehrlinge*), it is necessary to be in possession of an advanced qualification known as a *Meisterbrief*.

The working definition of *Mittelstand* firms is based on the quantitative criteria of turnover or employment. The extreme upper limits are companies with a turnover above DM100 million or over 500 employees. The 2 million Western enterprises in the *Mittelstand* with under 500 employees thus account for two-thirds of all private sector employment. They also train 80 per cent of all apprentices, and undertake 40 per cent of total investment. In the industrial sector, moreover, *Mittelstand* companies frequently dominate the world market for their product.

The TREUHANDANSTALT found it relatively easy to privatise the *Handwerker* and service sector companies and recreating an East German *Mittelstand* from this point of view was not difficult. But there remains a serious shortage of industrial concerns in this size category.

Mittelstand companies are less likely to be taken over by larger concerns than in the Anglo-Saxon world. This is because they are rarely floated on the stock market. *Mittelstand* companies would see this as undermining both their ownership and the degree of control they exercise. See DUALES SYSTEM.
(EOS)

Mittlere Reife See WEITERFÜHRENDE SCHULEN.

Modrow, Hans Hans Modrow (1928–) was Chairman of the GDR Council of Ministers in 1989–90. Born into a working-class family in Pomerania, Modrow served in the Home Guard during the final months of World War II and was interned in a Soviet prisoner-of-war camp until 1949. Soon after his release, he joined the SED and rose through the ranks as a youth movement official, a section head in the SED's Berlin regional organisation (1967–1971) and head of the Central Committee's Political Agitation department. He entered the Central Committee in 1958 and became a full member in 1967.

As First Secretary of the SED's Dresden regional organisation, he acquired a reputation for hard work, efficiency and a modest lifestyle. After Gorbachev came to power, Modrow became increasingly disturbed by the obduracy of Erich HONECKER and Günter MITTAG and sent out discrete signals of his support for a more flexible system of government.

The overthrow of Honecker removed the main obstacle to his career: in November 1989, he entered the *Politbüro* and became Chairman of the Council of Ministers (MINISTERRAT DER DDR). After Egon KRENZ's resignation in December, Modrow bore the main responsibility for stabilising the GDR and preserving it as an independent state. He introduced an ambitious economic reform programme, announced far-reaching political reforms and, in January 1990, entered into a dialogue with the RUNDER TISCH (Round Table). One month later, he tried to shore up his government by forming a 'government of national responsibility' with representatives from the new parties and movements.

However, with the economic situation deteriorating and the mass exodus showing no sign of abating, and with the Soviet Union unable to offer decisive aid, Modrow was forced to acknowledge, at the beginning of February 1990, that reformed communism had no future and that unification was unavoidable.

Although he lost power after the VOLKSKAMMER election in March 1990, he managed to enter the BUNDESTAG in December 1990. He did not seek re-election to the *Bundestag* in 1994, though remains active in politics as honorary chairman of the PDS.
See BÜRGERBEWEGUNGEN; DDR; SED.
(MD)

Moskauer Vertrag   The Moscow Treaty was signed as a non-aggression pact between the Federal Republic and the Soviet Union in 1970. The Moscow Treaty formed part of Willy BRANDT's eastern policy, or OSTPOLITIK, of 'normalising' relations with communist Eastern Europe. Negotiations were carried out by Egon Bahr between January and May 1970 and cemented by the Foreign Minister, Walter Scheel. Both the Soviet Union and the Federal Republic renounced the use of force. The Moscow Treaty entailed the Federal Republic committing itself to the inviolability of their borders including the ODER-NEISSE-LINIE between the GDR and Poland and the demarcation line between the Federal Republic and the GDR. Brandt was successful in excluding from the treaty any mention of the status of the GDR or the Soviet demand that the Federal Republic grant the GDR full diplomatic recognition. The Soviets insisted that the Treaty make no mention of German unification. However, Brandt's government presented a 'letter on German unity' to the Soviet government at the signing of the Treaty, reaffirming the Federal Republic's commitment to German unity. The aim behind this move was to quieten domestic opposition to the Treaty.

See ENTSPANNUNG.

(NM)

N

Nationale Front The National Front, to which all GDR political parties and mass organisations belonged, was the organisation responsible for the conduct of all elections to the VOLKSKAMMER and the GDR's other representative assemblies.

The election programme was drawn up by the National Front and was based on the overall policy of the SED. All candidates for election to the *Volkskammer* had to have the prior approval of the SED. The single list of candidates for elections which was ultimately presented to the electorate was identical with the result of the election. Other functions of the National Front included assisting the organs of state in the implementation of economic policy and in the election of lay judges.

The National Front was organised according to the territorial principle. In 1989, shortly before its dissolution, its 19 400 committees at regional, district and local levels had about 405 000 members, including 117 000 from the SED and 132 500 without party affiliation.

See MASSENORGANISATIONEN.

(MD)

Nationale Identität The definition of Germany's 'national identity' has been the subject of intense intellectual debate in German political life. The question of identity has always been problematic, due to the fact that Germany's territorial boundaries were not finally resolved until unification in 1990. Indeed, when 'Germany' was formed in 1870, it was not seen as a political entity, but rather as a cultural, ethnic and linguistic community, bound together by a common destiny (*Schicksalsgemeinschaft*).

Following defeat in two world wars and the experience of Nazi dictatorship, German national identity had to be rebuilt and reoriented. Put very simply, the debate may be subdivided into 'internal' and 'external' dimensions. The internal debate has included whether the collapse of Germany in 1945 should be seen as defeat or liberation. In addition, the broadly left-wing Frankfurt School (FRANKFURTER SCHULE) of philosophers, which include Theodor Adorno and Jürgen Habermas, argued that patriotism had found new expression in a broad, patriotic support for the GRUNDGESETZ (*Verfassungspatriotismus*, or 'constitutional patriotism').

Externally, Germany's identity has been, at times, contradictory. On the one hand, Germany has been at the forefront of the drive to transform the European nation–state, by proposing European economic, monetary and political union. On the other hand, the migration flows Germany has experienced have encouraged those on the far Right to conjure up a homogeneous German cultural identity (*homogene Kulturnation*), which requires its naturalised members to demonstrate attachment to German values.

With the collapse of the GDR, new issues of national identity have arisen: internally, the differences between Eastern and Western Germans have yet to be overcome (the so-called 'wall in the head, or MAUER IM KOPF); and externally, Germany's future role in the world, in particular in peace-keeping operations, has sparked political controversy.

See BLAUHELM-EINSÄTZE; EUROPAPOLITIK; HISTORIKERSTREIT; STAATS-ANGEHÖRIGKEITSRECHT; VEREINIGUNG.

(SG)

Nationale Volksarmee   The National People's Army was the GDR military from 1956–90. Although the GDR did not possess its own army until 1956, the Soviet occupation authority authorised, in 1946, the formation of 'garrisoned alert squads' or, as they soon became known, Garrisoned People's Police, which provided the basis for the *Nationale Volksarmee* (NVA). The decision to create the NVA and a Ministry of Defence was determined by the entry of the Federal Republic into NATO and of the GDR into the Warsaw Pact. The size of the NVA was originally fixed at 90 000. At the beginning of the 1980s, over 113 000 troops were in the army, over 38 000 in the air force and about 16 000 in the navy. In 1989, the total strength of the NVA stood at 173 000.

Military service did not become compulsory until 1962, once the building of the Berlin Wall made it easier for the SED to introduce such a controversial measure. In 1964, service in construction units was made an alternative to formal military service, an option which was, however, limited to a small minority. NVA conscripts served for a period of 18 months and reservists were obliged to perform active duties until the age of 50, or 60 in the event of an emergency.

In the 1960s and 1970s, the military doctrine was based on 'forward defence', which had as one of its aims reaching the Atlantic within 12 to 16 days. From about the mid-1970s, the Warsaw Pact began to downscale this doctrine, partly as a result of the CSCE (Conference on Security and Co-operation in Europe) process, culminating in the announcement in 1987 of a defensive military doctrine.

The SED exercised tight political and ideological control over the GDR military. Virtually all the officers and over one-third of warrant officers and NCOs were party members and thus subject to party discipline. Major military questions were controlled by top SED organs and a network of political organs and party organisations within the NVA-reinforced SED authority. The Main Political Administration (*Politische Hauptverwaltung*) directed political work in the armed forces. This included the political and ideological training of troops and the implementation and supervision of party directives and policies. A political organ was located in the NVA down to regimental level. The long-serving Minister of Defence Heinz Hoffmann (1960–1985) sat on the *Politbüro* (1973-1985), as did his successor Heinz Keßler. Hoffmann was regarded as a hardliner for his endorsement of the possibility of a 'just' nuclear war.

The Main Political Administration ceased its activities in January 1990 and a former construction soldier, Pastor Rainer Eppelmann, became Minister of Defence and Disarmament in the DE MAIZIÈRE cabinet. Plans to maintain a separate NVA were soon abandoned. The West German Defence Minister Stoltenberg assumed control over the East German forces after unification and the 90 000 NVA troops were incorporated into the BUNDESWEHR.

See ABRÜSTUNG; BERLINER MAUER; SMAD; WARSCHAUER PAKT.

(MD)

Nationalsozialismus National Socialism was a movement defined by its extreme nationalism, a racialist ideology dominated by anti-Semitism, its anti-democratic thrust, its anti-Communism and, perhaps above all, the leadership of Adolf HITLER. The National Socialist Party emerged from modest beginnings to become the largest party of the Weimar Republic and the only permitted political party during the Third Reich.

In 1919 the National Socialist Party (NSDAP, the *National-sozialistische Deutsche Arbeiterpartei*) was founded in München. Hitler, one of the earliest members, had become the leading figure by 1921 and proved adept in selling a message focused initially on resentment at the defeat of World War I and the the injustice of the Versailles Peace Treaty, and tempered with elements of anti-Semitism and anti-capitalism. Hitler led a somewhat farcical and hopeless uprising (the so-called 'Beer Hall Putsch') against the Weimar system in München in 1923, which led to a four-year jail sentence. He was released after eight months, during which period he had written *Mein Kampf* (My Struggle), an impenetrable and incoherent book which nevertheless presented a vivid outline of a hardening racialist and anti-Weimar ideology.

The following years saw the extension of the NSDAP from its heartland in Bavaria to become a nationwide organisation. Electoral success came following the economic collapse of the Great Depression in 1929–30. The NSDAP, drawing on Hitler's talents as publicist and propagandist, capitalised on the sense of crisis, contrasting renewed economic catastrophe amid weak and unstable government with a vision of strong leadership, economic revival, social solidarity, anti-communism and a new national assertiveness in foreign affairs. This vision had a widespread attraction, extending NSDAP support into probably the broadest range of social groups ever ranged behind one party in free electoral competition in Germany. As a result, the NSDAP was, by 1932, by far the largest political party of the Weimar Republic. As such, it was invited into government, with Hitler as Chancellor, in January 1933. Within three months, Hitler's government had dismantled the democratic constitution, laying the final foundation for the dictatorial rule of the Third Reich in the 'Enabling Law' (ERMÄCHTIGUNGSGESETZ) of March 1933.

The Third Reich saw the implementation of National Socialist ideology. This centred on the concept of *Volksgemeinschaft*, a racially defined national community, for which additional 'living space' (*Lebensraum*) for the German *Volk* needed to be secured, and from which racial 'impurities' – above all the Jews, but also gypsies, Slavs, the disabled and homosexuals – had to be removed. The ideologies of *Lebensraum* and racial 'purification' were reflected respectively in the military campaigns in Eastern Europe in World War II and in the stages of increasingly severe racial persecution which culminated in the HOLOCAUST.

Parties of the far Right in Germany (and elsewhere) still see Hitler as an icon and National Socialist ideology as an inspiration, although any propagation of the symbols and ideas of National Socialism is technically illegal in the Federal Republic.

See ANTISEMITISMUS; DRITTES REICH; VERSAILLER FRIEDENSVERTRAG; WEIMARER REPUBLIK.

(RW)

NATO-Doppelbeschluß The NATO dual track decision of December 1979 was the single most controversial military decision in post-war Germany. It brought anti-American feelings among many groups in society to a climax and led to many non-violent though intellectually aggressive demonstrations.

The decision was meant to act both as part of the *Nachrüstung*, or arms build-up, of intermediate range nuclear forces (INF) in Western Europe, as well as the starting-point of arms control negotiations with the Soviet Union which aimed at limiting the deployment of such weapons in the future. INF include those missiles with a range of between 1000–5500km. The deployment of the so called 'Euro-missiles' (Tomahawk Cruise and Pershing 2 ballistic missiles) in Italy, Belgium, The Netherlands, the UK and the Federal Republic began in 1983. The missiles were ground-based and US-owned and maintained.

The decision to deploy INF was born out of the concerns held in Western Europe about the absolute guarantee of the US deterrent in the actual event of nuclear war. Not convinced by new US targeting plans, European NATO members felt increasingly vulnerable in the face of the modernisation of Soviet SS20 missiles. The Federal Republic saw that the credibility of the Western deterrent could only be enhanced by establishing a truly European response to Soviet weapons modernisation. The initial decision as well as the deployment were met by a rising tide of anti-nuclear protest in Western Europe, and by an especially strong and vocal FRIEDENSBEWEGUNG (peace movement) in the Federal Republic. The then Chancellor Helmut SCHMIDT's own party (the SPD) also gradually turned against NATO strategy. Schmidt was able to push the INF decision through by trying to stress the arms control element and the connected processes of European *détente* and East–West dialogue.

The arms control negotiations laid down in the dual track decision ran from autumn 1980 until December 1987 in Geneva. After the breakdown of talks in 1983 real progress was made after Gorbachev came to power in the Soviet Union in 1985. The INF agreement was finally signed in December 1987 between the Soviet Union and United States. For the first time in arms control history an entire category of nuclear weapons was to be eliminated.

See ENTSPANNUNG.

(KL)

Neue Bundesländer   The new *Bundesländer* are those on the territory of the former German Democratic Republic: BRANDENBURG, MECKLENBURG-VORPOMMERN, SACHSEN, SACHSEN-ANHALT and THÜRINGEN. These were integrated alongside the existing Western BUNDESLÄNDER as component units of the German federal system upon German unification on 3 October 1990. Their boundaries correspond, with minor changes, to the *Bundesländer* abolished by the GDR in 1952. The former GDR capital city of East Berlin merged with West Berlin at the same point to create a unified *Bundesland* of BERLIN, though is not normally regarded as one of the new *Bundesländer*.

Upon their integration into the federal system, the new *Bundesländer* took on the full constitutional responsibilities hitherto fulfilled by the existing Western BUNDESLÄNDER (apart from a number of transitional exceptions set out in the EINIGUNGSVERTRAG).

Their capacity to do so was limited both by their inevitable lack of administrative experience in the practice of German federalism and by their economic and related financial weakness. Considerable steps have since been taken to remedy these problems, though uncertainties still exist as to the long-term impact the different profile and background of the new BUNDESLÄNDER will have on the operation of Germany's characteristic 'co-operative' federalism.

See FÖDERALISMUS.

(CJ)

Neue Soziale Bewegungen   The 'New Social Movements' (NSM) was a term coined in the 1970s to describe those social movements advocating 'post-materialist' values. The term is now used as a form of shorthand to describe a range of 'alternative' movements such as the Women's

Movement, Gay Rights organisations and environmentalist groups. A NSM can be described as a movement advocating autonomy from established hierarchies – such as the state, established religions, the economy and traditional left-wing organisations – and their ideologies such as nationalism, clericalism/anti-Clericalism, capitalism and socialism, in favour of more diffuse 'post-materialist' values focused on quality of life and lifestyle.

Many of the themes advocated by the NSMs have subsequently been co-opted by the mainstream political parties. This is especially true of environmentalism, which is no longer just the preserve of the GRÜNE and its supporters. As a result, NSMs now have a much lower profile than they enjoyed in the 1970s, although it is a matter of opinion whether this is indicative of their ultimate success or failure.

See APO; POSTMATERIALISMUS.

(CL)

Neues Deutschland   *Neues Deutschland* was published daily as the GDR-wide newspaper of the SED. The Party also published a newspaper in each *Bezirk* (district), for example the *Leipziger Volkszeitung*. *Neues Deutschland* contained authoritative statements by the SED and its leaders and was subject to an elaborate system of censorship and political control. It did, however, contain articles on a wide range of subjects, from sport to the theatre. In the early 1980s, it had over 1 million subscribers.

After the collapse of SED rule the newspaper lost most of its subscribers and restructured itself as the critical voice of the PDS. With a much reduced subscription list, the paper faces an uncertain financial future.

(MD)

Neues Ökonomisches System (NES)   The New Economic System of Planning and Management (NES) in the GDR was the first significant attempt at economic reform in the Soviet bloc. In order to stimulate economic growth and boost living standards as part of the SED's attempt to generate support after the construction of the Berlin Wall, ULBRICHT launched an economic experiment in 1963. Known originally as the NES, it was renamed in 1967 the Economic System of Socialism. By transforming the economy into a highly dynamic and more innovative system, it was hoped to demonstrate the superiority of the GDR's socialist system over capitalism. Innovation was promoted by reducing the number of compulsory state indicators imposed on the nationalised enterprises (VEBs) and by giving more weight to indirect steering techniques, notably prices, credits and interest. This meant that enterprises were given a greater say in economic decision-making. A gradual modification of the price system was initiated as the old system, which was based on 1944 levels, had become a serious impediment to innovation and efficiency. In addition to Ulbricht, the main proponents of NES were Günter MITTAG and Erich Apel. The latter, the head of the

State Planning Commission, committed suicide in 1965 when the reform encountered criticism and technical problems.

NES underwent a major overhaul in 1968 when a centrally directed structural policy was introduced. Priority was given to so-called structure-determining tasks which were believed to be necessary for the automation and rationalisation of production. The main beneficiaries of the new state investment policy included electronics, instrument building and machine tools.

The emphasis on structural tasks soon produced distortions for the neglect of non-priority sectors led to difficulties in supplies to priority areas. In 1970, the situation was exacerbated by bad weather and a growing, though still modest, hard-currency debt. Political opposition to the experiment had also grown, especially among those conservative politicians like Erich HONECKER and Willi Stoph who had close ties to Moscow. Although NES did not constitute a fundamental departure from the traditional Soviet-style economic mechanism, this group of politicians feared, particularly after the Prague Spring, that any economic and political experimentation might erode the SED's political monopoly. In December 1970, a Central Committee plenum terminated the experiment.

See PLANWIRTSCHAFT.

(MD)

Niedersachsen Lower Saxony is one of the constituent BUNDESLÄNDER of the Federal Republic. It is the largest *Bundesland* in terms of area (47,351km²) and fourth largest in terms of population (7.71m in 1994). Its capital city is Hannover. It has been beset by structural economic weaknesses arising originally from its long border with the former GDR, which cut off former markets after 1949, and later from over-dependence on declining industries: agriculture, chemicals and cars (the latter, especially in the form of VOLKSWAGEN, still forming the most important sector). Above-average unemployment (10.9 per cent in 1995) has resulted, along with – for West German standards – a relatively low GDP per head (39,760DM in 1995).

The leadership of Niedersachsen's LANDESREGIERUNG has fluctuated between periods of SPD control (1946–55, 1959–76 and 1990 onwards) and that of the CDU or allied parties (1955–59, 1976–90). The SPD's recent revival in LANDTAG elections owes much to the popularity of Gerhard SCHRÖDER, Minister–President since 1990 (1990–94 in coalition with the GRÜNE, from 1994 with an SPD majority), who is also one of the SPD's most prominent leaders at the federal level.

See MINISTERPRÄSIDENT.

(CJ)

Nomenklatur The 'nomenklatura' was an appointments system which acted as a key mechanism for maintaining the leading role of the ruling

Communist parties in the Soviet Union and Eastern Europe. Central to the operation of the system in the GDR was a comprehensive list of those posts and functions in the Party, government and the economic and social spheres which the SED regarded as crucial for the implementation of party policy and for the exercise of party control. The system also included a list of eligible candidates and the arrangements and criteria for the selection, deployment and dismissal of cadres. The posts and functions were classified into three grades according to the degree of their political significance and persons appointed were known as nomenklatura cadres. Decisions on the suitability of cadres were taken by the Party and other bodies at the appropriate level and detailed files were kept on individual cadres.

(MD)

Nordrhein-Westfalen   North Rhine-Westphalia is one of the constituent BUNDESLÄNDER of the Federal Republic. It is the fourth largest *Bundesland* in terms of area (34,068km²) and the largest in terms of population (17.81m in 1994). Its capital is Düsseldorf and its largest city is Köln. Nordrhein-Westfalen remains the economic powerhouse of Germany, especially strong in exporting, despite the significant contraction of the heavy industries of the *Ruhrgebiet* since the 1960s. Massive amounts have been invested in industrial restructuring and diversification, with a growing emphasis on smaller scale, but high-tech production. Despite this, unemployment remains above the national average (10.6 per cent in 1995). GDP per head was 43 320DM in 1995.

In LANDTAG elections, the CDU was the strongest party from 1947–66, to be replaced by the SPD thereafter. Johannes Rau has been SPD Minister–President since 1978, heading LANDESREGIERUNG coalitions with the FDP (1978–80) and the GRÜNE (from 1995) and a majority SPD government from 1980–95.

See MINISTERPRÄSIDENT.

(CJ)

Notstandsgesetze   The 'Emergency Laws' were a package of measures proposed by the Grand Coalition and approved by the BUNDESTAG in 1968, and were designed to enhance the Federal Government's ability to respond to domestic unrest. The origin of the Emergency Laws debate goes back to 1960, when the incumbent CDU/CSU-FDP coalition decided that the GRUNDGESETZ did not provide enough powers to the state in the event of a serious challenge to its authority. Draft amendments were proposed in 1960 and 1962, amid much controversy. Centrist and right-wing elements within the SPD supported the changes, calculating that it would underline their emerging credentials as a respectable party of government. However, the left of the SPD and more radical groups such as the APO were bitterly opposed to what they saw as a draconian extension of state power, especially in view of the way in which emergency powers had been employed to undermine the Weimar Republic. The result was a high-profile petition by over 1 000 Left intellectuals opposing the Emergency Laws, which delayed their enactment until the late 1960s.

Eventually, the *Bundestag* passed a watered-down version of the Emergency Laws in the spring of 1968, providing the basis for the robust state response to subsequent 'threats', such as terrorism in the 'German Autumn' of 1977 and the anti-nuclear protests of the late 1970s and 1980s.

See GROßE KOALITION; TERRORISMUS; WEIMARER REPUBLIK.

(CL)

NPD (National-Demokratische Partei Deutschlands) The National Democratic Party of Germany is one of the three main extreme right-wing parties in German politics, although its peak in strength and significance was during the late 1960s. It never gained seats in the Federal Parliament. Although formally a new party at its foundation in 1964, the NPD was a fusion of several extreme right-wing groups. From 1966–69, the NPD was able to make political capital out of the first German recession after World War II and the resulting unemployment, as well as from an 'opposition vacuum' created by the formation of the Grand Coalition in Bonn. The NPD was able to secure representation in several LANDTAGE from 1966–68, notably scoring 9.8 per cent in BADEN-WÜRTTEMBERG in 1967. In 1969, the NPD only narrowly missed the 5 per cent barrier to the BUNDESTAG election (4.3 per cent), although it returned to insignificance in the next election in 1972 (0.6 per cent).

Since 1969, the NPD has been unable to return to national prominence, and was largely outmanoeuvred by the DVU and the REPUBLIKANER in the late 1980s. In 1987, it formed an electoral alliance with the DVU, and although it was able to derive some short-term gain, the NPD slumped to 0.3 per cent in the 1990 *Bundestag* election.

The NPD is currently suffering from a serious decrease in its membership. From its peak of 25 300 in 1966 it has fallen to around 5 000 in 1992, and is on the verge of insignificance.

See FÜNFPROZENTKLAUSEL; GROßE KOALITION.

(SG)

NSDAP (Nationalsozialistische Deutsche Arbeiterpartei) See NATIONAL-SOZIALISMUS.

Numerus Clausus (NC) *Numerus Clausus* refers to the limits imposed on places available in certain subject areas at German universities. In 1964 Georg Picht, an influential education expert, predicted a *Bildungskatastrophe* ('educational catastrophe') for the Federal Republic if no efforts were made to give a larger slice of the population access to higher education. Measures to avert such a catastrophe lead to the *Bildungsboom* (educational boom) from the late 1960s onwards. In particular, the number of school leavers with ABITUR increased dramatically. Institutions of higher education, however, were not ready for this as the number of places was limited. Efforts to squeeze in ever-increasing student numbers soon reached their limits, particularly in the case of the most popular universities, and a form of rationing of places – the *Numerus Clausus* – was introduced. The average grade score in the *Abitur* now decides who receives a place in the most popular subjects, traditionally law, medicine, veterinary medicine and dentistry but also a number of other subjects which are more subject to fluctuation in application rates.

In 1974 the BUNDESLÄNDER founded the Central Office for the Allocation of University Places (*Zentralstelle zur Vergabe von Studienplätzen*, or ZVS) in Dortmund. The ZVS publishes criteria (i.e. the average required in the *Abitur*) for the award of places and allocate the places through a complicated application process. When applying for a place to study future students first have to find out whether the subject(s) of their choice are administered by the university they want to attend or else centrally by the ZVS in Dortmund. If a *Numerus Clausus* applies, certain criteria determine whether a student will receive a place: availability of places at any given institution, the average mark achieved in the *Abitur*, waiting time and in a few subjects tests and oral exams. Although students can name their three preferred places, they may be allocated a place elsewhere. It is of paramount importance that applicants follow the application procedures meticulously and hand in the required documents in time.

See BAFÖG.

(AW)

Nürnberger Gesetze   The Nuremberg Laws acclaimed at the Nuremberg Reich Party Congress of the National Socialist Party of September 1935 accelerated the discrimination against Jews in the Third Reich. There were two laws adopted at the Congress: the Reich Citizenship Law, which deprived Jews of the rights and protections conferred by German citizenship; and the Law for the Protection of German Blood and Honour, which forbade marriage and sexual relations between Jews and non-Jews. The Nuremberg Laws were the most prominent examples of hundreds of decrees and laws which gradually restricted the ability of Jews to participate in normal social and economic interaction in the Third Reich. They were a key milestone in a process of social exclusion by legal discrimination which left Jews isolated and powerless and open to the more radical, later stages of Nazi anti-Jewish policy.

See ANTISEMITISMUS; DRITTES REICH; HOLOCAUST; REICHSKRISTALL-NACHT.

(CJ)

Nürnberger Prozeß   See Entnazifizierung.

O

Oder–Neisse-Linie The border between Germany and Poland along the line formed by the rivers Oder and Neisse re-emerged as a subject of controversy during the unification process. During the negotiations on German unification, Chancellor KOHL refused to make any binding commitments about the German–Polish border until Germany was united. Kohl's position was partly determined by domestic politics as he feared a loss of votes to the far-right REPUBLIKANER in the 1990 BUNDESTAG election if he definitively conceded the former German eastern territories of Silesia, Pomerania and East Prussia. Despite much internal and external criticism of the Chancellor's equivocation, Germany's definitive recognition of the Oder–Neisse line as Germany's eastern border with Poland did not occur until the border treaty of 14 November 1990.

At the end of World War II the Oder–Neisse line had tacitly been agreed upon by the Allies as a national border at the Yalta Conference and then confirmed at Potsdam in July–August 1945. The Potsdam protocol placed 104 000 sq km of former German territory under Polish administration. This was in part due to the loss of Polish territory to the east to the Soviet Union. The protocol also permitted Poland to expel around 6 million ethnic Germans from this newly acquired territory. The GDR agreed to acknowledge and respect the border in 1950 whilst the Federal Republic did not do so until November 1970 as part of the OSTPOLITIK of Willy BRANDT. However, these agreements did not breach the rights of a future united Germany to make the final determination on the border, as outlined in the Potsdam protocol. The Oder–Neisse border issue kept some of its political saliency throughout the years of German partition.

See VEREINIGUNG.

(MD)

Öffentliche Schulen The vast majority of German schools are public (*öffentlich*). This means that they are co-financed by the BUNDESLÄNDER and local authorities and that every child has a right as well as an obligation to attend a school.

As a rule, children attend the school in their catchment area except where they have special needs or where the schools in their area do not offer a specialisation they wish to study.

Private schools are often non-fee-paying and have to deliver the curriculum required by the respective *Bundesland*. Such schools are maintained by the Churches or other organisations offering alternative forms of education.

See GRUNDSCHULE; INTERNATSSCHULEN; SCHULPFLICHT; WEITERFÜHRENDE SCHULEN.

(AW)

Öffentlicher Dienst The concept of 'public service' refers both to all the forms of direct or indirect employment by the state, and to the particular form of employment relationship between the public servant and the state.

Public service encompasses all those public employees working for federal, *Bundesland* and local authorities, as well as those in state agencies such as social insurance funds. In 1993, only 31.9 per cent of a total of 5 364 500 public servants were employed by the federal level, reflecting the greater role of the BUNDESLÄNDER and the local authorities they supervise in implementing laws in the Federal Republic. The most important group among the public employees are the BEAMTE, or administrative grade civil servants (a status also enjoyed by most teachers and university lecturers), comprising less than half the overall total. *Beamte* are typically university-educated, traditionally dominated by graduates in law, and representatives of a long-standing public service ethos in Germany. *Beamte* have the unique privilege of lifetime tenure, high salaries and other occupational benefits, which are awarded in return for the particular responsibilities and ethos expected in their posts: unswerving loyalty to the constitutional order generally and to the instructions of their superiors in particular, and a commitment to lifetime service. *Beamte* have no right to strike. Professional bans (BERUFSVERBOTE) can be imposed on *Beamte* whose political views do not support the constitutional order. Other categories of public servant have a less privileged employment position regulated in collective agreements between their employers and trade unions.

Current concerns to reduce public expenditure have important implications for both the level and conditions of employment in public service. The strength of the *Beamte* tradition is likely to mean, however, that the force of any changes will be felt by other public service categories.

See KOMMUNALE SELBSTVERWALTUNG; RADIKALENERLAß.

(CJ)

Opel Opel is a major car manufacturer, with a turnover of DM26 billion, 45 500 employees and profits of DM363 million in 1995 (West German figures only).

The first Opel car was produced in 1899 and the company was the first German manufacturer to use production-line techniques in 1924. It was acquired by General Motors in 1929, moving subsequently into commercial vehicle manufacture. Following the war, production of both private and commercial vehicles recommenced in Rüsselsheim, and further plants were opened in Bochum and Kaiserslautern in the first half of the 1960s. The company re-established a presence in East Germany when the Eisenach plant opened in 1990. By 1995, the Eisenach plant employed an average of 1 876 persons, with sales of almost DM2 billion. Annual output per employee was 59 vehicles – the highest in Europe.

The General Motors Corporation, Detroit, holds all the Company's stock, which consists of 950 registered shares each having a face value of DM1 million. Apart from Ford, such a direct and complete foreign stake is not typical of German capitalism.

Like many other of the top industrials, the company is heavily dependent on a continued expansion of foreign trade. Strategic markets are central Europe, Latin America and the Asia/Pacific region. The export share of total unit sales of the main company between 1991–95 climbed from 37.9 to 54.4 per cent. Because of an above-average growth of sales in 1995, the share of the domestic market also rose to 17 per cent.

See BMW; DAIMLER-BENZ; FINANZWESEN; INDUSTRIE; VOLKSWAGEN.

(EOS)

Orientierungsstufe 'Orientation level' is the term used for the two years following GRUNDSCHULE (primary school) during which a child is prepared for secondary school. At the end of this period the school gives a recommendation to parents as to which type of secondary school – *Hauptschule*, *Realschule* or *Gymnasium* – the child should go on to.

The *Orientierungsstufe* (also called *Förderstufe* in some BUNDESLÄNDER) was introduced in 1970. It put back the age at which the decision on which type of secondary school a child was to attend from the age of 9–10 to 11–12. This change was brought in on the grounds that a child would benefit from more time to develop skills and interests at the end of the *Orientierungsstufe* so that predictions on performance in secondary education could be better informed and therefore fairer.

In some *Bundesländer* the *Orientierungsstufe* is integrated into the *Hauptschule* only, in others it is integrated into all three types of school. In Berlin it forms part of the *Grundschule*.

See WEITERFÜHRENDE SCHULEN.

(AW)

Ossi 'Ossi' is the term popularly used to describe East Germans after unification. Divergent political cultures and patterns of socialisation, particularly among older East Germans, produced value orientations different to those of Westerners ('WESSIS'). These were only temporarily submerged by the initial enthusiasm for unification. Post-unification problems such as ABWICKLUNG (winding-up), high rates of unemployment, lower pensions and rising rents, an understandably greater concern about job insecurity and a feeling of being second-class citizens forever having to justify their lives as citizens of the former GDR created deep resentment among many *Ossis* against '*Besserwessis*' (West German know-alls).

Whilst the majority of *Ossis* do not regret the passing of the GDR, many are allergic to being 'wessified' and have developed a positive and conscious identification with certain aspects of the East, including their own local products. Although most *Ossis* recognise that living standards and the level of scientific and technological development in the GDR were inferior to those in West Germany, an Emnid Institute survey in 1995 revealed that most *Ossis* perceive the GDR as superior in areas such as social security, the equality of women, vocational training and protection from crime.

See MAUER IM KOPF.

(MD)

Osterweiterung   The eastern enlargement of the European Union to comprise (some of) the former communist states of Eastern Europe is a major priority of the European Union, and one in which Germany has a key interest.

New member states may accede to the European Union (EU) on the condition that they are democratic European countries. The EU currently has 15 member states and the last enlargement saw the successful applications of Sweden, Finland and Austria. Germany has always been a keen supporter of enlargement, although the Federal Government has repeatedly stressed the need to reinforce the internal workings of the institutions (known as 'deepening' or 'VERTIEFUNG'), to ensure the smooth functioning of the EU's policy-making processes.

Although Cyprus and Malta have been at the head of the queue for the next round of enlargement negotiations, events in Eastern Europe have in many respects overshadowed their applications. The collapse of communism and the subsequent political, economic and social transformations which have occurred, have presented the EU with a further (and potentially more problematic) set of candidates for membership. The states of central and eastern Europe all aspire to membership of the EU and Germany has consistently championed their cause.

Germany's commitment to enlargement is unlikely to falter, although it may insist on some form of differentiated membership to ensure that European integration does not grind to a halt, or even disintegrate, under the burden of 25 or more member states.

(PH)

Ostpolitik   *Ostpolitik* – eastern policy – was the defining characteristic of West German foreign policy under SPD Chancellor Willy BRANDT in the 1970s.

West Germany's *Ostpolitik* led to a 'normalisation' of relations with the GDR and an improvement of relations with the Soviet Union and individual countries in the Eastern bloc. *Ostpolitik* eroded the so-called Hallstein Doctrine which saw the Federal Republic as the only legitimate German state.

Although attempts had been made before 1969 to develop a new *Ostpolitik*, progress had been limited. It was only after the change in government to a SPD–FDP coalition that *Ostpolitik* really took off. The success of *Ostpolitik* under Chancellor Brandt was undoubtedly facilitated by the emerging period of *détente* between the superpowers. A further strength of Brandt's *Ostpolitik* was that he accepted that Europe would remain divided for the forseeable future. Whilst unification remained his ultimate foreign policy goal, Brandt realised that he would have to go some distance in meeting Moscow's desire to have its control over Eastern Europe unconditionally recognised if conditions in Europe were to be improved.

Brandt's *Ostpolitik* prioritised relations with the Soviet Union. In early 1970 the Federal Republic signed agreements to supply pipelines in order that the Soviet Union could export natural gas to the West. The Moscow Treaty of August 1970 basically recognised the Soviet Union as the guardian of the Eastern bloc and accepted the existing borders in Europe, implicitly acknowledging the GDR state.

The Moscow Treaty was followed by a number of bilateral treaties with individual Eastern European states. In the 1970 treaty with Poland the Federal Republic guaranteed the Oder–Neisse frontier (pending a final peace treaty regulating the outcome of World War II) and managed to secure exit permits for some 60 000 ethnic Germans living in Poland. Later in an agreement in 1973 with Czechoslovakia the Federal Republic accepted that the Munich Agreement of 1938 was now null and void.

In the Four-Power Agreement on Berlin of September 1971 Moscow reciprocated Brandt's concessions by agreeing that the Federal Republic could represent West Berlin diplomatically and by allowing (relatively) unimpeded civilian traffic between West Berlin and the Federal Republic. The climax of *Ostpolitik* came with the Basic Treaty (GRUNDLAGENVER-TRAG) between the GDR and FRG of 8 November 1972. This was followed by the membership of both the GDR and the Federal Republic in the United Nations in 1973.

Brandt's political concessions as well as the financial sweeteners accompanying the treaties were seen with concern by those who believed that the West owed it to its democratic principles in general and the GDR people in particular not to give an inch to the Soviets. It was feared that the ultimate goal of reunification had been jeopardised. In retrospect it has been argued that the facilitation of travel of goods and people actually imported Western values into the East and was the beginning of the demise of the Eastern bloc.

See ENTSPANNUNG; MOSKAUER VERTRAG; ODER–NEISSE-LINIE.

(KL)

P

Parlamentarischer Rat The Parliamentary Council was the body which drafted the GRUNDGESETZ in 1948–49. The decision to establish the Parliamentary Council was taken by the Western occupying powers, the USA, Great Britain and France in June 1948 against the background of their steadily deteriorating relations with the Soviet Union. The Council was charged with drawing up a constitution which would establish democratic and decentralised, or federal, government and which would protect individual rights and freedoms. These guidelines were incompatible with the form of centralised, one-party system which was emerging at the same time in the Soviet occupation zone. They represented a clear, if implicit recognition of the inevitability of the division of Germany in the new, Cold War era. The Council was composed of delegates from the parliaments of the western BUNDESLÄNDER and the later Federal Chancellor Konrad ADENAUER was elected its President. The Council first met on 1 September 1948, presenting a first draft *Grundgesetz* to the Western Allies in February 1949. A delay followed as the Allies entered a number of reservations on the question of decentralisation. A final compromise draft was then passed by the Council on 8 May 1949, accepted by the Allies on 12 May, and came into force on 23 May, formally establishing the Federal Republic of Germany.

See BESATZUNG; FÖDERALISMUS; KALTER KRIEG.

(CJ)

Parteienfinanzierung The question of financing political parties by the state or by private sources has become increasingly controversial in recent years. State assistance for parties in Germany takes the form of reimbursement of campaign costs, for which a party becomes eligible if it polls more than 0.5 per cent in a BUNDESTAG, LANDTAG or European election. However, the details have caused controversy over many years and have been the subject of no fewer than six rulings by the Federal Constitutional Court.

Private donations to political parties were also at the heart of the controversial Flick scandal of 1983, where the three main political parties, CDU/CSU, SPD and FDP all used front organisations to avoid paying tax on these donations. The scandal reached into the highest echelons of power and caused the resignation of the then Federal Economics Minister, the FDP's Otto Graf Lambsdorff.

The latest version of the Party Finance Law was passed in November 1993 and based the state subsidy not only on the share of votes the party received (as was the case previously), but also the number of members the party has. It is likely that this law, too, will sooner or later be brought for judgement before the Federal Constitutional Court.

See BUNDESVERFASSUNGSGERICHT.

(SG)

PDS (Partei des Demokratischen Sozialismus) The Party of Democratic Socialism is the successor to the SED, the former ruling party of the GDR. Following the collapse of communist rule in the GDR, the SED displayed almost unseemly haste in disavowing the old HONECKER regime and reconstituting itself as the Party of Democratic Socialism, under which name it fought the elections to the GDR VOLKSKAMMER in March 1990. Under the charismatic leadership of Gregor GYSI, the PDS began to carve out a niche for itself as the self-styled defender of the GDR's formerly privileged elites and all those in the East who have suffered from the effects of unification.

After five years of unity, the PDS has confounded expectations that it would fade away, and has consolidated its position as the regional party of protest in the NEUE BUNDESLÄNDER, where it garners around a third of the vote. However, its attempts to establish itself nationwide have proved unsuccessful, with the party securing negligible support in the West. Despite the personal 'modernising' appeal of Gysi, the party is still home to a significant number of unreconstructed communists. Nevertheless, the persistence of the PDS has led some observers to conclude that the party – and the constituency it represents – must be integrated as a legitimate part of the political system.

(CL)

Pfadfinder The scout movement was founded in Great Britain by Baden-Powell at the beginning of the twentieth century. The German Scout organisation is structured in a similar way to its British counterpart and is a constituent member of the world-wide scouting organisation. It also shares the values of self-discipline and personal effort together with a particular appreciation of nature.

(AW)

Pflegeversicherung Care insurance forms the newest pillar of social insurance (SOZIALVERSICHERUNG) in the Federal Republic, and helps to cover the costs of long-term care for those incapacitated by old age, disability or ill-health. Contributions to the care insurance system commenced in January 1995, and benefits and services paid from care insurance came fully on-stream in the middle of 1996. Care insurance is administered through the wider health insurance (KRANKENVERSICHERUNG) system. It is based on the same structure: equal contributions are made by employees and employers, which vary according to income levels. The contributions of those unable to, or out of, work are made by other welfare support bodies, such as the pensions insurance (RENTENVERSICHERUNG) funds. Payments are graded in relation to the degree of incapacity of those needing care. Support is also offered to carers who are prevented from full-time working by their care responsibilities.

Private care insurance taken out before the introduction of social care insurance may be continued as long as it offers at least the same level of support.

The introduction of care insurance at a time when the wider system of social welfare provision was already under immense financial strain was highly controversial. This was particularly the case among employers, whose obligatory contributions to the scheme further increased the already high social element in their labour costs.

See ARBEITLOSENVERSICHERUNG; SOZIALES NETZ; SOZIALPOLITIK.

(CJ)

Planwirtschaft   The planned economy of the GDR was based on the socialisation of the means of production and on an elaborate system of central planning. The model was the Soviet administrative-command system as it had emerged under Stalin in the 1930s.

Although a planned economy was at first rejected for Germany by the KPD in its programme of June 1945, the embryo of such a system appeared in the late 1940s and early 1950s. The country's first medium-term economic plan was introduced in 1949 for a period of two years and the State Planning Commission was established in 1950. Strategic decisions were taken by the higher organs of the SED, notably the *Politbüro*, and the Council of Ministers (MINISTERRAT DER DDR) was the main governmental organ responsible for their implementation. The State Planning Commission undertook the key tasks of preparing, drafting and implementing economic plans.

The broad guidelines of economic policy were laid down in perspective plans over a period of 10 to 15 years. The medium-range or five-year plans were enacted into law by the VOLKSKAMMER. As not all eventualities could be covered in this way, annual plans were issued after the State Planning Commission had co-ordinated proposals by ministries, enterprises and other units.

The planning system underwent many changes. For example, whereas in the 1960s the 'New Economic System' (NEUES ÖKONOMISCHES SYSTEM) placed great emphasis on indirect levers, the Honecker era saw a tightening of central controls. The sheer complexity of the planning process, the inadequacy of data-processing techniques and planners' lack of crucial information led not only to plan instability but also to the proliferation of slack plans. Enterprises attempted to hide key data from the central planners and to negotiate a slack plan in which output targets were held down and inputs minimised. With fulfilment of the plan as the primary goal, there was no urgent need to rationalise on labour. And as not all goals could be achieved within the framework of the state sector, a second economy developed in which the demand for certain goods and services was met by a small private sector.

See DDR; SED; SOZIALE MARKTWIRTSCHAFT; STALINISMUS.

(MD)

Pluralismus   Pluralism refers both to the existence of a wide range of interest groups (VERBÄNDE) representing different social or professional groups and to the influence of such groups on policy-making.

The concept of pluralism is related to wider theories of pluralist democracy, in which the general will is not assumed to be known by state institutions, but emerges as a result of interest group competition over which state institutions act as a neutral arbiter. Interest group activity in this sense is seen as a necessary and desirable force for the stabilisation of society. Preconditions are the free articulation of interests, and a lack of obstacles to participation of interest group representatives in social, economic, and political affairs.

The notion of pluralism has been of particular interest in Germany because it sets out an open and positive model of democratic participation clearly distinguished from German experiences of totalitarian forms of government in the Third Reich and in the GDR.

(ECM)

Politbüro   See SED.

Politikverdrossenheit   *Politikverdrossenheit* refers to popular apathy towards, or rejection of, the established norms and institutions of politics. The term first emerged in the late 1980s, in particular in the light of the strong electoral performance of the far-Right REPUBLIKANER in LANDTAG and European elections in 1989, and a steady, more general decline in voter turnout at elections.

In post-unification Germany, turnout levels at elections have continued to drop and occasional surges of support for far-Right parties continue to be recorded. Furthermore, the degree of trust in political institutions and politicians dropped to an all-time low in 1992–93.

The reasons for *Politikverdrossenheit* are many. Most prominently, there were a number of controversial scandals involving parties and politicians in the 1990s (especially the Flick 'affair' concerning party financing and the Barschel 'affair' over electoral irregularities in SCHLESWIG-HOLSTEIN), whose resonance has been perpetuated by a number of more minor examples of UK-style 'sleaze' in the 1990s, in particular the spectacle of politicians voting themselves substantial pay increases in times of economic hardship. More broadly, the lessening programmatic and ideological distance between the two main parties, the CDU/CSU and SPD has created the impression of an overly uniform political debate devoid of real choices, especially since party patronage ensures the influence of the parties extends into most public institutions, in particular the public service (ÖFFENTLICHER DIENST).

It should be stressed that the broader level of interests and involvement of Germans in political life has not decreased; rather, dissatisfaction exists about the way political *parties* operate. Thus it may be more appropriate to speak of *Parteien-* rather that *Politikverdrossenheit*.

See ENGHOLM, BJÖRN; PARTEIENFINANZIERUNG; POLITISCHE PARTEIEN.

(SG)

Politikverflechtung The 'entanglement' of politics refers to the relationship between the BUND, or federal level, and the BUNDESLÄNDER in decision-making in the German federal system. *Politikverflechtung* arises from the way in which decision-making powers are distributed in German federalism. This distribution of powers typically requires intense co-ordination and co-operation between the Federal and *Bundesländer* Governments. The necessity for co-ordination was enhanced in a number of constitutional changes in 1969–70 which established so-called Joint Tasks (*Gemeinschaftsaufgaben*) of *Bund* and *Bundesländer*, which are carried out by the governments at both levels. The co-ordination process is carried out in a vast range of both *Länder–Länder* and *Bund–Länder* co-ordinating committees. More recently, similar mechanisms of co-ordination have been established in European policy following further constitutional changes in 1992.

The practice of *Politikverflechtung* has been subject to considerable criticism for three main reasons. First, the parliaments of the *Bundesländer* have lost out as legislative powers they used to exercise have fallen under *Bund–Bundesländer* governmental co-ordination, in particular as a result of the constitutional changes in 1969–70. Second, the process of co-ordination between the Federal and *Bundesländer* Governments is carried out largely 'behind closed doors' and is subject only to limited parliamentary control in the BUNDESTAG and, in particular, the LANDTAGE. Third, the need for such extensive *Bund–Bundesländer* co-ordination arguably makes the decision-making process over-complex, inflexible and inefficient.

The question was frequently posed after unification whether the integration of the new *Bundesländer* into the federal system would lead to a breakdown of *Politikverflechtung*, with the different profile and interests of the eastern *Bundesländer* making such intense co-ordination increasingly difficult and leading to a 'disentanglement' of the decision-making process. However, although there have certainly been tensions among the *Bundesländer* and between *Bund* and *Bundesländer*, the system of intense co-ordination has remained intact.

See BUNDESREGIERUNG; EUROPAPOLITIK; FÖDERALISMUS; LANDES-REGIERUNG; LANDTAG; VERFASSUNGSÄNDERUNG.
(CJ)

Politische Bildung   Political education refers to those activities designed to stimulate political awareness and participation and, more broadly, a critical commitment to the 'rules of the game' of democratic government. It may take place inside or outside the formal education system.

The commitment to political education in the Federal Republic is – compared to other Western democracies – relatively strong. This reflects the failure of the first German democratic state, the Weimar Republic, and its replacement by the Third Reich. Political education was strongly encouraged by the Western occupying powers (BESATZUNGSMÄCHTE) as part of the post-war denazification process (ENTNAZIFIZIERUNG). The commitment to political education was continued following the establishment of the West German Federal Republic, reflecting perceptions of the limited rootedness of democratic values in West German society. An organisational structure for the provision of materials and courses in political education was established, with a federal centre (*Bundeszentrale*) and *Bundesland* centres (*Landeszentralen*) for political education. The structures were extended rapidly in the territory of the former GDR after unification to facilitate the emergence of a fuller democratic awareness following the experience of communist rule since World War II.

See EUROPAHAUS.
(CJ)

Politische Parteien   Political parties are recognised in the GRUNDGESETZ as institutions of the state and as mechanisms for representing the interests of the population. Political parties were instrumental in the formation of the Federal Republic and in the development of democracy in Germany in the 1950s and 1960s. In the course of this process, the influence of parties in public life grew strongly. In particular, recruitment to many senior positions in German public service (ÖFFENTLICHER DIENST) and other state institutions (like the public broadcasting services) is strongly influenced by party-political considerations. This development of the so-called 'party state' has been widely criticised, especially by former Federal President Richard VON WEIZSÄCKER. Public financing of political parties has also been the source of considerable controversy, especially in the light of a number of financial scandals in the last 15 years. All parties today suffer from an ageing membership. Moreover, in attempts to appeal to the same electorates, the programmatic differences between the parties have progressively become fudged. All these factors are held to have contributed to the development of POLITIKVERDROSSENHEIT – a sense of alienation from political life – in Germany.

Given that political parties are given special status in the *Grundgesetz*, they have to conform to democratic principles. If they do not, they can be forbidden by the Federal Constitutional Court. To date, this has happened to only two parties, the extreme right-wing SRP (*Sozialistische Reichspartei*) in 1952 and the communist KPD in 1956.

See BUNDESVERFASSUNGSGERICHT; CDU; CSU; FDP; GRÜNE; PARTEIEN-FINANZIERUNG; PDS; SPD.

(SG)

Postmaterialismus 'Post-materialism' is a term used to describe political values focused on 'quality of life' issues and opposed to the hierarchical structures of traditional forms of social and political organisation – the state, established religions, business, political parties, and so on. The emergence of post-materialism is closely associated with the 'Extra-Parliamentary Opposition' (APO) of the late 1960s, the 'New Social Movements' focused on feminism, pacifism and environmentalism which the APO spawned, and the GRÜNE.

There are conflicting views as to the origins and significance of post-materialism. Some attribute it to the huge leap in living standards in Western Europe – and especially the Federal Republic – in the first three post-war decades. They argue that, as the immediate material needs of the individual are satisfied, they are free to pursue more abstract post-materialist needs. Others argue that the mobilisation of disaffected middle-class radicals over post-materialist themes in the 1960s and 1970s reflected the failure of the state to allow these groups channels of influence. The first explanation implies a lasting shift in political values and orientations and the second a more transient phenomenon, which would be overcome if new channels for influence were created. The persistence of support for the *Grüne* would appear to support the first explanation.

In recent years, many post-materialist themes, such as the environment and feminism, have become mainstream concerns. However, opinion poll data demonstrate that post-materialism has not replaced traditional 'materialist' concerns (such as jobs, pensions and consumerism) but, rather, co-exists with it.

See FRAUENBEWEGUNG; FRIEDENSBEWEGUNG; NEUE SOZIALE BEWEGUNGEN; UMWELTBEWEGUNG; WERTEWANDEL.

(CL)

Presse See ZEITUNGEN UND ZEITSCHRIFTEN.

Pressefreiheit The freedom of the press (and all other media) is guaranteed by the GRUNDGESETZ. It is one of the inalienable rights of German democracy that everybody has the right of access to publicly available information. The press, radio and television have the right to disseminate such information. The dissemination and teaching of ideas which are against the constitution are, however, not allowed. The framework in which these rights and duties can be carried out are laid down by laws in the individual BUNDESLÄNDER.

See BUNDESPRESSEKONFERENZ; RUNDFUNK UND FERNSEHEN; ZEITUNGEN UND ZEITSCHRIFTEN.

(RW)

Preussag Preussag is now the fourteenth largest industrial group in Germany, as measured by sales. Originally *Preussische* Bergwerks- und Hütten *AG*, Preussag was a fully owned subsidiary of VEBA. It became officially known as Preussag in 1964. VEBA sold its remaining stake to WESTLB in 1969. By 1995, Preussag had a turnover of DM26 billion, with 65 000 employees and a net profit of DM349 million.

The group has five divisions: steel and non-ferrous metals (14 per cent of turnover, 1994/95); energy and commodities (8 per cent); trading and transport (52 per cent); plant engineering and shipbuilding (16 per cent) and building engineering and components (10 per cent). In contrast to VEBA, Preussag withdrew from information technology in 1995.

The broad aim of the group is to transform Preussag from a European-orientated organisation to an internationally active raw materials and technology group through mobilisation of its expertise in exploration, and geophysical capabilities.

(EOS)

Preußen Prussia emerged, together with Austria and Bavaria, as one of the most important of the many German states by the eighteenth century. The wars it successfully conducted against Austria, Denmark and France from 1866–71 led to the establishment of a united Germany (excepting Austria) in the form of the DEUTSCHES REICH, or German Empire. The Empire remained Prussian-dominated (with the Prussian King also acting as Emperor) through to its collapse at the end of World War I. Having been the main bastion of monarchical government in the Empire, the Prussian state (or *Land*), now led by the SPD, curiously became one of the main bastions of democratic government in the Weimar Republic. The dissolution of the SPD Prussian government in July 1932 is therefore seen as one of the key stages in the drift into Nazi dictatorship.

The role of Prussia as bastion of democracy may seem somewhat ironic given that the image of Prussia typically remembered is that of the German Empire: undemocratic, authoritarian and militaristic. This was certainly the view of the victorious Allies after World War II, which for these reasons formally abolished the Prussian state in February 1947. Memories of the authoritarian and militaristic Prussia still persist today (particularly in southern Germany), as was exemplified in the controversy about moving the post-unification seat of government (the so-called HAUPTSTADTFRAGE) from Bonn to Berlin, the old Prussian capital city.

See WEIMARER REPUBLIK.

(CJ)

Privatisierung There have been four waves of privatisation in the Federal Republic. Between 1959–65 'people's shares' were sold in PREUSSAG, VW and VEBA. The NIEDERSACHSEN government opposed the sale of shares in VW, in which it had a stake. Ultimately, it joined the Federal Government in the sale, retaining an equal share in 40 per cent of VW's capital. Preussag, on the other hand, was a subsidiary of the federally owned VEBA. Between 1983–89 budgetary policy led to federal holdings in VW, VEBA, VIAG and Salzgitter AG being sold. Salzgitter, which had been established in the Third Reich in the same industrial region as VW, was purchased by Preussag. In addition, federal holdings in the national airline, Lufthansa were reduced, albeit with modest proceeds.

Between 1990–94 the TREUHANDANSTALT rationalised, and/or sold off, or liquidated, 14 000 East German companies. It made a loss of DM300 billion, compared to an initially predicted profit of DM600 billion. The number of jobs in the East fell from 9 million to 6 million. Finally, in the second half of the 1990s, the privatisation of DEUTSCHE TELEKOM will be an international stock exchange event.

Deutsche Telekom issued DM15 billion in shares in 1996. A second issue will follow in 1999. The 1996 issue exceeded the total proceeds of the 1983–89 phase of privatisation by DM5 billion. It seems certain, given the public demand for its shares in the initial 1996 issue, that Deutsche Telekom's privatisation will increase the taste for shareholding as a means of raising finance.

See FINANZWESEN.

(EOS)

Promotion A doctorate can be obtained in virtually all subjects that a university offers. The candidate (called *Promovend* or *Doktorand*) must show that he or she can do independent research by writing a thesis in his/her main subject. This must contribute significant new insights. He or she must also undergo an oral exam to show a wide knowledge in their other subjects.

The title of 'doctor' has traditionally been – and largely remains – the prerequisite for teaching at university. Today there are also unwritten rules which make a doctorate a desirable if not an essential precondition to work in certain fields, e.g. physics, chemistry, and publishing.

A doctorate is not a taught course and it is up to the student together with their supervisor to agree on a timetable, usually three to four years, sometimes longer. Rules and regulations are set out by the university in a *Promotionsordnung*. The finished thesis is scrutinized by an examinations committee (*Promotionsausschuß*) and only if it is found to be satisfactory will the candidate be invited for the oral part of the examination. Universities may also confer honorary doctorates on distinguished persons.

See HABILITATION.

(AW)

R

Radikalenerlaß The Radicals' Decree of 1972 became a controversial example of the principle of 'militant democracy' (WEHRHAFTE DEMO-KRATIE) in the Federal Republic, i.e. that of limiting the basic rights in the GRUNDGESETZ in order to protect the democratic order as a whole.

The context for the Radicals' Decree was set by the new forms of radicalism of the late 1960s in the students' movement and the extra-parliamentary opposition (APO). These in part professed revolutionary left-wing ideas which, it was suggested, would be implemented in a 'long march through the institutions' of the Federal Republic, including those of the state. The Federal and *Bundesländer* Governments' reaction to this prospect was to review their regulations on the conditions for public service employment. The resultant Radicals' Decree tightened up earlier provisions by stating that those involved in organisations 'hostile to the constitutional order' (*verfassungsfeindlich*) would not be recruited to, or could be dismissed from, public service.

No more than a few thousand people have had applications rejected, or lost office, as a result of the Decree. It nevertheless proved extremely controversial, in part because it was applied inconsistently in different *Bundesländer*, in part because members of left-wing organisations were discriminated against more than those of right-wing organisations, and in part because of the sheer scope of the screening process. The status of public servant in the Federal Republic is held not just by officials in public administration at the federal, *Bundesländer* and local levels, but also by school and university staff, postal and railway workers. Information is in principle collected on all of these in the same way and under the same conditions, producing vast databases of information about individuals, and arguably, in the process, taking 'militant democracy' too far in the consequent invasion of individuals' rights to privacy and freedom of speech and association.

The controversy over the Radicals' Decree gradually dissipated in the 1980s, though has recently flared up again in muted form in the policies of some *Bundesländer* of refusing employment to members of the ex-communist PDS.

See DATENSCHUTZ; GRUNDRECHTE; ÖFFENTLICHER DIENST; STUDENTEN-BEWEGUNG.

(CJ)

Rat für Gegenseitige Wirtschaftshilfe (RGW)   The Council for Mutual
Economic Assistance (COMECON), founded in 1949, was established to
promote economic relations between communist states. The GDR did not
join COMECON until almost two years after the organisation was founded as a response to the MARSHALL-PLAN of the West. COMECON was virtually moribund until the late 1950s and various attempts, notably by
Khrushchev in the early 1960s, to create an integrated, supra-national
community foundered on the diverging economic and political interests
and the uneven level of economic development of the member states.
However, forms of co-operation such as the co-ordination of national economic plans did increase after the 1971 agreement on a so-called complex
programme on economic integration.

The GDR came to enjoy a relatively high share of intra-COMECON
trade and it was usually involved in all major investment projects. As the
member with the most advanced technological base, the GDR was usually
to the forefront in production specialisation agreements and a regular
advocate of integration measures in science and technology.

The formal dissolution of COMECON in 1991 and the restructuring
of economic relations between former member states deprived East
German enterprises of many of their traditional markets in Eastern
Europe and the Soviet Union, compounding the wider problems of declining production and rising unemployment in the post-unification transformation process.

See DDR; PLANWIRTSCHAFT; WARSCHAUER PAKT.

(MD)

Real existierender Sozialismus   'Real existing socialism' was a term used by
the former Soviet bloc communist states to describe their ideological system, which had as its basis the teachings of Marx and Lenin. It was also
used by these states as a defensive term in response to their description in
the West as authoritarian and totalitarian.

When the term is used today it is often with an ironical undertone,
referring to the mismanagement of the planned economy (particularly in
the former GDR) and shortages of widely desired consumer goods.

See DDR; MARXISMUS-LENINISMUS; PLANWIRTSCHAFT.

(RW)

Realschule   See WEITERFÜHRENDE SCHULEN.

Rechtsstaat   The rule of law is one of the fundamental and unamendable
constitutional principles of the GRUNDGESETZ. The principle of the rule of
law is closely linked to the guarantees of basic rights (GRUNDRECHTE) in
the *Grundgesetz*. State institutions, like individuals, must abide by the constitution and by laws passed in accordance with the constitution. In particular, they may not infringe the guarantees offered by the *Grundrechte* or

infringe the principle of equal treatment in accordance with the law. The principle of the rule of law was given prominence in the *Grundgesetz* in reaction to the experience in the Third Reich, when abuses of basic rights were carried out with the authority of the state.

A further important component of the principle is the separation of powers (GEWALTENTEILUNG), which is intended to ensure that none of the major state institutions is in a position to exert – or, potentially, abuse – power without being subject to controls by other state institutions.

See DRITTES REICH.

(CJ)

Referendariat The *Referendariat* is a practical training period for future teachers and lawyers/barristers following their theoretical studies (and the first state examination, the *Erstes Staatsexamen*) at university.

For 18 months or two years (depending on the rules of the BUNDES-LAND concerned), students combine theoretical seminars with practical experience at their future workplace. They are observed and assessed regularly whilst in class (teachers) or working on cases (lawyers/barristers). They must also write a dissertation. During the *Referendariat* students receive a modest salary and the status of BEAMTE. Their final qualifying degree is the second state examination. This is also called the *Assessorexamen* for law students. Successful completion of *Referendariat* and examinations does not guarantee a job.

See STUDIENABSCHLÜSSE.

(AW)

Reichskristallnacht The 'Night of the Broken Glass' describes the nation-wide pogrom of the Jews organised in the Third Reich on 9–10 November 1938. The 'broken glass' refers to the glass which littered the streets following the violence of the pogrom. The pogrom was launched on the pretext provided by the supposed need to avenge the murder of a German diplomat by a Jew in Paris on 7 November. It was organised through the National Socialist Party and failed – despite extensive exhortations – to secure extensive public involvement. Nevertheless the pogrom was carried out across the Reich, from the largest cities to rural backwaters, leaving 91 murdered, thousands of businesses smashed and looted, most of Germany's synagogues burnt, many thousands beaten, and around 30 000 Jews shipped off to concentration camps.

Beyond the events of *Reichskristallnacht* itself, the pogrom had the wider significance of marking a radicalisation of Nazi anti-Jewish policy. This was focused on the exclusion of Jews from German economic life, and set the stage for subsequent policies directed at the forced removal of Jews from German soil.

See ANTISEMITISMUS; DRITTES REICH; HOLOCAUST; KONZENTRATION-SLAGER; NÜRNBERGER GESETZE.

(CJ)

Reichspräsident   The Reich President was the German head of state during the Weimar Republic. The Weimar constitution created overlapping executive powers shared between President and Chancellor. In routine matters, the Chancellor exercised executive authority, though could be dismissed (and appointed) by the President. In an emergency situation, however, the President had the power to rule by decree. Rule by decree increasingly became the norm after 1930, when no effective governing majority could be constructed in the REICHSTAG.

The personality of the then President, Paul von Hindenburg, the former World War I Field Marshall, had an important influence on how these powers were exercised. Hindenburg was not a democrat, favouring an authoritarian or monarchical system of government. This shaped the way in which he appointed Chancellors and issued emergency decrees after 1930. Presidential decrees were used purposefully to undermine the democratic system and introduce authoritarian government. This trend was fateful. The last Chancellor Hindenburg appointed was Adolf HITLER on 30 January 1933, and the Weimar system was effectively abolished just two months later with Hitler's 'Enabling Law' (ERMÄCHTIGUNGSGESETZ). Hindenburg was by then a very old man and was not able to stand up to Adolf Hitler.

The problem of overlap between the executive powers of President and Chancellor in the Weimar Republic was one of the central issues addressed by the framers of the GRUNDGESETZ, who demoted the Presidency to a mainly ceremonial role while establishing the Chancellor as the unrivalled seat of executive power.

See BUNDESKANZLER; BUNDESPRÄSIDENT; GEWALTENTEILUNG; WEIMARER REPUBLIK.

(CJ)

Reichstag   The *Reichstag* was the parliament of the German Empire and of the Weimar Republic. Although directly elected by universal male suffrage in the German Empire, the *Reichstag* had only limited powers to amend and reject, but not to initiate legislation. In the Weimar Republic it was endowed with powers of legislation and control of the executive, although these were qualified in certain circumstances by the powers of the President (REICHSPRÄSIDENT) to rule by Emergency Decree and to appoint and dismiss the Chancellor.

The fire in the *Reichstag* on 27 February 1933 played a symbolic role in the demise of the parliamentary democracy of the Weimar Republic. Whether started by the National Socialists or by the Communists (as the Nazis argued), it gave the newly appointed Chancellor, Adolf HITLER, the pretext to sweep away some of the basic rights guaranteed in the Weimar constitution and set the stage for the 'Enabling Law' (ERMÄCHTIGUNGSGE-SETZ) of March 1933, which gave Hitler the power of rule by decree and effectively abolished democratic government.

The *Reichstag* building in Berlin will house the parliamentary authorities of the Federal Republic following the transfer of the seat of government from Bonn to Berlin in the year 2000.

See BUNDESTAG; DEUTSCHES REICH; DRITTES REICH; WEIMARER REPUBLIK.

(CJ)

Renaissance   See STILE.

Rentenversicherung   Pension insurance finances the costs of providing pensions in old age or in case of invalidity. Pension insurance is organised on similar lines to the other main branches of social insurance (SOZIALVERSICHERUNG): costs of care are covered by insurance contributions, and not out of general taxation. Half the contributions are paid by the insured persons on a sliding scale in proportion to income, and half by their employers. Additional private insurance can be taken out, means permitting. Insurance contributions and payments are administered by a range of state-regulated pension funds (*Versicherungsanstalten*).

The normal pension age is 65 years. The size of the pension awarded is normally two-thirds of net earnings, upgraded regularly in line with the wider wage situation in the economy. The level of the pension falls if a person has not been insured for a sufficient number of years, or if he or she had less than average earnings. If a pensioner dies, his or her bereaved have a right to a widow(er)'s (or orphan's) pension.

The extension of the pension insurance system to East Germany after unification has done much to smooth the difficulties of transition for the elderly. Federal Republic pensions typically assure a higher standard of living than those of the GDR did. Moreover, pension levels in the East have rapidly begun to approach those of the West (rising from an average 40 per cent of the Western level in 1990 to 79 per cent in 1995).

However, the pension system as a whole is under considerable pressure due to the ageing of the population, which means that the relation of those contributing to and those drawing from the pension funds is moving out of balance. Reforms in pension arrangements to take account of this will become unavoidable.

See ARBEITSLOSENVERSICHERUNG; KRANKENVERSICHERUNG; SOZIALES NETZ.

(CJ)

Republikaner, Die   The 'Republicans' are a far right-wing party which has scored some notable electoral successes in recent years. The party was founded in 1983 as a right-wing breakaway party from the CSU in BAYERN, and initially saw itself as a conservative alternative to the CSU. However, the party veered to the Right under the leadership of Franz Schönhuber, who replaced Franz Handlos in 1985. The party attained national significance in the late 1980s with its anti-foreigner and anti-asylum rhetoric, and scored over 7 per cent in both the BERLIN and European elections in 1989.

Republikaner issues were sidelined during the process of German reunification, and the party scored only 2.1 per cent at the 1990 BUNDESTAG election. However, in summer 1991, with anti-foreigner riots in Rostock and Hoyerswerda, its xenophobic message fell on fertile ground, and its support rose correspondingly, peaking in April 1992, when the party attained 10.9 per cent in the BADEN-WÜRTTEMBERG election. Following an amendment to the GRUNDGESETZ in July 1993, which limited the flow of asylum seekers, the issue of asylum lost prominence in the public's minds, and the party's appeal as a protest force was effectively removed.

Most of the far-Right parties in the Federal Republic's history have been single-issue protest parties (e.g. the BUND DER VERTRIEBENEN in the 1950s and the NPD in the 1960s). Once the issue has lost its relevance, the party's support has withered. It seems that the *Republikaner* may be following this pattern.

By the mid-1990s, they had been weakened by internal quarrels over leadership (with Schönhuber dismissed as party leader in October 1994) and steady falls in membership. Their attempts to mobilise new support around Eurosceptical opposition to European Economic and Monetary Union have as yet been unsuccessful.

See ASYLRECHT; AUSLÄNDERFEINDLICHKEIT; DVU; EUROPAPOLITIK.
(SG)

Rheinland-Pfalz   Rhineland-Palatinate is one of the constituent BUNDESLÄNDER of the Federal Republic. It is a medium-sized *Bundesland* with an area of 19.849km² and a population of 3.95m (1994). Its capital city is Mainz and its largest city is Koblenz. Heavily agricultural in the 1950s, and still the leading wine-producing area in Germany, Rheinland-Pfalz has undergone a patchy economic modernisation process but still contributes at a below-average rate to German GDP, although unemployment is below the western average at 8.5 per cent (1995).

The MINISTERPRÄSIDENT of Rheinland-Pfalz was provided by the CDU from 1947–90, when a governing coalition of SPD and FDP under *Ministerpräsident* Rudolf SCHARPING took over. Scharping used this base to stand as SPD candidate for Federal Chancellor in 1994, as Helmut KOHL had done for the CDU in 1976. The most recent LANDTAG election in 1996 renewed the SPD-FDP coalition under *Ministerpräsident* Kurt Beck.

See BUNDESKANZLER; LANDESREGIERUNG.
(CJ)

Richtlinienkompetenz   See BUNDESKANZLER.

Rokoko   See STILE.

Romanik   See STILE.

Römische Verträge   The Rome Treaties established the European Economic Community (EEC) and the European Atomic Energy Community (Euratom), although only the EEC Treaty is normally known as the Treaty of Rome. The Rome Treaties were signed in Rome on 25 March 1957 by Germany, France, Italy, Belgium, the Netherlands and Luxembourg to establish an economic community and customs union among the member states in which the free movement of goods, services, people and capital would be ensured, and a community to manage the development of atomic energy. The difficulties which surrounded the work of the latter contributed to its relative insignificance as an institution of European integration. The Treaties established the framework for the development of the Economic Community and common institutions to ensure effective decision-making and management. The major revisions to the Rome Treaties occurred in 1985 with the Single European Act (with the intention of completing the Internal Market) and in 1991 with the Maastricht Treaty (which established the European Union).

The most recent, though rather less far-reaching, revision of the Treaty of Rome was undertaken under the auspices of the 1996–97 Intergovernmental Conference of the EU. The German Federal Government once again played a key role, producing a series of joint proposals (with the French government) on the content and direction of further integration among EU member states.

The challenge of enlargement is the main problem facing the Treaty of Rome today, in particular how to ensure its continued applicability, suitability and effectiveness in an enlarged EU.

See BINNENMARKT; EUROPAPOLITIK; OSTERWEITERUNG.

(PH)

Rote-Armee-Fraktion   See TERRORISMUS.

Rühe, Volker   Volker Rühe is currently Federal Defence Minister. A career politician, Rühe became a CDU member of the *Bürgerschaft* (LANDTAG) in HAMBURG as soon as he qualified as a teacher in 1970. Joining the BUNDESTAG in 1976, he rose quickly, becoming CDU General Secretary in 1989. Widely tipped as a possible successor to Helmut KOHL, Rühe's career was effectively put on hold in 1992, when he was appointed Defence Minister, a post normally considered a political backwater (akin to the Northern Ireland Office in the UK).

However, Rühe has managed to retain a relatively high profile, with his period as Defence Minister witnessing the successful restructuring of German armed forces following unification. More importantly, he has presided over the first out-of-area missions by German armed forces since 1945, in Somalia and Bosnia Herzegovina. His competent handling of these politically sensitive issues has earned him widespread respect and a renewed, outside chance of replacing Helmut Kohl as CDU leader when he retires.

See BLAUHELM-EINSÄTZE; BUNDESWEHR.

(SG)

Ruhrkohle Ruhrkohle was the sixteenth largest industrial company in Germany in 1995, with a turnover of DM25 billion and 102 000 employees. It was formed in the Ruhrgebiet – Germany's largest hard (or bituminous) coalfield – in 1968 from 21 coal-mining companies as a defensive measure in face of the critical state of the industry, in particular an over-production crisis. Some 65 per cent of Ruhrkohle's total sales are made to the electricity-supply industry, with most of the rest going for iron smelting. The present-day direct and indirect shareholdings in the company roughly reflects these interests: VEBA (40 per cent) and VEW (*V*ereinigte *E*lektrizitäts*w*erke AG, Dortmund – 30.2 per cent), together with THYSSEN (12.7 per cent) and KRUPP-HOESCH (8 per cent). Even with considerable subsidisation, overall output and the number of pits have fallen. By 1995, 15 pits were producing 43 million tons of coal. The labour force has been halved over the last decade and productivity has risen rapidly.

The electricity supply industry committed itself in 1977 to purchasing a fixed amount of domestically produced coal until 1995. Power generators then received subsidies financed from a levy added to electricity bills and related to the amount of electricity consumed. The levy was raising DM6 billion annually when it was declared unconstitutional by the Federal Constitutional Court in 1994. Under another subsidy agreement the Federal and BUNDESLÄNDER Governments compensated for the difference between the costs of producing domestic coking coal and the world prices at which it was sold to the steel industry. This arrangement is due to expire in 2000.

Total subsidisation of the coal industry reached DM10 billion in 1994. The coal industry's subsidy was therefore in the order of DM100 000 per employee. It is unclear how long this generous subsidy regime can be continued. However, given that Germany has virtually no indigenous oil and negligible natural gas reserves, its hard and brown coal reserves may well retain importance. Long-term subsidisation of coal therefore seems on balance a plausible policy option in terms of national interest.

See BUNDESVERFASSUNGSGERICHT.

(EOS)

Runder Tisch The Round Table was a forum for bringing together the forces of the old regime with those of the new order in the final months of the SED-led government in the GDR. In keeping with the opposition groups' concept of dialogue and the renewal of the GDR from below,

Round Tables proliferated at local and regional levels. The most significant one was the Central Round Table, which, chaired by Church representatives, held its first meeting in East Berlin on 7 December 1989 and its
last on 12 March 1990. The Round Tables in the GDR, as elsewhere in
Eastern Europe, constituted a forum for bringing together the old and
new forces as well as for facilitating the relatively peaceful, albeit difficult,
transition from one system to another.

The parties of the old regime, including the SED and the GDR-CDU
were allowed three representatives, whereas the new groups such as
Democracy Now, the Green Party and the SDP had two and New Forum
three. The Central Round Table originally saw itself as a control and
supervisory body but with the eventual involvement of members of the
opposition in Hans MODROW's Government of National Responsibility and
the acquisition of a legislative function it began to act as a co-government,
though with limited powers. The rapidity of political change altered the
balance of forces on the Round Table and eroded its functions.

A key aspect of the Round Table's work was the drafting of a model
for a new constitution and a social charter. The latter was approved at the
final session in March 1990 and sought to spell out the GDR's fundamental interests and principles: the right to work, as high a level of employment as possible, equality between the sexes, state control over rents, and
the retention of the network of pre-school institutions.

See BÜRGERBEWEGUNGEN.

(MD)

Rundfunk und Fernsehen   Radio and television services in Germany are provided by both public and private broadcasters. These are independent of
the state, though are required by law to transmit politically balanced and
varied programmes. Whereas public broadcasting is financed through fees
as well as advertising, private broadcasting is financed solely by advertising.

There are two public broadcasting corporations: the *ARD*
(*Arbeitsgemeinschaft der öffentlich-rechtlichen Rundfunkanstalten Deutschlands*) which comprises broadcasting agencies in the BUNDESLÄNDER
(*Landesrundfunkanstalten*) and produces both radio and TV programmes;
and the ZDF (*Zweites Deutsches Fernsehen*), which produces TV programmes only. Their rights and obligations are laid down in a periodically
reviewed treaty among the *Bundesländer*. The *ARD* produces TV programmes for nationwide broadcasting (Channel One, or *Erstes Programm*)
as well as *Bundesländer*-specific programmes (on Channel Three, the
Drittes Programm) on a regional basis. The *Drittes Programm* also includes
school's TV and Open University programmes.

Radio broadcasting has the additional task of presenting a balanced
and comprehensive picture of German life and politics both within and outside the national borders. Foreign language programmes have included the

Deutsche Welle, Deutschlandfunk and *RIAS (Rundfunk im Amerikanischen Sektor)*. Since 1994 *Deutschlandfunk, RIAS* and the former GDR channel *Deutschlandsender Kultur* have been merged under the umbrella of *Deutschlandradio*.

There are over 100 private local radio stations but these do not normally broadcast a full-time service. Around 80 per cent of all households have access to new, and mainly privately owned, cable and satellite TV technologies. Channels provide mixes of news and entertainment (*SAT1, Pro7, RTL*) sport (*DSF, Eurosport*) and culture (*3SAT* and *Arte*).

Public TV also offers teletext services which, alongside established news and information services, now offer shopping and banking services.

See PRESSEFREIHEIT.

(RW)

RWE   RWE *(Rheinisch-Westfälisches Elektrizitätswerk AG)* was the fifth largest industrial enterprise in Germany in 1995 with sales of DM64 million, 137 000 employees and net profits of DM750 million. RWE was established as an electricity producer in Essen in 1898. From 1905 power was supplied for tramways, and from 1928 for household appliances. Between 1914–38, vertical diversification added brown coal (lignite) and hydro-power to hard coal as primary energy sources. Horizontal diversification into construction, gas and water also took place. The network of gas pipelines was sold to what is now Ruhrgas in 1926. Mineral oil and chemicals were added by the acquisition of Deutsche Texaco in 1989 (RWE-DEA AG).

RWE operates six divisions: energy (electricity) supply, petroleum and chemicals, mechanical and plant engineering, construction, mining and raw materials, and waste management. Turnover trebled between 1980–95.

Apart from some construction projects and, more marginally, engineering, RWE's activities are essentially confined to the domestic economy. It therefore has a particular interest in Germany's competitive viability. The rising external value of the DM and labour costs are sources of concern. More positively, the abolition of coal subsidies from 1996 was seen as a means of purchasing hard coal at world prices and passing on the cost savings to consumers.

As with all power generators, environmental issues unsurprisingly present RWE with major problems. More specifically, long-running opposition to nuclear power stations in RHEINLAND-PFALZ and HESSEN, along with the fact that half the company's electricity is generated from highly pollutant brown coal, are symptomatic of the policy issues involved. However, the group opened the second phase of Europe's first solar energy project in 1996.

Telecommunications promise to become a growth area. RWE formed a consortium with British Telecom and will be seeking to compete with Deutsche Telekom.

See PRIVATISIERUNG; RUHRKOHLE; VEBA.

(EOS)

S

SA (Sturmabteilung) The 'Storm Detachment', or more commonly, Stormtroopers or 'brown-shirts', were the paramilitary wing of the National Socialist Party (NSDAP) in the Weimar Republic. Founded in 1921, the SA was used to protect NSDAP meetings from disorder, organise demonstrations and (violently) disrupt the meetings of political opponents. The organisation largely disintegrated in the mid-1920s, but re-emerged with great force in the Great Depression years. Under the leadership of Ernst Röhm, a close friend of Adolf HITLER, its membership expanded from 70 000 in 1930 to 170 000 in 1931 and a staggering 4.5 million by the end of 1933. Its purposes were much the same as in the earlier years: stewarding Nazi meetings, intimidating opponents and, increasingly, engaging their KPD and SPD opponents in brawls on the streets.

The swelling of the SA's size created disciplinary problems. It had attracted a yob element which was unused to the hierarchical structures of command expected in the Nazi movement. This was revealed in particular after the NSDAP's move into government in 1933, after which SA units were wont to take the law into their own hands. Röhm encouraged this, seeing his SA as the guarantors of the revolutionary spirit of National Socialism. Hitler, on the other hand, saw such excesses as a liability which alienated conservative and nationalist opinion and, more importantly, the army. The army was perhaps the only force which could have unseated Hitler, and it was extremely uneasy about the millions-strong uniformed force of the SA posing a challenge to its own functions. In a display of extreme ruthlessness, Hitler ordered the arrest and execution of over 70 SA leaders, including his friend Röhm, on 20 July 1934 to appease conservative and military opinion. Following this 'Night of the Long Knives', the SA's significance plummeted, to be displaced as a Nazi security force by the rapidly expanding SS empire.

See DRITTES REICH; NATIONALSOZIALISMUS; WEIMARER REPUBLIK.

(CJ)

Saarland The Saarland is one of the constituent BUNDESLÄNDER of the Federal Republic. It joined the Federal Republic in 1955 following the ending of French control under a special agreement of the post-war occu-

pation regime. It is the smallest *Bundesland* outside the city–states of
BERLIN, BREMEN and HAMBURG in terms of area (2,569km²) and second
smallest after Bremen in terms of population (1.08m in 1994). Its capital
city is Saarbrücken. It has faced serious economic problems resulting from
the decline of its dominant coal-mining and steel industries since the
1960s. It has not yet successfully restructured and remains economically
weak with an above-average unemployment rate of 11.7 per cent (1995).

From 1956–85, the leadership of Saarland's government (LAN-
DESREGIERUNG) was in the hands of the CDU. Since then, the SPD has taken
control under MINISTERPRÄSIDENT Oskar LAFONTAINE, who also stood
unsuccessfully as SPD candidate for Federal Chancellor in 1990. In each
of the last three elections, Lafontaine has led the SPD to an absolute
majority of LANDTAG seats.

See BESATZUNGSMÄCHTE; BUNDESKANZLER.

(CJ)

Sachsen   Saxony is one of the constituent BUNDESLÄNDER of the Federal
Republic and one of the NEUE BUNDESLÄNDER on the territory of the former GDR. Its capital city is Dresden and its biggest city is Leipzig. It is
18 338km² in size and with a population of 4.58m (1994) is the most popu-
lous *Bundesland* in Eastern Germany. It has long been one of Germany's
major industrial centres, and despite the industrial contraction characteristic
in the East since unification ranks higher than the other *neue Bundesländer*,
and also the SAARLAND in the West, in its contribution to German GDP.
Unemployment remains, however, high at 14.4 per cent (1995).

Saxony has emerged as the biggest CDU stronghold in the East, with
the party winning an absolute majority in the LANDTAG elections in 1990 and
1994, and forming a single-party government since 1990 under the extremely
popular MINISTERPRÄSIDENT Kurt Biedenkopf. The only other parties represented in the LANDTAG after the 1994 election were the SPD and PDS.

See LANDESREGIERUNG.

(CJ)

Sachsen-Anhalt   Saxony-Anhalt is one of the constituent BUNDESLÄNDER of
the Federal Republic and one of the NEUE BUNDESLÄNDER on the territory
of the former GDR. Its capital city is Magdeburg. It is 20 455km² in size
and has a population of 2.80m (1993). Saxony-Anhalt possessed a strong
industrial base in vehicles production, metallurgy, mining and chemicals,
but has seen much of its industry close down following the transition to
the free market in 1990. The chemicals industry has produced a problem
of severe environmental degradation, especially in the area around Halle
and Bitterfeld. Unemployment is the highest of all the *Bundesländer* at
16.5 per cent (1995).

Following its first LANDTAG election in 1990, Sachsen-Anhalt was
governed by a coalition of CDU and FDP. The second election in 1994 pro-

duced a change of government. Both CDU and FDP lost heavily, and the
SPD under MINISTERPRÄSIDENT Reinhard Höppner formed a minority
coalition with the GRÜNE, 'tolerated' by a strengthened PDS. The co-
operation of the 'red–green' minority coalition with the former communist
PDS proved highly controversial, especially in Western Germany, where
the PDS is still seen as beyond the pale of political respectability.

See LANDESREGIERUNG.

(CJ)

Scharping, Rudolf Rudolf Scharping is a leading member of the SPD, and is
currently leader of the SPD parliamentary grouping (FRAKTION) in the
BUNDESTAG. Born on 2 December 1947, Rudolf Scharping followed the
usual route taken by German politicians, rising doggedly up the local SPD
hierarchy in his native RHEINLAND-PFALZ. He was a member of the
Rheinland-Pfalz parliament from 1975–94, becoming Chief Whip
(*Parlamentarischer Geschäftsführer*) in 1979, leader of the parliamentary
grouping from 1985–91, leader of the SPD in Rheinland-Pfalz from
1985–93 and MINISTERPRÄSIDENT of Rheinland-Pfalz from 1991–94. In
1993, Scharping was elected leader of the SPD and was the party's
Chancellor-Candidate in the 1994 BUNDESTAG elections. He lost to Helmut
KOHL after fighting what was generally regarded as a poor campaign.
Following his election failure, Scharping was attacked for his low-key style
of leadership, especially by the abrasive *Ministerpräsident* of NIEDER-
SACHSEN, Gerhard Schröder. Nevertheless, it was not Schröder but Oskar
LAFONTAINE who finally ousted Scharping as party leader at the SPD's
annual conference in November 1995.

Although no longer party leader, Scharping still exercises considerable
power as leader of the SPD parliamentary grouping in the *Bundestag* and as
the most prominent member of the SPD's centre-right.

See BUNDESKANZLER; LANDTAG.

(CL)

Schäuble, Wolfgang Wolfgang Schäuble is former Federal Interior Minister,
and is now leader of the CDU/CSU parliamentary grouping (FRAKTION) in
the BUNDESTAG. Born in 1942 in Freiburg, he became a CDU *Bundestag*
deputy in 1972. He soon became a confidant of Helmut KOHL and from
1984–89 was head of Kohl's Chancellor's Office (BUNDESKANZLERAMT). In
1989 he became Federal Interior Minister, a post he held until 1991, when
he was appointed to lead the parliamentary party. As Interior Minister, he
was the West German signatory to the Unification Treaty (EINIGUNGSVER-
TRAG) and had a substantial role in its negotiation.

Since 1991, Schäuble has been confined to a wheelchair following an
assassination attempt. An extremely astute political operator, he is seen as
Kohl's most likely successor, although much will depend on the timing of

Kohl's retirement. Schäuble is a firm supporter of Kohl's European policy, in particular Economic and Monetary Union, and his control of the parliamentary party will be crucial in delivering support for this to Kohl.
See EUROPAPOLITIK.
(SG)

Schein A *Schein*, or certificate, is a form filled in by a university student and his/her tutor as evidence of attendance and achievement in a university course (LEHRVERANSTALTUNGEN). A *Schein* often carries a mark on a scale of one (the best) to six, but sometimes only a pass.

A student 'collects' *Scheine* by attending courses in the areas prescribed by the exam regulations and fulfilling the requirements to gain evidence of achievement. When students matriculate for their exams they have to present their *Scheine* to the examinations officer. *Scheine* are normally given for a semester's work but sometimes there may be one *Schein* for the year's work in one course. Academic achievement can be demonstrated through a paper delivered orally and/or in writing, a written exam or by passing an oral exam.
See STUDIUM.
(AW)

Schengen The Schengen Accord over open borders within (part of) the European Community and over European police co-operation was signed in 1985 by Germany, France and the Benelux countries.

The Schengen Accord set out to eliminate internal border controls within the EU, and includes measures for the co-ordination of visa policies, police co-operation and computerised information exchange systems.

Between 1990 and 1996 most other EU members, with the exception of Britain, Ireland and Denmark, joined the Schengen group, with the aim of working together against illegal immigration, a common problem viewed to be a fundamental threat to the social and economic stability of the EU. Several computerised networks now make police information available to all member states, and numerous forms of active police cooperation are being put into operation, some of which are centred around the newly-founded EUROPOL.

The EUROPOL is a German initiative for a nucleus of a European police force. Based in The Hague, it is empowered to handle drug-related crime throughout the EU, and further expansion of its authorities is being discussed.

Recent terrorist activities have put on hold the full implementation of the Schengen open-borders system. After a series of bombings in 1995 France unofficially suspended some of the Schengen articles relating to the free movement of people across its border with Germany. The

German authorities are pushing for a widening of the EUROPOL mandate to more areas of law enforcement.

Once EUROPOL is given not only the legal mandate but also extensive funds and facilities, it may develop to be a truly European investigative police force. This process is, however, dependent on the harmonisation of criminal laws in the EU member states.

(SS)

Schießbefehl The shoot-to-kill policy at the Berlin Wall and along the German–German border has re-emerged as a highly controversial issue since unification. Although no shoot-to-kill law or specific written instruction to this effect have been uncovered, there did exist a series of instructions and binding regulations authorising border guards to use firearms if they could not otherwise prevent flight across the border. The guards were trained to obey these orders unconditionally; disobedience could lead to a prison sentence of up to five years.

The Unification Treaty (EINIGUNGSVERTRAG) provided the legal basis for placing former border guards and their officers as well as the responsible politicians on trial. GDR law was held to apply to crimes committed before unification and Federal Republic law thereafter. The first border guard trial began in September 1991 and ended in the conviction of two soldiers for killing Chris Gueffroy in February 1989. In this trial, the judge asserted that standards of human rights prevailed over the laws of a state according to the principle that 'what is law is not always right'. In 1992, the ex-GDR Defence Minister, Heinz Keßler, together with other members of the GDR National Defence Council, were charged with having had 'unlimited influence' in determining how the GDR's borders had been fortified, including the use of firearms. These three defendants and, subsequently, Erich HONECKER, were accused of 'collective manslaughter'. In September 1993, Keßler and Streletz were found guilty for being 'instigators' in the border deaths and Albrecht for being an accessory. In passing sentence, the presiding judge asserted that they realised that the killings were wrong since GDR law recognised the primacy of human life over serving state interests and that the guards should have used milder means. In July 1994, in its review of the case the *Bundesgerichtshof* (Federal Law Court) also stressed the defendants' individual culpability. During Honecker's trial, it was noted that at a meeting of the National Defence Council in May 1974 he had supposedly endorsed the 'unhampered use' of firearms to prevent escapes. This trial was terminated without judgement in 1993 on account of Honecker's serious illness.

In December 1995, Egon KRENZ and six other former members of the SED *Politbüro* were indicted not for their participation in the shootings policy but rather for not actively seeking to prevent the crimes.

See BERLINER MAUER; GERICHTE.

(MD)

Schleswig-Holstein   Schleswig-Holstein is one of the constituent BUNDES-
LÄNDER of the Federal Republic. It is the northernmost *Bundesland* and
has coasts on the North and Baltic Seas. It has an area of 15 731km² and a
population of 2.76m (1994), and its capital city is Kiel. Schleswig-Holstein
has been beset by structural economic weaknesses arising from its peripheral location and its over-dependence on declining industries, in particular, agriculture, fishing and shipbuilding. It has slightly above-average
unemployment (9.1 per cent in 1995) for a Western *Bundesland*.

From 1950–87, the LANDESREGIERUNG was dominated by the CDU.
This dominance was broken only in 1988 after the CDU MINISTERPRÄSI-
DENT Uwe Barschel was allegedly involved in electoral irregularities and
subsequently committed suicide. The SPD has led the *Landesregierung*
since, from 1993 under Germany's first female Minister-President, Heidi
Simonis. Following the most recent LANDTAG election in 1996, Simonis
heads a *Landesregierung* coalition of SPD and GRÜNE.

See ENGHOLM, BJÖRN; POLITIKVERDROSSENHEIT.

(CJ)

Schmidt, Helmut   Helmut Schmidt is the last living former SPD Chancellor
(1974–82). Born on 23 December 1918 in Hamburg, Schmidt served as a
young man in the German army from 1937–45. After the war, he carved
out a political career in his native BUNDESLAND of HAMBURG, first serving
as a political secretary in the office of the Senator for Economics and
Transport from 1949–53 before holding the post of Senator for Internal
Affairs from 1961–65. He was a member of the BUNDESTAG from 1953–61
and 1965–87. Following the formation of the coalition of SPD and FDP in
1969, Schmidt became Federal Defence Minister, holding the post for
three years until taking over the Federal Finance Ministry in 1972.
Following the resignation of Willy BRANDT in 1974, Schmidt became
Chancellor. Schmidt's Chancellorship was dogged by the economic problems of the mid-1970s and domestic terrorism and, perhaps a little unfairly, is not referred to by his party with the same nostalgia accorded to the
Brandt Chancellorship. By the same token, Schmidt never achieved the
same talismanic status within the SPD enjoyed by his predecessor.

See BUNDESKANZLER; SOZIALLIBERALE KOALITION.

(CL)

Schröder, Gerhard   Gerhard Schröder is MINISTERPRÄSIDENT of NIEDER-
SACHSEN and a leading figure within the SPD. Born on 7 April 1944,
Schröder rose through the SPD's youth wing, holding the post of chairman
from 1978–80. He headed the SPD's parliamentary grouping in the
Niedersachsen LANDTAG from 1986–90, when he became *Ministerpräsident*.

Schröder has, perhaps unfairly, a reputation as an opportunist and a
maverick in his party, and became renowned for his often outspoken
attacks on his own party's policies when Rudolf SCHARPING was SPD

Candidate for Chancellor in the 1994 BUNDESTAG election. Nevertheless, he enjoys a great deal of popularity both in Niedersachsen and among the German population as a whole and cannot be discounted as a future SPD Chancellor-Candidate.

See LAFONTAINE, OSKAR.

(CL)

Schulpflicht School attendance is obligatory from the age of six onwards and then for a minimum of nine years. Those who chose to do an apprenticeship after these nine years are obliged to attend special schools for a further three years.

Compulsory schooling was increased from eight to nine years in the 1960s so as to give more time to young people to find a career. Some BUNDESLÄNDER now offer a tenth year at the *Hauptschule*. This not only enables students to get a higher school-leaving qualification (*Mittlere Reife*) but also reduces youth unemployment.

See DUALES SYSTEM; GRUNDSCHULE; WEITERFÜHRENDE SCHULEN.

(AW)

SED (Sozialistische Einheitspartei Deutschlands) Founded in April 1946, the Socialist Unity Party of Germany (SED) was the ruling party of the GDR. The SED was founded as a result of a merger between the KPD and SPD. The Social Democrats, though not without some sympathy for the principle of co-operation, were subjected to such severe pressure by Soviet occupation authorities to unite with the German Communists that many regard the union as a shotgun marriage. During 1948, the SED was transformed into a 'party of a new type' led by a small *Politbüro*. The parity of status between ex-Communists and ex-Social Democrats was abolished to the detriment of the latter. This re-organisation, plus a series of purges between 1948 and 1953, affecting in particular former Social Democrats and those former Communists suspected of opposition views, not only virtually halved the size of membership but also produced a disciplined party more in line with the Soviet model.

The SED's constitutionally proclaimed leadership role was buttressed by a tightly knit network of party organs based on the application of the principle of democratic centralism. State functionaries and party members were bound to party decisions and factions were banned. Party members (2.3 million in 1986) were obliged to spend considerable time at party meetings and on ideological training.

The SED was based on a hierarchical and territorial basis. On the lowest level were the basic and residential district party organisations. Above these were the 263 district (*Kreis*), the 15 regional (*Bezirk*) and the central party organisations. Although the *Parteitag*, which from 1971 onwards met once every five years, was in theory the SED's highest organ, it was restricted to ratifying policies which were determined in advance by party elites.

According to party statute, the Central Committee was the highest organ between congresses. A plenum had to be held once every six months. Whilst the Central Committee represented a wide range of party interest groups, it met too infrequently to perform a policy-making role and under HONECKER discussion was kept to a minimum. A more important body was the small Secretariat of the Central Committee (11 members throughout the 1980s) which was responsible for the direction of party work, above all for the selection of party cadres and the implementation of party directives.

The *Politbüro*, the key decision-making body, concerned itself at its weekly meetings with the basic questions affecting the SED, the government and the economy. Its size fluctuated between 14 and 27 members and candidates. Power usually resided in the First/Central Secretary. In the late 1980s, an overcentralisation of decision-making and an ageing leadership reduced the capacity of the *Politbüro* to respond flexibly to the growing problems in society and accelerated the party's demise.

On 1 December 1989, the VOLKSKAMMER removed the SED's leadership claim from the Constitution. With the party split between reformers and traditionalists and confronted by a mass exodus of members, an extraordinary congress was held on 8 and 15 December 1989 which elected a new party executive with Gregor GYSI as chairman. The SED did not dissolve itself, partly because it did not wish to surrender its vast assets; instead it compromised on a change of title to SED-PDS (Party of Democratic Socialism). The prefix was dropped two months later.

See BLOCKPARTEIEN; DDR; MARXISMUS-LENINISMUS; MASSENORGANISATIONEN; PDS; SMAD.

(MD)

Siemens   Siemens is one of the largest employers in Germany. It has also been profitable – in stark contrast to AEG, its rival in electrical and electronic engineering. In the mid-1990s, its world-wide sales were nearing DM90 billion, together with a gradually decreasing employment level of then 375 000.

Initially concerned with telegraphic systems, Siemens diversified into electrification in the last quarter of the nineteenth century. Together with AEG, Siemens subsequently dominated the entire German electrical industry. Today, Siemens' operational divisions are: energy, industrial systems, telecommunications, information technology, transport systems, medical technology, components and, through its wholly owned subsidiary Osram, lighting. A household appliance subsidiary is jointly owned with BOSCH. With its large liquid reserves, Siemens embarked on a process of diversification and international expansion in the 1980s. It acquired Nixdorf, Plessey and Bendix. Siemens Nixdorf subsequently passed from losses to profits. This was reflected in the proportion of sales in Germany decreasing from 50 to 40 per cent during the first half of the 1990s.

(EOS)

Sinatra-Doktrin   The 'Sinatra-Doctrine' refers to the release of the communist countries of Eastern Europe from the threat of Soviet armed intervention in their domestic affairs (the so-called Brezhnev Doctrine).

In October 1989, during Gorbachev's visit to Finland, the Soviet Foreign Ministry spokesman Gennadi Gerasimov declared that the Brezhnev Doctrine had been replaced by the Sinatra Doctrine. This implied that the communist countries of Eastern Europe could, in the words of the song by Frank Sinatra, 'do it their way', that is, they were able to decide on political, social and economic reforms free of Soviet interference.

See BRESCHNEW-DOKTRIN.

(MD)

SMAD (Sowjetische Militäradministration in Deutschland)   The Soviet Military Administration in Germany (SMAD) was the agent of direct Soviet control over the post-war Soviet Occupation Zone. As in the three western zones, a military administration was set up in the Soviet Zone following World War II. SMAD's headquarters were at Berlin-Karlshorst and its first head was the commander-in-chief of the Soviet occupation forces, Marshal Zhukov. The overall strength of SMAD declined from about 50 000 in late 1946 to 31 500 in August 1948.

The Central Administration, the key organ of SMAD in Berlin-Karlshorst, was responsible for the administration of the Soviet Zone as well as being responsible for the questions affecting Germany as a whole which were dealt with in the Allied Control Council. Numerous specialist departments were created to enable SMAD to perform its governmental function, among which the most important were the Political Administration and the Propaganda Administration.

Corresponding to the division of the Soviet Zone into five *Länder*, SMAD established Military Administrations in the *Länder* and provinces; these oversaw local and district *Kommandaturas*. This system did not operate as smoothly as was once thought: some departments were understaffed. STALIN, though the undisputed master, tended to issue ambiguous policy directives which could be interpreted in a variety of ways; and disputes arose over competencies between local commandants and SMAD departments in Berlin and between Karlshorst and ministries and organisations in Moscow.

Despite these problems, SMAD was undoubtedly the dominant influence in the restructuring of the Soviet Zone where even loyal German Communists like ULBRICHT and Pieck had to accept a subordinate position. SMAD played the key role in crucial developments such as the founding of the SED, the creation of nationalised enterprises, the land reform of 1946, the establishment of German administration, and the denazification process.

On SMAD's orders, former concentration camps were reopened in the zone for the internment of former members of the Nazi Party and the armed forces. Also interned were actual and suspected opponents of Soviet policy, some of whom had also opposed the Nazis. Between 1945 and 1950, when the last camps in Bautzen, Buchenwald and Sachsenhausen were closed, possibly over 200 000 Germans had been interned in the 11 camps. At least 42 000 – some estimates give 100 000 – had died there, mainly of malnutrition and disease such as tuberculosis.

On 10 October 1949, SMAD dissolved itself and was replaced by the Soviet Control Commission.

See BESATZUNG; DDR; STALINISMUS.

(MD)

Solidaritätszuschlag See STEUERLÜGE.

(MD)

Solidarpakt The Solidarity Pact was concluded in 1993 to revive the East German economy. With the East German economy still contracting, the public deficit rising, wages increasing and the CDU's popularity in decline, Chancellor Helmut KOHL proposed, in September 1992, a Solidarity Pact among unions, employers, local and regional governments, the federal government and the SPD. Such a pact was envisaged as the main instrument for mobilising political support and additional resources to cope with the unification crisis until the BUNDESTAG election in October 1994.

To the surprise of most observers, the pact was concluded in March 1993 between the coalition government, the SPD, labour, business, banks and the BUNDESLÄNDER, a demonstration of the consensual approach which had typified the old (western) Federal Republic. The Federal Government, under pressure from the SPD, abandoned its aspirations to make deep cuts in social security and agreed to provide the *Bundesländer* with about DM20 billion in extra tax revenues to enable them to pay transfers from the East. This was done by raising VAT receipts from 37 to 44 per cent. Rather than push through deep spending cuts to reduce the public deficit, the taxpayers were called upon to dig deeper into their pockets. From January 1995, appreciable increases were made in income and wealth taxes. The TREUHANDANSTALT's borrowing limit was increased and the Bank for Reconstruction was empowered to raise its borrowing from DM30 billion to DM60 billion to finance housing modernisation in East Germany. Large manufacturing and retail firms agreed to set a target of doubling the value of their East German purchases by 1995, DM2 billion were released for job creation measures and Kohl intimated that the 'industrial cores' of East Germany would be kept afloat and renewed.

See STEUERLÜGE; TRANSFORMATION.

(MD)

Soziale Marktwirtschaft A socially responsible market economy offers equal weighting to the principles of freedom, efficiency and equity. The notion of *Soziale Marktwirtschaft* originated just prior to 1933. After the war it also represented an alternative to the communist economic system but it should not be confused with *laissez-faire* market economics. The economic role for state intervention is for an active anti-trust policy, a strong monetary policy in order to assure macroeconomic stability (via the DEUTSCHE BUNDESBANK) and the setting of a social framework and safety for those who are not able to compete in the market (e.g. children, the elderly, the sick, the unemployed).

Employers blame the high non-wage labour costs, which result from the social element of the *Soziale Marktwirtschaft* for the decreasing competiveness of domestic production (*Standort Deutschland*). Yet the system has been Europe's most successful wealth creator.

See SOZIALES NETZ; SOZIALSTAAT.

(EOS)

Soziales Netz   The social (safety) net in the Federal Republic is the collection of measures of social policy (SOZIALPOLITIK) designed to offer protection against the disadvantages individuals might experience in a free market economy.

The social net is based on three principles. The first is the *Versicherungsprinzip*, the 'insurance principle' that each should contribute through insurance contributions to the costs of social policy provision. A range of compulsory social insurance schemes accordingly exist to provide protection, for example against the consequences of unemployment, ill-health and old age (SOZIALVERSICHERUNG). Supplementary protection is also provided outside the framework of social insurance schemes – and therefore financed by general taxation – according to the *Fürsorgeprinzip* (welfare principle). Policy instruments under the welfare principle include SOZIALHILFE (social assistance for those with otherwise insufficient sources of income), FAMILIENPOLITIK (family policy, in particular *Kindergeld*, or child benefit, which offers a contribution to the costs of raising children) and WOHNUNGSPOLITIK (housing policy, in particular *Wohngeld*, or housing benefit, which is designed to ensure adequate housing conditions for those on low incomes). The third principle of the social safety net is the *Versorgungsprinzip* (principle of provision) which awards additional protection to groups such as war victims and civil servants deemed to be entitled to special support, again financed through general taxation, in reflection of their wider contribution to society.

See SOZIALSTAAT.

(CJ)

Sozialhilfe   Social Assistance has become increasingly important in recent years as a last resort in the social safety net (SOZIALES NETZ) for those unable to maintain a satisfactory standard of living on the basis of their own resources.

Social Assistance is not part of the social insurance system. Instead, it is based on the *Fürsorgeprinzip* (welfare principle) of German welfare provision, which does not require previous insurance contributions by the recipient to qualify for support, and is financed by general taxation. It is designed to ensure that those in difficulty (*Notlage*) have sufficient means to pay for essential outgoings such as food, housing, heating and clothing. Social assistance is administered by local government in accordance with federal legislative guidelines.

The number of recipients – and the costs of support – have risen dramatically. The main categories of recipient are: the unemployed who have made insufficient contributions to the unemployment insurance (ARBEITS-LOSENVERSICHERUNG) system and thus do not qualify for insurance-financed support; pensioners whose pensions are insufficient to cover essential living costs, in particular rents, which have increased substantially in recent years; and – in reflection of increasing divorce rates – the growing number of single-parent families without sufficient means of support. Further demands on Social Assistance have been made since unification as the problems of economic transition in the East have reduced the income of many Easterners below a satisfactory minimum subsistence level (*Existenzminimum*).

See FAMILIENPOLITIK; SOZIALVERSICHERUNG; WOHNUNGSPOLITIK.

(CJ)

Sozialistischer Realismus   Socialist Realism is a literary theory which was adopted as the yardstick for literary creativity in the Soviet Union in 1934 and then in the other Soviet satellite states.

Socialist Realism requires the author to portray the general rather than the individual and exceptional, to aim at a large audience, to portray the social struggle – in accordance with the teachings of Marxism–Leninism – and to convey a sense of optimism in human progress, particularly by choosing (working-class) heroes who would typify this hope.

In the former GDR this led to the so-called *Aufbauromane* and *Betriebsromane* (reconstruction and workplace novels). These were not very exciting in literary terms but reflected the writers' belief that socialism as Marx had meant it was to come in their lifetimes.

See MARXISMUS-LENINISMUS; REAL EXISTIERENDER SOZIALISMUS.

(RW)

Sozialliberale Koalition   The Social–Liberal Coalition was the federal government coalition between SPD and FDP between 1969–1982 under the successive Chancellorships of Willy BRANDT (1969–74) and Helmut SCHMIDT (1974–82).

Following the BUNDESTAG elections of 1969, the new coalition, led by Brandt, saw its main tasks as undertaking social reform and – its greatest achievement – improving relations with the GDR, the Soviet Union and the wider communist bloc in a new OSTPOLITIK. The 1972 *Bundestag* elections endorsed the coalition's policies by bestowing upon the SPD its largest ever share of the vote (45.8 per cent) and giving the FDP a respectable 8.4 per cent. However, the 1973 oil price shock, the resignation of Brandt in 1974 and a shift to the left within the SPD (especially its youth wing) combined to put an increasing strain on the coalition. The SPD and FDP's share of the votes was reduced in the 1976 *Bundestag* elections to 42.6 per cent and 7.9 per cent respectively. The Schmidt period was dominated by the management of the economic problems produced by the oil crisis, the introduction of robust internal security measures in response to domestic terrorism, and the growth of new social movements (NEUE SOZIALE BEWE-GUNGEN). The coalition remained in power following the 1980 *Bundestag* elections but was becoming increasingly fractious as the SPD rank-and-file pushed for a more overtly left-wing agenda while the FDP moved to the Right, especially on economic issues. Finally, on 17 September 1982, the FDP left the coalition, endorsing a constructive vote of no-confidence (KONSTRUKTIVES MIßTRAUENSVOTUM) in Schmidt which installed Helmut KOHL as Chancellor and leader of a new CDU/CSU-FDP coalition.

A new social–liberal coalition is often cited by observers as an alternative to the CDU/CSU-FDP coalition in power since 1982. However, the weakness of the FDP in the mid-1990s has made a new social–liberal coalition extremely unlikely. Moreover, on the SPD side, memories of the 'betrayal' of September 1982 are still bitter in some quarters, whilst at the same time many members would prefer the GRÜNE to be their first choice of coalition partner.

See ENTSPANNUNG; FRIEDENSBEWEGUNG; NATO-DOPPELBESCHLUß; TERRORISMUS.

(CL)

Sozialpartnerschaft   Social Partnership describes the priority given to the commonality of interests in the relationship between employers and unions. The period of post-war reconstruction saw the trade union movement accept a system of industrial relations in the Federal Republic based upon the accommodation of competing interests between employers and employees. This represented a clear move away from the theoretical Marxist approach of social democracy which held the belief that class conflict was irreconcilable. Although conflict in the form of strikes and other forms of industrial action occurs in the pluralist system of industrial relations, the system aims to institutionalise such conflict and place it within clearly defined parameters. The system brought real material improvements for employees on the back of the economic miracle in the Federal Republic. Even with recession, unemployment, changes in the structure of industry and the introduction of new technology the system – based upon free collective bargaining (TARIFAUTONOMIE) and collective agreements has brought rises in real incomes for employees and social peace for employers.

German reunification (with the transfer of the western system of industrial relations to the NEUE BUNDESLÄNDER) posed a major test for social partnership. So far the system has survived in the West and developed with remarkable success in the East.

With employers increasingly trying to reduce labour costs to retain competitiveness, rising unemployment and a stagnation in real incomes, enormous strain remains on the system of industrial relations which embodies social partnership. The system has become so institutionalised in the Federal Republic, however, that new compromises will be looked for, at least in the short term.

See GEWERKSCHAFTEN; KORPORATISMUS; PLURALISMUS; UNTERNEHMER-VERBÄNDE; WIRTSCHAFTSWUNDER.

(SRF)

Sozialpolitik   Social policy, broadly defined, refers to those policy fields in which forms of protection and assistance are offered to those who experience disadvantage in the operation of the free market economy. In the Federal Republic, social policy somewhat unusually has a constitutional foundation in the form of the principle of the social state (SOZIALSTAAT).

Social policy in the Federal Republic provides an extensive social (safety) net (SOZIALES NETZ) designed to protect individual welfare and wider social cohesion in the face of problems such as ill-health, unemployment, old age, poverty, inadequate housing, the costs of raising a family, and so on. The safety net is government-regulated, though only partly government-financed through taxation. The bulk of the costs of the safety net are provided by social insurance schemes (SOZIALVERSICHERUNG). Both the insurance-financed and tax-financed elements of social policy allow for a redistributive element, where richer citizens on average contribute more to the system than they receive from it.

A general problem in social policy in western democracies has been the increasing cost of providing an extensive safety net. This problem has been exacerbated by German unification. The method of social policy unification was, as elsewhere, the wholesale adoption of the existing West German model. This has proved extremely beneficial in some respects, in particular by offering some low-income groups in the East – e.g. pensioners and the unemployed – a relatively generous 'cushion' for the problems of transition. It has, though, produced a cost explosion which has had to be financed largely by the increasingly disgruntled West German taxpayers. Some have also argued that the process of West–East social policy transfer swept away the old GDR system in too wholesale a manner, ignoring its positive aspects, such as near-comprehensive pre-school child-care.

The cost issue remains at the forefront in the 1990s. As elsewhere in Europe, the social policy budget remains difficult to control, let alone reduce, which has a knock-on effect regarding the achievement of other policy goals (in particular the quest to qualify for European Economic and Monetary Union). A further problem are the high levels of contributions employers have to make through the social insurance funds, which raise labour costs and can reduce competitiveness. As a result, the wider principle of comprehensive social policy provision itself has come under attack.

See EUROPAPOLITIK; GEWERKSCHAFTEN; WIRTSCHAFTS-, WÄHRUNGS- UND SOZIALUNION.

(CJ)

Sozialstaat The social state is one of the fundamental and unalterable constitutional principles of the GRUNDGESETZ. The principle of the *Sozialstaat* implies a commitment on the part of the German state to intervene to offer protection to its citizens against the disadvantages which may occur for some in a free market economy. This protection is offered in the various fields of SOZIALPOLITIK and underlies the notion of the social market economy (SOZIALE MARKTWIRTSCHAFT) in Germany.

The *Sozialstaat* has become the most contested of the fundamental principles of the *Grundgesetz*. The economic recessions of the 1970s and 1980s raised doubts about the state's ability in the long term to fund an extensive *Sozialpolitik*. In addition, the ideas of neo-liberalism have provoked a polarised debate about the desirability and effectiveness of an extensive *Sozialpolitik*.

The controversy surrounding the *Sozialstaat* principle has intensified after unification. The cost of offering social protection to those disadvantaged in East Germany by the adaptation to a free market economy has been extremely high. Increased *Sozialpolitik* expenditures have both resulted in unpopular tax rises, while also causing Germany difficulties in meeting the criteria for Economic and Monetary Union in the European Union. The consequence has been increasing pressure to reduce expenditures and, by implication, undermine the substance of the *Sozialstaat* principle.

(CJ)

Sozialversicherung Social insurance is one of the central principles of social policy (SOZIALPOLITIK) provision and the social safety net (SOZIALES NETZ) in the Federal Republic. Compulsory membership in and contribution to social insurance schemes provides a right to financial support should the risk against which the insurance protects occur. The main forms of social insurance are KRANKENVERSICHERUNG (health insurance), RENTENVERSICHERUNG (pension insurance), ARBEITSLOSENVERSICHERUNG (unemployment insurance), PFLEGEVERSICHERUNG (care insurance) and *Unfallversicherung* (accident insurance). Contributions, set at a percentage of salary, are paid half by the individuals concerned and half by their employers, with the exception of accident insurance, which is covered wholly by employers. Additional private insurance can be taken out in the fields of health, pensions and care (income allowing). In contrast to private insurance, social insurance provides protection for all on an equal basis, regardless of the total sum contributed. This means that those on higher incomes, and making higher contributions, subsidise the services provided to those with lower incomes and lower contributions, and is known as the *Solidarausgleich*, or 'solidarity balance'.

The scale of the contributions made by employers to social insurance schemes has become controversial, with many arguing that the additional labour costs thus imposed have undermined German economic competitiveness. Some major German companies have set up operations abroad, at least partly from the motivation of avoiding the high cost of social insurance within Germany.

(CJ)

SPD (Sozialdemokratische Partei Deutschlands) The Social Democratic Party of Germany is the oldest political party in Germany, dating back to 1848. It was the largest political party for most of the Weimar Republic before being suppressed by the National Socialists in 1933. The SPD was reconstituted after 1945, under the leadership of Kurt Schumacher, as an anti-communist, pacifist party of the Left with a strong commitment to national unity. In this role, the SPD was fundamentally opposed to the direction the nascent Federal Republic was taking, especially with regard to Konrad ADENAUER's foreign policy stance and Ludwig Erhard's economic management. By the mid-1950s, it was clear that the SPD had lost the argument over these issues and underwent an ideological re-think that culminated in the Bad Godesberg Programme of 1959, which re-oriented it as a pragmatic centre-left *Volkspartei*, or 'catch-all' party. The SPD's reorientation was confirmed when it entered into a Grand Coalition with the CDU/CSU in 1966. In 1969, the SPD formed a new coalition with the liberal FDP and Willy BRANDT became the first SPD Chancellor of the Federal Republic. Brandt was succeeded as Chancellor in 1974 by Helmut SCHMIDT, who presided over the coalition until it was dissolved in 1982.

Since losing office, the SPD has struggled to find a clear political direction and has steadily lost electoral support. The party has been unable to solve the dilemma of both winning back the political centre-ground from the CDU/CSU, whilst responding to the challenge from the Left of the GRÜNE (who have taken a substantial share of young and Left-oriented voters from the SPD). Moreover, the SPD has not been able to field a candidate for Chancellor who has been able to match the popularity and political skills of Chancellor Helmut KOHL.

The SPD's problems have continued since unification, with uncertainties over its leadership and programme as well as its failure to unseat the CDU/CSU-FDP coalition in both the 1990 and 1994 elections.

See GROßE KOALITION; LAFONTAINE, OSKAR; SCHARPING, RUDOLF; SCHRÖDER, GERHARD; SOZIALLIBERALE KOALITION.

(CL)

SS (Schutzstaffel) The black-shirted 'Protection Corps' was established as Adolf HITLER's personal bodyguard within the National Socialist paramilitary organisation, the SA, in the Weimar Republic. Its leader from 1929 was Heinrich Himmler.

The SS played a key role in the violent suppression of the SA in July 1934. Emerging with his and his organisation's prestige enhanced, Himmler sought subsequently to concentrate internal policing and security functions under the SS banner. Over time, the GESTAPO (secret state police) and the whole judicial and criminal constabulary fell under SS control, as well as new, quasi-judicial functions such as running the concentration camps. The SS security empire's power lay in the fact that it stood outside normal state structures and was directly responsible to Hitler as *Führer* of the Reich.

It was able to expand its military role in World War II from that of elite bodyguard and special force to become a supplementary regular army. This *Waffen-SS* was reserved for those considered to be racially pure Germans. The SS also massively expanded the concentration camp network in the occupied territories in World War II, developing immense economic muscle from the exploitation of slave labour, and organising the mass murder of Jews and others in the extermination camps of eastern Europe.

See DRITTES REICH; HOLOCAUST; KONZENTRATIONSLAGER; NATIONAL-SOZIALISMUS.

(CJ)

Staatsangehörigkeitsrecht   Citizenship law in Germany is based on the principle of descent, or bloodline (*ius sanguinis*), as opposed to the principle of territory, or birthplace (*ius soli*). The legal basis of German citizenship remains the Imperial Citizenship Law (*Reichs- und Staatsangehörigkeitsgesetz*, or *RuStaG*) of 1913.

The *RuStaG* was the first law to define a national German citizenship. As it defined citizenship by descent, it enabled Germany to take in the millions of German refugees from eastern Europe after World War II. Even today, around 220 000 ethnic Germans per year enter Germany from the former USSR under this provision. Although the GDR created its own citizenship, the Federal Republic continued to adhere to the all-German 1913 law to avoid creating a separate West German citizenship, which would have implicitly acknowledged the legitimacy of the GDR.

The principle of descent has been called into question ever since the arrival of the first 'guest workers' (GASTARBEITER) in 1955. After the more permanent settlement of *Gastarbeiter* in Germany following the recruitment stop in 1973, the principle of descent hindered their integration by failing to grant children born in Germany automatic citizenship. As a consequence, a third generation of 'foreigners' is thus currently growing up in Germany today.

Although it is possible to obtain German citizenship, the procedure is complex and dual citizenship is not normally permitted. The numbers of foreigners awarded German citizenship has been correspondingly low (annually around 0.5 per cent of the total foreign population).

In the course of the 1990 reform of the Foreigners' Law, a legal right to citizenship was introduced for certain groups of foreigners. Although this has resulted in greater numbers of applications for citizenship, large numbers of foreigners are still excluded from the law's provisions. A planned reform of the *RuStaG* before the next federal election in 1998 is unlikely to bring any fundamental changes in the direction of the principle of territory.

See AUSLÄNDERPOLITIK; NATIONALE IDENTITÄT.

(SG)

Staatsrat der DDR The GDR Council of State was created as 'collective head of state' after the death of Wilhelm Pieck in 1960. The first Chairman of the Council of State, Walter ULBRICHT extended the body's powers at the expense of the Council of Ministers (MINISTERRAT DER DDR). Article 79 of the 1968 Constitution proclaimed the Council of Ministers as functioning on the basis of the laws and decrees of the VOLKSKAMMER (parliament) but also of the decrees and decisions of the Council of State. The latter's decrees and decisions enjoyed legal force and its activities covered all important domestic affairs. Ulbricht used his position as Chairman of the Council of State to enhance his own power and authority. Article 69 of the Constitution empowered the Chairman to direct the work of the Council and to represent the *Volkskammer* in international relations.

After Ulbricht's resignation as party leader in 1971, the Council of State lost much of its authority to the Council of Ministers and many of its remaining rights and functions were essentially ceremonial. On Ulbricht's death in 1973, Willi Stoph became Chairman of the Council of State; he was replaced by Erich HONECKER three years later.

(MD)

Stadtstaat See BUNDESLÄNDER.

Stalin, Josef Stalin (1879–1953) was the Soviet dictator whose policies were instrumental in shaping the structure of the Soviet zone and the GDR. Stalin, a Georgian by birth, emerged by 1929, after a series of fierce internal struggles, as the master of party and state in the Soviet Union. He subsequently consolidated that position to the point of absolutism. The Red Army's victory against Nazi Germany gave a further boost to Stalin's reputation even though the effort exhausted the Soviet Union economically and cost the lives of millions of soldiers.

Stalin's policy towards Germany after the war remains a matter of lively debate, despite the availability of new archival materials. It is still unclear whether and/or when Stalin aspired to divide Germany and to what extent his policies at a given moment were determined by his perception of Soviet interests. These interests in the immediate post-war era concerned drawing upon Germany, especially the Ruhr, for reparations and securing the Soviet Union against any future German threat. These considerations probably persuaded Stalin of the advisability of operating within the four-power system of control over Germany while at the same time protecting Soviet security interests and tightening Soviet control over its zone. Once the Americans had made their expected withdrawal from Germany, Stalin may have entertained the hope that the social order of the Soviet zone might eventually become attractive as a model for Germany. He did not, however, openly aspire to implant the Soviet-style system in Eastern Germany until four-power control became unworkable – hence the aspiration in 1945 to establish a so-called anti-fascist democratic order and the SED's advocacy in February 1946 of a specific 'German Road to Socialism'. Undesirable from Stalin's point of view – but partly of his own making – was the emergence of the West German state, which was incorporated into an American–West European system of alliances. In this situation, Stalin pursued the dual track policy of promoting the Soviet-style system in the GDR while professing a commitment to German unity. The latter was intended to prevent the closer integration of the Federal Republic into the Western system and may well have been the main motive behind Stalin's proposals in March 1952 for unification based on free elections. Stalin's seeming readiness to accept the dismantling of the GDR in return for a neutral Germany was not put to the test as the Western powers and Chancellor ADENAUER were unwilling to enter into serious negotiations.

See DDR; MARXISMUS-LENINISMUS; STALINISMUS.

(MD)

Stalinismus Stalinism was the system of rule and pattern of political action which assumed its characteristic shape during Stalin's period in power and which was transposed to the countries of Eastern Europe after the end of World War II.

Although the revolutionary period after 1917 is often regarded as the embryo of Stalinism, it was not until the mid-1930s that the system was fully developed in the Soviet Union. In Eastern Europe, the high tide of Stalinism extended from 1947 to 1956. The Stalinist system was associated with the cult of the personality of the leader, a high level of coercion and physical terror, the destruction of civil liberties, ideological conformity to the principles of Marxism–Leninism, a hierarchical and bureaucratic system of government, albeit without clear criteria for rational decision-making, a ruling Communist party, the collectivisation of agriculture, the nationalisation of industry with an emphasis on basic industries, and the elimination of the market in favour of a rigid system of central planning of the economy.

The Stalinist system was implanted in the Soviet Union's Eastern European satellites after the World War II, at first gradually but accelerating from 1947/48 onwards. In the Soviet Zone/GDR, Stalinisation was inaugurated by the transformation of the SED into a Soviet-type party in 1948/49 and consolidated by the construction of socialism programme of 1952. Although Khruschchev's de-Stalinisation campaigns and Brezhnev's pragmatic real existing socialism modified the Stalinist heritage, for example its terroristic excesses, the basic administrative–command structure remained in place until the advent of Gorbachev.

See MARXISMUS-LENINISMUS; NOMENKLATUR; PLANWIRTSCHAFT; REAL EXISTIERENDER SOZIALISMUS; STALIN.

(MD)

Ständige Konferenz der Kultusminister der Länder der Bundesrepublik Deutschland (KMK) The Standing Conference of the Ministers of Culture of the BUNDESLÄNDER exists to co-ordinate policy among the *Bundesländer* in their core field of competence in education and cultural affairs (*Kulturhoheit*). In 1949 the *Bundesländer* decided to found the KMK as a working party of the ministries concerned with education. After reunification, the NEUE BUNDESLÄNDER joined in 1990. The KMK's seat is in Bonn.

The task of the KMK is to work out recommendations and come to decisions which are then presented to the individual LANDTAGE so that they can be incorporated into laws or regulations. Its work mainly covers the timing of the school year, holidays in the different *Bundesländer* (e.g. staggered summer holidays), recognition of school-leaving certificates, recognition of certain degrees, recognition of German schools abroad and foreign qualifications.

See FÖDERALISMUS.

(AW)

Stasi (Ministerium für Staatssicherheit) The Ministry of State Security (*Stasi*) was responsible for protecting the GDR state from perceived internal and external threats. Although a secret police force was created in the Soviet Occupation Zone soon after the end of World War II, a separate Ministry of State Security was not founded until 1950. The direct involvement of its first two ministers, Zaisser and Wollweber, in attempts to unseat Walther ULBRICHT created considerable turmoil in the service. However, the appointment of Erich Mielke as minister in 1957 inaugurated an era of stability and organisational efficiency.

The organisational structure of the Stasi reflected its mission to protect the GDR and the SED from internal and external enemies. Among the twelve main departments (*Hauptverwaltungen*) were those for combating political–ideological sabotage and political underground activity and protection against internal spying. Numerous units engaged in activities ranging from observation of the Churches to the protection of party and state installations. A Central Reconnaissance Administration, presided over for

34 years by Markus Wolf, was concerned with foreign espionage. The Central Evaluation and Information Group collected and assessed the information it received and drew up detailed and realistic situation reports for the state and party leadership.

The full-time staff, which numbered about 4 000 in 1952, grew quickly after Erich HONECKER came to power: from 52 700 in 1973 to about 100 000 in 1989. There was also a rapid increase under Honecker in the various categories of Stasi collaborators, a reflection of the mania for a comprehensive surveillance of GDR citizens to combat hostile–negative tendencies and forces, a category which was interpreted in its broadest sense. 'Security' took precedence over the law. In 1988, it is estimated that there were about 109 000 unofficial collaborators, 32 000 people who put their apartment at the disposal of the Stasi for secret meetings and a similar number of 'societal collaborators for security'. *In toto*, there was one part-time Stasi employee per 120 East Germans. The veritable army of full-time and unofficial collaborators left behind 178 kilometres of files and documents. Files were kept on 6 million GDR citizens and 2 million West Germans.

After Honecker's fall, MODROW's attempt to reorganise the state security system soon foundered on popular opposition and the whole system was dismantled by the DE MAIZIÈRE government.

(MD)

Steuerlüge   Chancellor KOHL was accused of a 'lie about taxes' in giving the impression that taxes would not have to be raised to fund the reconstruction of the GDR. During the March 1990 VOLKSKAMMER election and then throughout most of the remainder of the year Kohl assured East and West German electors that no increases in taxes would be necessary for German unity. This assurance was based on a belief in the efficacy of market instruments to transform the socialist system, hopes of a high level of private investment, a rapid recovery by the East German economy and a resulting increase in tax revenues. However, escalating unemployment, the collapse of East German industry, rising wages and the adoption of the West German social security system resulted in a dramatic increase in public transfers from West to East Germany. The government bowed to the inevitable and announced a tax package at the end of February 1991. The most important measures were a 7.5 per cent surcharge on income tax and corporation tax liabilities from 1 July 1991 to 30 June 1992, a 25 per cent increase in the tax on tobacco from 1 January 1992, an increase by 1.5 per cent net of contributions to social insurance funds and an appreciable rise in various fuel and energy taxes from 1 July 1991. The revenue from the solidarity surcharge amounted to about DM22 billion in 1991 and 1992 and the surcharge was extended by a tax amendment law in 1993. It was reintroduced at the start of 1995 and yielded receipts of about DM26 billion. The surcharge has proved highly unpopular, testimony to the reluctance of West Germans to make major sacrifices to rebuild the East.

The increase in the burden of taxation is indicated by the overall rate of taxation and social insurance contributions. This stood at about 24.5 per cent of GDP at the end of 1995, or 4.5 per cent above the 1990 level.

See SOLIDARPAKT; TRANSFORMATION; WESSI.

(MD)

Stiftungen Foundations seek to promote excellence in academia and research by financing students, academics and academic projects and by offering a wide range of seminars where members can meet, learn and exchange their ideas.

Some of the best known are the following: the *Alexander-von-Humboldt Stiftung*, which enables German academics to research abroad and foreign academics to come to Germany for their research by offering scholarships; the *Stiftung Volkswagenwerk*, which promotes research and development in research institutions and supports conferences; the *Carl-Duisberg-Gesellschaft*, which supports German and foreign new blood in the area of economics; the *Studienstiftung des deutschen Volkes*, which gives scholarships to outstanding German students and graduates working on a doctorate (applicants need to be excellent in their field of work as well as be politically and socially conscious); the *Cusanus-Stiftung*, which promotes Catholic students who are excellent in their work as well as socially active (the equivalent foundation for Protestant students is the *Evangelisches Studienwerk*); and the *Deutsche Stiftung für internationale Entwicklung*, which concentrates on rural development, sending Germans to Third World countries to develop training facilities and also helping people from the Third World to come to Germany for training.

Party-political foundations, which may also support academic work, are the *Friedrich-Ebert-Stiftung* (SPD), the *Konrad-Adenauer-Stiftung* (CDU), the *Hanns-Seidel-Stiftung* (CSU), the *Heinrich-Böll-Stiftung* (*Grüne*), and the *Friedrich-Naumann-Stiftung* (FDP).

A complete list of foundations and their aims can be found in the handbook *Pro-Wissenschaft* published by the *Stifterverband für die deutsche Wissenschaft*.

(RW)

Stile Styles of architecture in Germany vary in respect of historical eras and fashions. The oldest buildings in Germany, Switzerland and Austria are built in the Romanesque style (*Romanik*). Their walls are thick and the windows relatively small because such buildings also had to serve as a fortress in times of war. Among the most famous Romanic buildings are the Cathedral of Trier and that of Speyer. The gothic style (*Gotik*) was first developed in France in the twelfth century. It is playful and decorative, with high windows giving light rooms. Probably the most famous gothic cathedral is that of Köln. In the north-east of Germany and former East Prussia buildings were often built with red clay bricks and the gothic style is here called *Backsteingothik* (e.g. the Cathedrals of Lübeck, Ratzeburg, Rostock and Gdansk). Although the renaissance style (*Renaissance*) had started in Italy in the fourteenth century it only became fashionable in Germany around 150 years later. As its name indicates, it goes back to the more simple and linear Roman style but with the building techniques which had been developed in the meantime. Examples of this architecture exist in many German cities such as the Patrician houses in Regensburg and other Bavarian and Swabian towns along with houses and churches in the former GDR (e.g. Halle). Again, Northern German cities had their own Renaissance style in red clay bricks. The baroque style (*Barok*) is even more playful than the gothic style but emphasises horizontal lines as well as vertical ones. Such buildings thus look 'heavier'. In the south of Germany most churches are baroque and are characterised by their onion-shaped tower. Older churches were often changed to what was the fashionable style around the eighteenth century. A number of palaces were also built in this style, e.g. Linderhof near Garmisch-Partenkirchen. The *Rokoko* style of the second half of the eighteenth century brings a shift from the pompous and theatrical to smaller, more intimate spaces. This was the era when small Apollo and Venus statues were put into the parks of the palaces and the aristocracy built their amusement and hunting lodges, e.g. in the Nymphenburger Park in München and the Ermitage in Bayreuth. The classicist style (*Klazzisismus*) of the latter half of the eighteenth century is another attempt to go back to the antique precepts by using stereometric design where ornaments do not form an integral part of the whole. The Brandenburg Gate is probably the most famous surviving building but good examples of city architecture can also be found in Karlsruhe and Koblenz.

See JUGENDSTIL.

(RW)

Strauß, Franz Josef Franz Josef Strauß was leader of the CSU from 1961, and Minister-President of Bavaria from 1980 through to his death in 1988. Probably the most colourful figure in post-war German politics, he elicited intense dislike from his opponents and great affection from his supporters, and yet commanded the respect of both. As Federal Defence Minister in ADENAUER's government, he was the centre of the so-called 'Spiegel Affair' in 1961, which resulted in his resignation from the Federal Government. He returned as Finance Minister in the Grand Coalition in 1966. His often autocratic style brought him into frequent and prolonged political conflict with the CSU's sister party, the CDU.

In 1980, Strauß became the Chancellor-Candidate of the CDU/CSU. In a characteristically aggressive campaign, he attempted to secure an absolute majority for the CDU/CSU, but succeeded only in losing votes to the FDP. Following this defeat, he became MINISTERPRÄSIDENT in Bavaria, where he remained until his death in 1988. During this time, he remained an active figure in national politics, even pursuing a prominent role on the international stage from his Bavarian base.

Strauß was considered an arch-conservative, and his presence on the national stage thus had great influence in binding voters with otherwise more extreme tendencies into the CDU/CSU camp. He was also a key figure in the negotiation of loans to the GDR, and enjoyed excellent contacts with its leadership. Recently, allegations and, in some cases, evidence of sleaze and even outright illegal activities have surfaced, ranging from arms deals to tipping off fraudulent business associates. Since his death, the CSU's leadership has found it hard to emulate his dynamism, charisma and ability to infuriate his party's federal coalition partners.

See BAYERN; BUNDESKANZLER; ZEITUNGEN UND ZEITSCHRIFTEN.

(SG)

Streik   Strikes in Germany are carried out under strict legal conditions and can be seen as an instrument of last resort for trade unions in dispute with employers. Strike rates in the Federal Republic of Germany are generally low. Between 1986 and 1990, days lost through strikes were, for example, almost a third of those lost in Britain. Trade unions have a monopoly on the right to call strikes, and strikes are only allowed on issues concerned with wages and working conditions, not on political matters.

The favourable strike record is due to the pragmatic, comparatively unideological attitude of trade unions. The structures of MITBESTIMMUNG (co-determination) ensure a framework for positive co-operation between business and trade unions. Moreover, civil servants have no right to strike.

See GEWERKSCHAFTEN; TARIFAUTONOMIE.

(ECM)

Studentenausweis   See IMMATRIKULATION.

Studentenbewegung   The Student Movement originated in the mid- to late 1960s with the involvement of the Socialist German Students' League (SDS), and its fiery leader Rudi Dutschke, in the Extra-Parliamentary Opposition (APO). The initial Student Movement arose from feelings among the young generation that, helped by the wealth creation of the WIRTSCHAFTSWUNDER, the older generation was trying to hide the guilt of the Nazi past and remain in their old hierarchically oriented ways of political and social thinking. Protests by socialist and Marxist student groups included sit-ins, boycotts and graffiti in universities as well as protest marches in university cities. The action focused against the proposed Emergency Laws (NOTSTANDSGESETZE) as well as the hierarchical structure of the universities in Germany. At the same time anti-American protest marches against the Vietnam War were organised.

After the fragmentation of the APO, the student movement ceased to have the same notoriety, with the notable exception of West Berlin which remained a hotbed of radical student activity. The peace and squatters' movements of the late 1970s and early 1980s, although not exclusively associated with the Student Movement, provided temporary focus points around which it was able to mobilise.

Many of the original '68ers' (as veterans of the 1960s student movement are called in Germany) went on to join the GRÜNE and slowly became establishment figures. The student movement today is a more modest affair, although German campuses are still full of posters for forthcoming demonstrations on a whole range of issues. The participants, although fewer in number, appear to be just as idealistic as their more notorious predecessors.

See BÖLL, HEINRICH; FRANKFURTER SCHULE; FRIEDENSBEWEGUNG; GRASS, GÜNTER; GROßE KOALITION; HOCHSCHULRAHMENGESETZ; NEUE SOZIALE BEWEGUNGEN; TERRORISMUS; VERGANGENHEITSBEWÄLTIGUNG.
(CL)

Studentenwerk The *Studentenwerk* is an organisation which is obliged by law to provide certain facilities for students. The *Studentenwerk* runs student canteens (*Mensa*), plans and administrates student halls of residence (*Wohnheime*), may offer child care facilities, helps students find accommodation and gives grants for students in financial difficulties.

Students have no automatic right to a place in a hall of residence and in the old BUNDESLÄNDER only about 10 per cent of all students have such a place. The number is higher in the new *Bundesländer* where students used to live in boarding school-type accommodation. Most halls have waiting lists and each semester there are deadlines for applying for a place in the following semester. The time a student can spend in a hall is limited to a certain number of semesters. Rents are often cheaper than in the private sector and the level set according to BAFÖG.
(AW)

Studentenwohnheim (SWH) See STUDENTENWERK.

Studentische Verbindungen Student associations have existed since the seventeenth century, typically offering support to students from the same country or region by living together in a community (*Burschenschaft*).

In the nineteenth century *Burschenschaften* were linked with the nationalist struggle and were outlawed to be followed by the unpolitical *Korps*. *Korps* offer a rigid organisation, their own rituals and often symbols, lifelong membership, an old members' network as well as the obligation to help each other. Today there are both officer corps-like duelling societies with their rather doubtful code of honour and non-duelling societies.

From 1841 onwards *Korps* were founded which rejected duelling on Christian grounds (*UV Unitas-Verband, CV Cartell-Verband, KV Kartell-Verband*). The academic women's movement led to the foundation of a number of groups which organised themselves in the *Deutscher akademischer Frauenbund*.

After World War I groups with quite different aims were founded, such as *Hochland, Quickborn, Neudeutschland* and *Heiland* (women only), which wanted to help generate academics who would be willing and able to take on responsibilities in public life, motivated by Christian ethics. After World War II these groups gave new and decisive impulses to student life. The *Christopherus* is a more recent Catholic group (1946) which formed around a number of prominent theologians (Guardini, Kahlefeld, Thilman) and has been open to men and women from the very beginning. In addition, after World War II, political parties established their own student organisations.

(AW)

Studienabschlüsse   There are two types of degrees: academic degrees conferred by the university itself and the *Staatsexamen* (state examination) which is conferred by the university on behalf of the state. *Staatsexamen* is the degree necessary for going into the public sector: Teachers, lawyers and medical doctors all have to have *Staatsexamen I* and *II* to carry out their profession. Academic degrees are Diploma, Master's and PhD (*Diplom, Magister*, PROMOTION) and are the essential qualifications for a career within a research institution or where *Staatsexamen* is not available.

Academic and state degrees have a similar structure: prospective candidates have to enrol for their exams at given dates and times. They need to show their *Studienbuch* with their record of achievement (SCHEINE). There are three parts to *Staatsexamen, Magister* and *Diplom*: a thesis (*Staatsarbeit, Magisterarbeit, Diplomarbeit*, sometimes also called *Zulassungsarbeit*) in the main subject, a number of unseen exams, and an oral exam in each subject. Each part of the exam is marked on a scale of 1 to 6, with 1 being the best mark, and the final mark is calculated according to the respective exam regulations (*Prüfungsordnung*). The duration of the whole process from enrolment to completion is also laid down in the exam regulations but will usually be one to two years.

Depending on the BUNDESLAND and the university, a certain level of competence in Latin (*kleines Latinum, großes Latinum*) may be mandatory for enrolment in exams in certain degrees.

(AW)

Studiendauer   For generations, students at German universities have been able to spend as many semesters studying for their first degree as they wanted or their finances allowed. However, this has been a subject of debate ever since the large increase in student numbers in the 1970s.

The two main concerns are: first, given the constantly high numbers of school-leavers wanting to study, resources are permanently strained. Second, compared to other countries, students in Germany take much longer before completing their first degree. They are therefore older when they qualify and often have to compete with much younger graduates from other countries.

In the 1970s, the concept of *Regelstudienzeit* (standard period of study) was introduced, indicating how long it should take students to gather their SCHEINE before they could matriculate for their final exams. It also indicated to departments what they had to offer in terms of courses and numbers of places in labs and practicals. Students receiving BAFÖG are penalised for taking longer than the *Regelstudienzeit* of their subject.

The Mindeststudiendauer is the prescribed minimum number of semesters a student has to spend studying towards a degree. This is set in order to ensure that a candidate achieves sufficient breadth and depth in a subject.

The debate about *Studienzeitverkürzung*, i.e. setting a maximum number of semesters is controversial. Although the financial constraints imposed by students who never finish but remain registered are generally recognised, it is unclear how a prescriptive approach should work, given the diverse federal nature of the German system of higher education and also in the face of inadequate resources in many institutions (e.g. lab places) for accommodating a whole year of students within one semester for certain courses. Besides, candidates choosing a complicated subject matter for their final thesis would be at best discouraged and at worst discriminated against.

Proposed solutions so far have included forced deregistration or charging fees from students after a certain number of semesters, paying premiums to students for finishing early, or shortening the exam period (currently at least 1 year but often much longer) by scheduling certain parts of the exams earlier in the course.

See GRUND- UND HAUPTSTUDIUM; LEHRVERANSTALTUNGEN; STUDIEN-ABSCHLÜSSE; STUDIUM.

(AW)

Studium   Study at university is meant to provide the first phase of qualification for the academic professions. Students are expected to take part in appropriate courses and work on their own initiative. Prerequisites for university study are the ABITUR or a certificate of the same standing.

Faced with ever-growing student numbers and demands by industry for more relevant or vocational curricula, study today is increasingly directed at getting students to a first degree in the shortest time possible even though, unlike in the Anglo-Saxon countries, the exact duration and contents of courses have not yet been fixed. The student's way towards a degree is now mapped out rather rigidly through a standard period of study (*Regelstudienzeit*), curricula for each subject, differentiation between foundation and main studies (GRUND- UND HAUPTSTUDIUM), and prescribed pieces of evidence of academic achievement. A core principle is that every appropriately qualified person should be able to enter university and acquire an academic degree. Thus no fees are payable for studying at a German university. Only a *Sozialbeitrag* (social contribution) is due each semester. This includes accident insurance and a contribution to the student body and in some *Länder* also the right to use public transport for free. The amount of the *Sozialbeitrag* varies between *Länder*.

As far as the students' living expenses are concerned, the state mainly relies on parents' contributions; an increasing number of students work, even during term time. Some receive BAFÖG or are funded by scholarships promoting gifted students.

See HOCHSCHULE; IMMATRIKULATION; SCHEIN; STIFTUNGEN; STUDIENABSCHLÜSSE; STUDIENDAUER; VERFAßTE STUDENTENSCHAFT.

(AW)

Stunde Null   'Zero Hour' is the way in which 1945 is viewed in the history of the Federal Republic as a new beginning or fresh start. *Stunde Null* refers to Germany in ruins and signifies a radical break with the past and a forced re-think of German national identity, values and society.

Given the obvious foreign and domestic policy disasters of the Third Reich and the magnitude of attrocities conducted by the Nazis, 1945 represented an opportunity to forge a new political culture, internal institutions as well as better foreign relations for Germany. But *Stunde Null* was also informed by the broader negative legacy of German state building since 1871: the forging of the first German nation–state under Bismarck, and the 14-year experiment with democracy in the Weimar Republic, the weakness of which was the wellspring for Hitler's Third Reich.

Linked to *Stunde Null* is the notion of VERGANGENHEITSBEWÄLTIGUNG or 'coming to terms with the past' which concerns the place and role of historical experiences, especially the Third Reich in contemporary German consciousness.

See DRITTES REICH; WEIMARER REPUBLIK.

(KL)

Sturm und Drang   Storm and Stress refers to a period in German thought between the age of Enlightenment and Classicism, from around 1765 to 1790. Though originally the title of a play by F.M. Klinger (1776), the term was quickly extended to describe the whole movement. Its representatives are, among others, Lichtenberg, Herder and Lavater (philosophy) as well as the writers Goethe (*Werther*), Lenz, Klinger and the young Schiller (*Die Räuber*). Whilst rejecting the rationalism of the Enlightenment, they strove towards the holistic liberation of the individual person through emotional spontaneity, sensual perception, and access to life and original creativity through the experience of nature. For the author, this implied a faith in genius and original creativity. The period is therefore also sometimes called *Geniezeit* (period of the genius). Some literary critics (e.g. Lukács) see *Sturm und Drang* as an extension of the Age of Enlightenment whereas for others (e.g. Korff, Pascal) it was the precursor movement to Romanticism. German and Anglo-American newspapers occasionally use *Sturm und Drang* more loosely and even jokingly, referring to a young person revolting against institutional pressure or established opinion (*'die Stürmer und Dränger'*).

(RW)

Subsidiarität Subsidiarity is a principle derived from social philosophy, in particular that of the Catholic Church, which demands that decisions be taken as close as possible to the citizen. It is often presented as a rule guiding the operation of federalism, where decisions should be taken as far as possible by sub-national political institutions, and only where it is absolutely necessary by institutions at the national level.

Subsidiarity is not explicitly mentioned in the GRUNDGESETZ as a rule guiding the operation of German federalism, where most decision-making powers are held by federal-level institutions. The term is used more frequently and accurately in relation to European integration policy as a hitherto very loose guide for when decisions should be taken by the institutions of the member states or those of the European Union. This definition of subsidiarity was incorporated into the *Grundgesetz* in a number of constitutional changes amending the formulation of European integration policy in Germany in 1992.

See EUROPAPOLITIK; FÖDERALISMUS; VERFASSUNGSÄNDERUNG.

(CJ)

T

Tag der Einheit The Day of Unity is the official date of the unification of the Federal Republic and the GDR. At 0.00 hours on 3 October 1990, Germany was united in line with the decision reached by the VOLKS-KAMMER on 23 August of that year that the GDR would accede to the jurisdiction of the Federal Republic of Germany according to Article 23 of the GRUNDGESETZ. Thus 3 October has been designated as a public holiday.
See FESTE UND FEIERN; VEREINIGUNG.
(MD)

Tarifautonomie *Tarifautonomie* is the right of trade unions and employers' associations or individual employers to conclude collective agreements (*Tarifverträge*) regulating wages and workplace conditions free from the intervention of third parties. Following the disastrous experiences of state intervention in industrial disputes in the Weimar Republic, *Tarifautonomie* was established with the creation of the Federal Republic. It allows the collective bargaining partners to negotiate freely within a framework of labour laws and has led to the development of multi-employer bargaining and a system based upon collective agreements which set minimum pay and conditions across whole branches of industry (*Flächentarifverträge*).

Although the concept of *Tarifautonomie* itself is widely accepted, there have been calls for its jurisdiction to be restricted. This arose largely following economic collapse in the new BUNDESLÄNDER where collective agreements based on political necessity rather than economic reality were seen as responsible for causing plant closures and unemployment by maintaining too high labour costs. There were subsequently threats by the Federal Government to pass laws which directly intervened in collective bargaining. This was the case in 1993 where the government proposed to initiate a law in the new *Bundesländer* allowing collective agreements to be terminated before their legal date of expiry. Such threats remained just that, however, and there have been no direct attempts to intervene in *Tarifautonomie*. Despite increasing competitive pressures, the bargaining partners are likely to be left to negotiate new solutions themselves. The incentive for them to do so is the threat of direct government intervention in *Tarifautonomie*.

It is important to stress the vast number of workers covered by collective agreements. In 1994, 81.14 per cent of workers in West Germany were covered by collective agreements.

See BETRIEBSRAT; GEWERKSCHAFTEN; KONZERTIERTE AKTION.

(SRF)

Technische Hochschule (TH)   Technical universities were first founded in the late eighteenth century in order to satisfy the growing demand for technically qualified personnel during the industrialisation process. Among the oldest THs in Germany are Darmstadt and München (1836), Aachen and Hannover (1870). A TH initially only offered education in disciplines like engineering, metallurgy and materials sciences.

In recognition of the wider impact of technology in contemporary life, THs have broadened their mission. They now also offer degrees in psychology, medicine, education and other subjects. Students study for at least 8 semesters and gain a *Diplom* at the end of their course.

See STUDIENABSCHLÜSSE; UNIVERSITÄT.

(AW)

Terrorismus   Terrorism is a form of political extremism. The Federal Republic has been faced with terrorist acts since 1970. Terrorist groups have traditionally been supporters of left-wing causes perpetrating violent acts against prominent business and political figures.

The first generation of terrorists, the so-called *Baader-Meinhof-Gruppe* (after their leaders, also called the *Rote-Armee-Fraktion*) emerged from the student revolts in the late 1960s. Their aim was to undermine what the group called the 'imperialist' power base in politics and business in order to bring about a workers' revolution. Their terrorist activities deeply shocked the nation but the group never had serious support for their aims. Following the arrest and sentencing of leading members of the group, three of them committed suicide in 1977 as a protest against being held as what they termed 'political prisoners'.

A second generation of terrorists, the so-called 'Revolutionary Cells' (*Revolutionäre Zellen*) started a further wave of terrorist attacks in 1977 murdering, among others, a board member of the Deutsche Bank, and the head of the main German employers' association. The latest victim of left-wing terrorism was the President of the TREUHANDANSTALT, Detlef Rohwedder in 1991. After reunification it was found that the former East German regime had allowed several terrorists wanted in the Federal Republic to start a new life there in impunity. More recently, right-wing extremist groups in post-unification Germany have undertaken terroristic acts of violence against foreigners and, more rarely, disabled people.

See AUSLÄNDERFEINDLICHKEIT; STUDENTENBEWEGUNG.

(RW)

Theater Germany has over 460 theatres. Although between 30 and 35 million tickets are sold each year, most theatres also need substantial public subsidies. The theatres best known for their inspired as well as controversial productions are in Berlin, Stuttgart, München, Essen and Bayreuth (where the Wagner Festival takes place).

German theatre can trace its roots back to the Middle Ages. During the Renaissance there was a strong influence from both French dramatists and Shakespeare. In the eighteenth century even the smallest kingdom or principality felt it necessary to have its own theatre. In the nineteenth century these theatres were taken over by public authorities, laying the foundation for the theatre landscape as it exists today.

Recent closures of theatres, particularly in Berlin, owing to budgetary pressures have caused widespread protest both because going to see a play, opera or ballet is a popular pastime and because limitations to the freedom of artistic expression have been feared.

(RW)

Thierse, Wolfgang Wolfgang Thierse (1949–) is a leading East German Social Democrat. Born in Breslau, the son of a lawyer, Thierse studied German and Cultural Sciences at the Humboldt University, Berlin. In 1976, he was dismissed from his post in the GDR Ministry of Culture after protesting at the expatriation of Wolf Biermann, a protest singer critical of the regime, from the GDR. In the following year, he became a member of the Central Institute for the History of Literature at the Academy of Sciences. During the WENDE, he was active in New Forum before joining the SPD in January 1990. A member of the VOLKSKAMMER from March–October 1990, he replaced the discredited STASI informer Ibrahim Böhme as Chairman of the East German SPD in June of that year.

After the union of the East and West German SPD parties in September 1990, Thierse became a Deputy Chairman of the party. He entered the BUNDESTAG in December 1990 and was re-elected four years later.

See BÜRGERBEWEGUNGEN.

(MD)

Thüringen Thuringia is one of the constituent BUNDESLÄNDER of the Federal Republic and one of the NEUE BUNDESLÄNDER on the territory of the former GDR. Its capital city is Erfurt. It is some 16 200km² in size and has a population of 2.52m (1994). It has a less large-scale and more diversified industrial profile than neighbouring SACHSEN and SACHSEN-ANHALT which, despite the industrial contraction characteristic in the East since unification, has left it relatively well placed in the post-communist economic reconstruction process. Unemployment, however, remains high at 15 per cent.

The CDU has been the strongest party in Thüringen since 1990, providing the MINISTERPRÄSIDENT (since 1993 the former RHEINLAND-PFALZ *Ministerpräsident*, Bernhard Vogel) following LANDTAG elections in both 1990 and 1994. The LANDESREGIERUNG is currently a coalition of CDU and SPD. Following the 1994 election, the PDS was the only other party still represented in the *Landtag*.

(CJ)

Thyssen Thyssen was the seventh largest industrial company in Germany in 1995 with a turnover of DM39 billion, 127 000 employees and a net income of DM478 million. Thyssen was a pioneer in the integration of coal, iron and steel production at optimal locations. It was also active in establishing RWE. In the attempt to deal with the problems of over-capacity and diminished demand after World War I Thyssen led efforts to concentrate the steel industry in the Thyssen-dominated *Vereinigte Stahlwerke*. Initial co-operation with the National Socialists was replaced by repression of Thyssen family members. After World War II, an Allied condition for restoration was the deconcentration of *Vereinigte Stahlwerke*. A series of mergers and acquisitions, many of which involved other former Thyssen family concerns, restored the company to its former pre-eminence. By 1965, Thyssen had become Europe's largest steel producer. It had also re-entered the market for lifts and escalators and, unlike KRUPP, a traditional competitor, shipbuilding. On the downside, with corporate growth it inherited problems of structural decline in the coal industry from 1958 and, a decade later, over-capacity in steel.

Profitability in 1995 contrasted with a loss in 1993 and a net income of only DM90 million in 1994. A dividend was not paid in either year. The group now consists of three divisions: capital goods and manufactured products (Thyssen Industrie/Budd USA/Wülfrath), trading and services (Thyssen Handelsunion), and steel (Thyssen Stahl). Thyssen Telekom, which is three-quarters owned by Handelsunion, is another company which aspires to capturing part of the large deregulated telecoms market in 1998. German, French and Dutch financial institutions purchased the other quarter of Telekom for DM1 billion and the company is already active in eight separate branches of the industry. Thyssen is now quoted on all the German and Swiss Stock Exchanges, together with Paris and London.

Like Krupp-Hoesch, Thyssen was dependent on the German market for over half of total sales in 1995 – with the other members of the EU accounting for almost a further quarter. Less than one-third of the labour force is employed outside of Germany. If the anxieties about Germany's competitive viability are valid, a greater degree of internationalisation would be advisable.

(EOS)

Transformation   Transformation is the process whereby the GDR, like many other client states of the USSR, is undergoing a fundamental change from the communist socio-economic and political order. From October 1989 to January 1990, the reform of the existing system was high on the agenda in the GDR. Various combinations of market and socialist elements within an independent, reformed GDR were proposed by the reformed SED and groups such as New Forum and Democracy Now. These soon succumbed to the notion of a radical and rapid transformation via the incorporation of the GDR into the institutional system of the Federal Republic. The advantages of this route were that the GDR would be adopting a proven system and drawing on the extensive financial resources and the political and managerial skills of West Germany. This made the GDR's transition distinct from that experienced by other former communist states.

On the other hand, the 'big bang' approach had a devastating effect on GDR firms and employment, the consequence of an ailing and radically different economic system suddenly being confronted with the pressures of external competition. The appreciation of the GDR Mark, literally overnight, by 300 per cent exposed the GDR's low productivity and obsolete capital in a merciless manner. Domestic production fell by more than 40 per cent from 1989–1991 and the number of gainfully employed persons declined from about 9.9 million to 6.25 million between 1989 and spring 1992. Heavy financial transfers from West Germany – DM178.5 billion gross in 1993 and DM180.0 billion in 1994 – helped to ease the pain by creating or preserving jobs and subsidising pensions, unemployment benefit and wages.

Signs of an upturn in the East German economy were observable in 1994 and capital investment rose rapidly from 1991. Productivity in agriculture approaches West German levels thanks to a modernisation of plant, a drastic cut in labour and a reduction in the area under cultivation. Productivity in construction has risen to about 75 per cent of that in the West. However, progress in the processing industries is much more modest.

The East German economy has not attained self-sustaining growth and is still heavily dependent on public transfers. Furthermore, the East German party system, significantly shaped by the PDS, is proving more polarised and fragmented than in the West.

See BÜRGERBEWEGUNGEN; MAUER IM KOPF; SOLIDARPAKT; STEUER-LÜGE; TREUHANDANSTALT; VEREINIGUNG.

(MD)

Treuhandanstalt   The 'Trustee Agency' was the controversial public holding company set up to privatise and restructure the state-owned assets of the GDR. The *Treuhand* created by the *Treuhand* Act in June 1990 was the fundamentally different successor to the body with the same name established by the Modrow government in March. The legal status of the second *Treuhand* was that of an independent entity in public law answerable to the Finance Ministry. The *Treuhand* Act transferred all state-owned enterprises and property to the agency, in particular, the combines (KOM-BINATE, encompassing about 8 000 enterprises before they were subdivided), 40 000 smaller service outlets such as shops and bars, the property of the STASI and considerable real estate.

The *Treuhand* was organised into 15 regional offices and, at central level, it had a Management Board which reported to the Supervisory Board. The latter was dominated by West German businessmen and specialists. In addition, there were eight sections, one each for personnel and finance and six industrial departments. The key office of President was occupied by Birgit Breuel after the assassination of her predecessor, Detlev Rohwedder, in April 1991.

The function of the agency was defined in the *Treuhand* Act as the privatisation and use of state-owned assets based on the principles of the market economy and the restructuring of the economy to meet market demands by developing viable firms into competitive enterprises and then transferring them into private ownership. Priority was given to complete and rapid privatisation of firms in the belief that this was the most effective way to restructure them. The sale of profitable firms would, it was hoped, provide funds for investment in potentially viable firms. A purchaser was usually committed to binding assurances regarding investment levels and work places.

It soon became apparent, however, that the Federal Government and the *Treuhand* had over-estimated the viability of *Treuhand* enterprises and the blessings of market instruments and had underestimated the obstacles to privatisation arising from the Unification Treaty's commitment to restitution of property and compensation to former owners. Inherited debt, overmanning and low productivity were some of the other main obstacles.

The *Treuhand* attracted fierce criticism for the lack of transparency in its dealings, for corruption among some of its staff and for its responsibility for rocketing unemployment and massive deindustrialisation. This criticism and the problems of disposing of uncompetitive firms, especially the industrial dinosaurs in chemicals, prompted a modification, though by no means a fundamental shift, in policy towards active restructuring. These measures included a greater emphasis on investments for the modernisation of its enterprises, and co-operative arrangements with the new BUNDESLÄNDER and the unions.

The *Treuhand* was wound up at the end of 1994, having privatised over 14 000 firms and sold around 25 000 shops, restaurants and small sale outlets. After the transfer of debts to the newly-established Redemption Fund for Inherited Liabilities at the beginning of 1995, its balance sheet showed a cumulative debt of about DM205 billion.

See ABWICKLUNG; NEUE BUNDESLÄNDER; PRIVATISIERUNG; TERRORIS-MUS; TRANSFORMATION; VEREINIGUNG.

(MD)

Trümmerfrauen *Trümmerfrauen* is the name given to those women who participated in the debris-clearing and rebuilding of the Federal Republic after the war. *Trümmerfrauen* have acquired a symbolic status, personifying the rise from ruins and complete reconstruction of the Federal Republic after the war.

(KL)

U

Ulbricht, Walter   Walter Ulbricht (1893–1973) was First Secretary of the SED and Chairman of the GDR Council of State. The son of a Leipzig tailor, Ulbricht joined the SPD in 1912. He was drafted into the army in 1915 and was courtmartialled in 1918. A founder member of the KPD, he rapidly rose through the party's ranks entering the *Politbüro* in 1928 and heading the party' s Berlin–Brandenburg regional organisation (1929–1933). Exiled in Moscow for most of the Third Reich, he co-founded the National Committee for Free Germany and played an active part in shaping communist plans for the post-war order.

He returned to Germany on 30 April 1945 as leader of one of the three initiative groups of KPD functionaries who were commissioned to assist the Soviet authorities in the reconstruction of the Soviet zone. Ulbricht carried out his task with ruthless efficiency, ensuring that German Communists were appointed to key posts in the civil administration. Although obliged to concede the post of SED chairman to Wilhelm Pieck, Ulbricht was appointed as a deputy-chairman and in 1950 became First Secretary (from 1953 onwards General Secretary) of the Central Committee of the party.

A dedicated and experienced administrator with a firm hand on the party *Apparat*, Ulbricht soon emerged as the dominant force in the SED. However, his autocratic methods and his advocacy of the rapid construction of socialism antagonised many colleagues and in 1953 and 1956 two abortive attempts were made to unseat him. In 1960, he consolidated his position by acquiring the chairmanship of the National Defence Council and the Council of State. The cult of his personality was fostered throughout the following decade.

After the building of the Berlin Wall, he sought to legitimise SED rule by introducing the New Economic System, fostering new developments in science and technology and propagating the notion of the GDR as a harmonious human community in contrast to the exploitative capitalist society of West Germany. His portrayal of the GDR as a model for other socialist societies and his stubborn insistence on Western recognition of the GDR's full sovereignty as a precondition for formal negotiations with Bonn, thereby jeopardising Soviet *détente* plans, aroused the ire of the

Soviet leadership. This paved the way for an alliance between the anti-Ulbricht faction in the SED and Brezhnev to dethrone the ageing General Secretary in 1971.

See DDR; HONECKER, ERICH; NEUES ÖKONOMISCHES SYSTEM; STAATS-RAT.

(MD)

Umweltbewegung The environmental movement arose from a growing awareness of the need for environmental protection in the highly industrialised and successful economic landscape of the Federal Republic during the 1970s. It was based on citizen's initiatives (BÜRGERINITIATIVEN) at local level and the umbrella organisations the *Bundesverband Bürgerinitiativen Umweltschutz e.V* (Federal Association of Environmental Citizen Initiatives – BBU) founded in 1972 and the *Bund für Umwelt und Naturschutz Deutschland e.V* (Association for environmental and nature protection in Germany – BUND) founded in 1975. The movement gained impetus from opposition to the nuclear power programme initiated by the social–liberal coalition in response to the oil crises. The organisations' goals have been centred on changing industrial and energy policy to reduce pollution and promote new environmentally responsible technology and processes.

The influence of the movements is best seen in the electoral success of the GRÜNE at the federal level and in the BUNDESLÄNDER. Environmental concern has become an important political issue, taken on by all major parties and reflected in stricter environmental legislation.

An ecological movement also developed in the former GDR during the 1980s. This can be attributed to high levels of pollution in the GDR and the right of environmental protection embodied in the state's constitution, on which basis the environment become a focus for wider opposition.

Unification has posed a major challenge for the environmental movement with the need to reduce pollution from East German plants and to replace brown coal as a source of energy. At the same time environmentally-related plant closures raise the issue of the relationship between ecology and jobs, a theme which caused the labour movement major policy difficulties in the 1980s.

(CL)

Universität The first German universities were founded in the Middle Ages (Prag, Leipzig, Wien, Heidelberg, Köln, Erfurt). Theology, and the *Trivium* (grammar, rhetoric and dialectics) and *Quadrivium* (arithmetic, geometry, music and astronomy) were the core of the curriculum. Philosophy, law and medicine were added from the sixteenth century onwards. The big universities such as München, Berlin, Bonn, and Hamburg were founded in the nineteenth century and it was then that the sciences became recognised university subjects.

Because of a vast increase in student numbers in the 1970s new universities were founded (including Essen, Dortmund, Bayreuth, Bamberg,

Regensburg, Augsburg, Passau), while in the 1980s and early 1990s many former colleges were granted university status.

German universities typically have no campus and because of the increase in student numbers – in some cities such as Berlin, München and Köln to over 100 000 – departments may be spread over several parts of the city.

See HOCHSCHULE; STUDIENABSCHLÜSSE.

(AW)

Unternehmerverbände   Employers' Associations represent the interests of business *vis-à-vis* political decision-makers and in national industrial relations. The Federation of German Industry (*Bund Deutscher Industrie*, or BDI) and the Federation of German Employers (*Bundesvereinigung der Deutschen Arbeitgeber*, or BDA) are the umbrella organisations of German business. Whereas the BDI has a broader political focus, the BDA concentrates on negotiating with trade unions on wages and employment conditions for its members. Both have very high membership rates.

German employers' associations are seen as particularly successful and politically powerful in comparison to other interest groups and to equivalent organisations in other countries. They play an important role in German corporatism.

See KORPORATISMUS; TARIFAUTONOMIE.

(ECM)

V

VEBA (Vereinigte Elektrizitäts- und Bergwerks AG) VEBA was the fourth largest industrial company in Germany in 1995 with a turnover of DM72 billion, 125 000 employees and a net income of DM2.1 billion. In 1929, the Prussian state holdings in electricity and coal mining were consolidated into the *V*ereinigte *E*lektrizitäts- und *B*ergwerks- *A*ktiengesellschaft. VEBA's principal activities remained in power generation and coal mining until the early 1960s. During the various phases of the company's privatisation (1965–1987), VEBA transferred its mining interests to RUHRKOHLE, in which it still holds a 40 per cent stake. It also sold off its shareholding in PREUSSAG. On the other hand, it acquired Gelsenberg (petroleum products) and the remaining shares in HÜLS (chemicals). Following full privatisation, VEBA was reorganised into four independent operating divisions: electricity, chemicals, oil and trading/transport/services.

The internationalisation of the company's shareholder base, along with its experience of Anglo-American capital markets, has led to the adoption a shareholder-value culture. The financial reporting and disclosure policy has been progressively aligned with international standards.

Over a ten-year period the share of foreign sales has increased from 25 to 30 per cent. But this still leaves the company with an untypically low export share compared to similar concerns. However, investment in electricity has dominated strategy and VEBA's subsidiary Preussenelektra supplies 25 per cent of the population within one-third of the country's surface area.

VEBA aspires to become DEUTSCHE TELEKOM's strongest competitor. Attractive growth rates are predicted because of Germany's large (23 per cent) share of Europe's telecoms market. VEBA obtained a 10.5 per cent shareholding in Cable and Wireless (C&W) for DM2.2 billion, whereas C&W was to have paid a total of DM1.9 billion by 1997 for a 45 per cent share in VEBACOM which was formed in 1994. Activities in the EU and Switzerland were to be channelled through the equally owned subsidiary, C&W Europe. Following a policy disagreement, RWE announced in October 1996 that it was leaving the BT/VIAG telecoms venture in order to join VEBA/C&W. In early 1997, C&W sold its stake in VEBACOM, whereas VEBA retained its holding in C&W.

(EOS)

Verbände   Interest groups mainly evolved to represent the interests of social groups emerging from the industrialisation process in interactions with other interest groups, government, parliament, parties and the public.

Historically, interest groups were viewed with suspicion in their pursuit of the sectional interests of their members rather than wider national interests. A more positive view emerged under the influence of Anglo-Saxon theories of pluralism which suggested that interest groups were part of the fabric of a democratic society, providing individuals with access to political decision-making processes and allowing for the consensual resolution of conflicting group interests.

Classic, industrialisation-related interest groups are employers's associations (UNTERNEHMERVERBÄNDE) and trade unions (GEWERKSCHAFTEN). Newer, issue-based forms of interest group have since emerged, including consumer associations (VERBRAUCHERVERBÄNDE) and citizen's initiatives groups (BÜRGERINITIATIVEN) in such fields as environmental protection. (ECM)

Verbraucherverbände   Consumer associations are directed at the protection of the interests of consumers. Consumer associations in Germany provide information services for customers and represent their interests. Examples include the *Arbeitsgemeinschaft der Verbraucher* (AgV), *Verbraucherzentralen* (Consumer Advice Centres) and *Stiftung Warentest* (Foundation for Product Testing). Associations are largely funded by the Federal Government and the *Bundesländer*. *Stiftung Warentest* is self-financed through its monthly publication (like *Which?* magazine in the UK) on product quality.

The major justification for consumer associations is that capitalist markets have a tendency towards a reduction of competition in which producers are increasingly powerful, and to which consumer associations provide a useful counterbalance. (ECM)

Vereinigung   Unification between the GDR and the Federal Republic took place in October 1990 on the basis of a series of treaties between the two German republics and agreements with the four victor powers. Dismissed by Erich HONECKER as like trying to mix fire and water, German unification unexpectedly became a possibility as the SED regime collapsed in late 1989 and as the popular cry on the streets of the GDR changed from 'We are the people' to 'We are one people' soon after the opening of the Berlin Wall. Minister–President MODROW's proposal on 17 November 1989 for a contractual community between the two German states was countered by Chancellor KOHL's ten-point plan for German unity and the unexpected offer on 7 February 1990 of rapid monetary and economic union.

After the East German electorate's endorsement in March 1990 of the quick route to economic, monetary and social union with the Federal Republic, the East and West German governments started negotiations in late April. The first State Treaty was signed on 18 May 1990 and came into force on 1 July. Wages, salaries, rents and pensions were converted at a rate of 1DM:1GDR Mark. Pensions were raised to 70 per cent of West German levels. Personal savings were converted at 1:1 up to 2 000 Marks for children under 14, 4 000 Marks for people aged 15 to 59 and 6 000 Marks for those over 60. Financial assets and liabilities were generally converted at two GDR Marks to one DM, thus putting a heavy debt-service burden on the state-owned enterprise sector. The West German social market economy was made the basis of the economic union. This meant GDR acceptance of private ownership of the means of production, the free establishment of prices and the freedom of movement of labour, capital goods and services. Finally, the GDR agreed to accept, though with some modifications and in stages, West German labour, trade union, welfare and tax legislation.

The State Treaty failed to lay down detailed privatisation guidlines on property rights. An inter-governmental agreement in July 1990 stipulated that expropriations would not be reversed but compensation would be determined by an all-German government. Second, expropriated or state-administered land and real estate would in principle be returned to the previous owners or their heirs, as was the case with companies expropriated after 1949. The right to restitution and the lack of clear ownership rights to many properties severely impeded private investment and redevelopment.

The legal unity of Germany was completed by the Treaty of Unification which was signed by the West and East German representatives, Wolfgang SCHÄUBLE and Günther Krause, on 31 August 1990 and came into operation on 3 October 1990 in accordance with Article 23 of the West German GRUNDGESETZ. This article allowed for the simple accession of the newly-constituted five Eastern German BUNDESLÄNDER rather than the use of Article 146, which would have entailed the adoption of a new constitution on the basis of a general debate. The BUNDESRAT was to be reconstituted according to a new allocation system, giving seats to each *Bundesland* according to population from a minimum of three to a maximum of six. Existing GDR laws on abortion were to apply for two years pending new legislation.

The Compensation Law of September 1994 helped to clarify some of the main problems relating to the compensation of former owners of property and the rights of present incumbents. However, a similar balance was not struck between compensation and restitution.

See DDR; FONDS 'DEUTSCHE EINHEIT'; MAIZIÈRE, LOTHAR DE; TAG DER EINHEIT; TRANSFORMATION; TREUHANDANSTALT; VOLKSKAMMER; ZEHN-PUNKTE-PLAN; ZWEI-PLUS-VIER-VERTRAG.

(MD)

Vereinte Nationen　The United Nations Organisation was founded by the victorious Allies of World War II in 1945. It was envisaged as an effective replacement for the League of Nations, helping to maintain international peace and security. The Security Council, with five permanent and 13 temporary members, is the UN's most important body, the only one entitled by international law to authorise international military action to maintain peace.

Divided Germany, as the defeated party of the war, did not become a member of the UN at its inception. The main reasons were initially perceptions about Germany as constituting a threat to international peace, and Germany's division into two separate states. Only after the 1973 Basic Treaty (GRUNDLAGENVERTRAG) between the two German states did both the Federal Republic and the GDR become full members of the UN. Since then Germany has participated in most UN agencies and forums.

Despite successes of peace-keeping missions in the 1960s and 1970s, the UN's recent failures in Somalia and former Yugoslavia cast a doubt on the ability of the organisation to adapt itself to the new post-Cold-War international environment.

Until very recently, constitutional restrictions limited German participation in UN peace-keeping missions. These restrictions were eased by the 1993 Federal Constitutional Court ruling on the matter. German forces have since participated in UN missions in Somalia, Cambodia and former Yugoslavia.

The main question in German politics today regarding the UN is the issue of participation in peace-keeping operations, which ties in with the issue of a German permanent seat in the Security Council. Wide circles within the German centre–right political spectrum maintain that Germany should, by virtue of its new role in world affairs and its economic importance, be granted a permanent seat in this exclusive club.

See BLAUHELM-EINSÄTZE; BUNDESVERFASSUNGSGERICHT; JUGOSLAWIEN-KRISE.

(SS)

Verfaßte Studentenschaft (VS)   The *Verfaßte Studentschaft* represents all students of a university and is similar in some respects to a British Students' Union. It consists of three bodies: the General Student Committee (*Allgemeiner Studenten-Ausschuß*, or ASta), the Student Parliament (*Studentenparlament*, or Stupa) and some universities also have a representative body for each department (*Fachschaft*). Each of the three bodies is elected by the students.

The *ASta* and *Stupa* are responsible for sending representatives to the Senate, faculties, and appointments committees. They have a vote in decisions taken by these committees. While relations between student representatives and other groups on such committees used to be confrontational during the years of the Students' Movement (STUDENTENBEWEGUNG), it is now more co-operative even though student representatives still perceive their interests to be opposed to those of university teaching staff.

The *ASta* is responsible for counselling students (BAFÖG, study courses), offering extra-curricular activities (sport, language courses, summer schools) and supplying practical help (photocopying facilities, lecture scripts, introduction for freshers).

The *Fachschaft* is a student body representing students' views in committees of each department, including on appointments.

See AKADEMISCHE FREIHEIT; HOCHSCHULLEHRER.

(AW)

Verfassungsänderung   Constitutional changes to the GRUNDGESETZ are possible in certain circumstances. They provide a means of ensuring that the *Grundgesetz* remains sufficiently flexible to take account of changing conditions not necessarily foreseen when it was drawn up.

Constitutional changes are enacted in a special legislative procedure requiring the support of two-thirds of the members of the BUNDESTAG and two-thirds of the votes in the BUNDESRAT. They can be introduced on the initiative of *Bundestag* or *Bundesrat* or as a requirement of decisions of the Federal Constitutional Court. Changes cannot be made which undermine the fundamental principles of the *Grundgesetz*: guarantees of basic rights (GRUNDRECHTE), the democratic principle, the rule of law (RECHTSSTAAT), federalism and the social state (SOZIALSTAAT).

By December 1993, 40 acts of amendment to the *Grundgesetz* introducing constitutional changes had been passed, the most recent amending the procedures for making European policy (December 1992), limiting the scope of the right to asylum (June 1993), and introducing a number of changes proposed by a Joint Constitutional Commission of *Bundestag* and *Bundesrat* set up to explore the need for reforming the *Grundgesetz* following German unification in 1990 (December 1993).

See ASYLRECHT; BUNDESVERFASSUNGSGERICHT; EINIGUNGSVERTRAG; EUROPAPOLITIK; FÖDERALISMUS.

(CJ)

Verfassungsbeschwerde   Constitutional complaint is a right open to citizens of the Federal Republic should they feel that their basic rights (GRUNDRECHTE) or other rights guaranteed in the GRUNDGESETZ have been infringed by state institutions. It is an important component of the rule of law (RECHTSSTAAT) and offers protection to the citizen against the abuse of state power.

Constitutional complaints are addressed to the Federal Constitutional Court (BUNDESVERFASSUNGSGERICHT). They are the last right of appeal against alleged infringements of rights and can only be made after all other appeal procedures available in the legal system have been exhausted. Most are rejected.

See GERICHTE.

(CJ)

Vergangenheitsbewältigung   'Coming to terms with the past' is an issue which every country has to deal with. Confronting and learning lessons from historical experience everywhere contributes inherently to how countries deal with problems in the present and approach the future. *Vergangenheitsbewältigung* has been, however, an especially difficult problem in the Federal Republic and in those other countries which formed part of the the Third Reich, the GDR and Austria. The enormity of the crimes of the Third Reich, in particular the mass murder of Jews and other groups designated as racially inferior, and its responsibility for unleashing World War II provide an especially weighty and uncomfortable historical legacy. Unlike the GDR and Austria, the Federal Republic approached the problem of coming to terms with this National Socialist past with a high degree of openness.

Conscious efforts were made to extend the patchy results of the denazification and re-education policies of the period of post-war occupation into a more diffuse and extensive political education in democracy and anti-racism (although these efforts themselves were also very patchy until the late 1960s). Such efforts have been reflected in school curricula, local history groups, the materials and courses provided by institutions of political education (POLITISCHE BILDUNG), through to the external projection of German experience in confronting the past by institutions such as the GOETHE-INSTITUT.

The National Socialist past remains, however, a permanent and potent legacy which, some would argue, imposes too much of a burden on younger generations who had nothing to do with the Third Reich. This feeling was given potent illustration – though was also forcefully rejected – in the second half of the 1980s in the so-called HISTORIKERSTREIT (Historians' Dispute).

A new problem of *Vergangenheitsbewältigung* emerged after unification as East Germans began to come to terms with their past in the GDR. Their problem was compounded by revelations of the scope of popular involvement in the STASI and has done much to entrench the feeling that a 'wall in the head' still divides OSSI from WESSI long after the concrete walls which divided Germany have been demolished.

See ANTISEMITISMUS; DRITTES REICH; ENTNAZIFIZIERUNG; KONZENTRATIONSLAGER; MAUER IM KOPF; NATIONALSOZIALISMUS.

(CJ)

Vermittlungsausschuß   The Mediation Committee of the *Bundestag* and *Bundesrat* plays an important role in the federal-level legislative process. It currently has 32 members, half of whom are members of the BUNDESTAG, nominated in proportion to party-political strengths in the *Bundestag*, and half of whom are nominated by the BUNDESRAT (one per BUNDESLAND).

Its function is to seek compromise in cases where the *Bundestag* and *Bundesrat* fail to agree on legislative bills. It can be convened after the

Bundesrat has rejected a bill passed on to it by the *Bundestag*. Where bills require the consent of the *Bundesrat* to become law (*Zustimmungsgesetze*), it can be convened by any of the *Bundestag*, *Bundesrat* or Federal Government (BUNDESREGIERUNG). In all other cases, it can only be convened by the *Bundesrat*.

The Mediation Committee has been convened most frequently in periods when the party-political majority in the *Bundesrat* is different from that in the *Bundestag*. This was the case throughout the period 1969–82, when a *Bundestag* majority coalition of SPD and FDP faced a majority of CDU and CSU in the *Bundesrat*, and again for most of the period since 1990, when a majority of CDU/CSU and FDP in the *Bundestag* has faced an SPD majority in the *Bundesrat*. In both eras, mediation has been largely successful, with few bills failing to make it through the legislative process.

See GESETZGEBUNG.

(CJ)

Versailler Friedensvertrag   The Versailles Peace Treaty set out the terms of the peace Germany had to follow after its defeat in World War I. It was signed on 28 June 1919 in Versailles, near Paris, on the authority of the first elected assembly of the Weimar Republic.

It was widely regarded as excessively punitive in Germany and as failing to keep to the spirit of the US President Woodrow Wilson's 'Fourteen Points' for shaping the post-war order. It stripped Germany of all overseas colonies in Africa and elsewhere, along with some 27 000 square miles of territory and 6 million inhabitants in Europe (mainly in favour of Poland, but also of Belgium, Czechoslovakia, Denmark, France and Lithuania). It prohibited the accession of the German-speaking parts of the old Austro-Hungarian Empire (present-day Austria and the Czech Sudetenland) to Germany. In addition, the German army was to be restricted to 100 000 men and forbidden certain types of weaponry. Finally, Germany was required to pay massive war reparations to compensate the victorious powers for war damage and their war efforts. This was justified in the so-called 'war guilt' clause, requiring Germany (and its allies) to accept responsibility for loss and damage caused by 'German aggression'. The whole of German territory west of the Rhine as well as the Ruhr area was to be occupied for 15 years as security against the payment of reparations.

The German government – now democratically elected and disassociated from the old order which had led Germany into war – was forced to accept these harsh terms, fearing both an allied invasion in case of rejection and the breakdown of social order in the near-revolutionary situation at home if the allies' partial blockade on imports into Germany were not soon lifted.

The result was the stigmatisation of the new democratic Republic. The German public had not been fully informed of the course of the war and the parlous state of the German military by the autumn of 1918. The surrender in November 1918 and the Versailles Treaty were consequently regarded as a national betrayal by the new democratic politicians who had 'sold out' Germany. Thus started the 'stab-in-the-back myth' (*Dolchstoßlegende*). This myth tarnished the new democratic system, imposing on it a legacy of perceived treachery which it could never shake off, and playing into the hands of those on the extreme Right – including the National Socialists – who were committed to the destruction of the Weimar Republic.

See NATIONALSOZIALISMUS; WEIMARER REPUBLIK.

(CJ)

Vertiefung   The so-called 'deepening' of integration among Member States of the European Union (EU) implies the strengthening of the supranational element of the EU's institutions, procedures and policies. It is usually contrasted with the 'widening' (*Erweiterung*) of the membership of the Union.

Deepening and widening are inextricably linked as both the practical and political implications of enlargement of membership require some form of internal reinforcing of institutions and procedures within the EU. Germany, as a central member of the EU, and a protagonist of ensuring the process of integration maintains its momentum, has been a key advocate of deepening throughout the history of the integration in Europe. The most significant attempts to deepen integration occurred with the Single European Act of 1986 (establishing the Internal Market) and with the Treaty on European Union (TEU) in 1991 (establishing the EU).

The Member States of the EU considered the deepening and widening debate in an intergovernmental conference (IGC), established to review the functioning of the TEU in 1996–97. The German Federal Government, often in alliance with its French counterpart, was conspicuous in its active pressure for reform, for example in proposing greater 'flexibility' in the workings of the EU, which implies different speeds of integration for different groups of Member States.

The main problems facing the EU today derive from the challenge of enlargement in Eastern Europe. Many Member States perceive that the EU will cease to function effectively or efficiently if it fails to reinforce its internal mechanisms – i.e. to deepen – in the face of a larger membership. However, the implications of deepening, particularly in terms of the erosion of the sovereign powers of national governments, are highly controversial in some Member States, notably Great Britain.

See BINNENMARKT; OSTERWEITERUNG.

(PH)

VIAG   VIAG is the tenth largest industrial group in Germany in 1995, with external sales of DM42 billion, 84 000 employees and a net income of DM1.3 billion. *V*ereinigte *I*ndustrie-Unternehmungen *AG* was founded in

Berlin by the German government in 1923. Until 1986, 87 per cent of VIAG was owned by the Federal Government, the remainder of the share capital being owned by the Federal Government's *Kreditanstalt für Wiederaufbau.* As part of its privatisation programme, the Federal Government then reduced its share to 47 per cent before complete privatisation in 1988. VIAG has had a dynamic growth pattern resulting in an increased turnover of 366 per cent between 1986–95.

The group consists of four divisions: energy, chemicals, packaging and logistics. Energy constitutes 25 per cent of sales but 50 per cent of pretax profits. A further 25 per cent of profits is derived from an identical proportion of packaging sales. Chemicals also yields identical proportions (of 10 per cent) in both sales and profits. The remaining 15 per cent of profits and 40 per cent of sales are attributable to logistics. VIAG's has also expanded into telecommunications (within a 'strategic alliance' also consisting of British Telecom and RWE) in competition with DEUTSCHE TELEKOM.

Like the other two large energy utilities (RWE and VEBA), VIAG has a stake in the East German electricity supplier VEAG (22.5 per cent). Also like RWE and VEBA – and, indeed many other German companies – VIAG seeks a stable, above-average income growth on a long-term basis. Similarly, its corporate policy is now one of 'shareholder value'. None the less, within a decade of partial privatisation, ordinary share values increased from DM165 to DM600 and dividends doubled from DM6 to DM12.

The group is heavily dependent on domestic energy sales. Over 50 per cent of its total sales are generated within Germany.

See PRIVATISIERUNG.

(EOS)

Volkshochschule (VHS) *Volkshochschulen* offer courses both for pleasure and personal advancement, including certificate courses. They are co-financed by the respective *Land* and the local council and charge modest fees from course participants.

In the nineteenth century the aim of the VHS was defined in terms of educating the people to take care of their own affairs by offering courses in practical fields such as business, politics, and literature. The idea behind the VHS was to provide a democratic education.

Today *Volkshochschulen* still offer courses for people's personal advancement in subjects such as cooking and flower arranging but they also provide further training or retraining for professionals, language courses, courses for school-leavers without a school leavers' certificate or for those wanting to obtain a higher certificate. Their importance is in providing opportunities for citizens to have training or further training regardless of their previous schooling.

Whilst non-professional courses can be taught by lay people, all those leading to certificates are taught by properly qualified full-time and part-time staff. Language courses are often taught by native speakers spending a year or more in Germany.

See ZWEITER BILDUNGSWEG.

(AW)

Volkskammer The *Volkskammer* (People's Chamber, or parliament), although in theory the supreme organ of state in the GDR, was a relatively powerless body. It comprised 500 deputies (463 until 1963) who were elected after 1971 for a period of five years. The distribution of seats among the political parties and mass organisations was determined in advance in a unitary list of candidates prepared by the NATIONALE FRONT. The standing committees met on average only three times per year and plenary sessions of the Chamber were not only infrequent but only lasted for just one or two days.

During the WENDE, the *Volkskammer* became a lively debating chamber which inflicted humiliation on veteran SED leaders such as the Minister of State Security, Erich Mielke. The March 1990 election, the first competitive election in the history of the GDR, provided a popular mandate for rapid unification, a policy advocated by the East German CDU and its partners in the ALLIANZ FÜR DEUTSCHLAND. The CDU attracted support across all social strata; in fact, its support among the manual workers (49.8 per cent) was higher than its share of the overall vote. The PDS, the reformed successor to the SED, scored over 16 per cent of the vote but recruited its voters primarily from white-collar employees and functionaries of the old regime, not the working class. The SPD, which had entertained hopes of victory, scored a disappointing 21.9 per cent.

After the March 1990 election, the *Volkskammer* was reduced to 400 members. Once Germany had been unified in October 1990, 144 deputies from the defunct East German Parliament joined the BUNDESTAG until the all-German election in December 1990.

See BUND FREIER DEMOKRATEN; BÜNDNIS '90; BÜRGERBEWEGUNGEN; STAATSRAT DER DDR.

(MD)

Volkspartei The term 'people's party' is often used to describe the two largest parties, the CDU/CSU and the SPD. The term refers to political parties which manage to attract substantial numbers of votes from all sections of the population. The CDU/CSU is often cited as the archetypal *Volkspartei*, in view of its success in appealing to broad sections of the electorate beyond its traditional core support among practising Christians. The SPD has pursued a similar strategy from the late 1950s.

In the 1960s and 1970s, the two *Volksparteien* together accounted for between 80 and 90 per cent of all votes cast. However, since the rise of the

GRÜNE in the early 1980s, the two *Volksparteien* have been losing votes and in 1990 commanded the support of less than 80 per cent of voters for the first time since 1953.

The special status of political parties in Germany means that the two *Volksparteien* have a substantial say in many public appointments; indeed, such posts are normally shared out between the two on an alternate basis. It was this wide-ranging influence in public life that former Federal President Richard von WEIZSÄCKER criticised in 1993. Moreover, with both *Volksparteien* competing for the same electoral ground, the political programmes have converged, leaving voters little real choice and promoting a sense of popular alienation from politics (POLITIKVERDROSSENHEIT).

See PARTEIENFINANZIERUNG.

(SG)

Volkspolizei The German People's Police (*Deutsche Volkspolizei*, called the *Vopo*) was the police force of the GDR. It was established in the Soviet zone in 1945, although it was not until 1968 that it was put on a legal footing. From 1949 onwards, the DVP was under the jurisdiction of the Ministry of the Interior. It was divided into several administration branches: passports and police registration, transport police, criminal police, traffic police and the security force. The latter included ward commissioners who usually held a lower officer rank and were responsible for various neighbourhood tasks. In addition, there were 177 500 volunteer assistants (1989) who were recruited by the ward commissioners and assisted with traffic control at peak hours and crime prevention tasks. In 1989, the total strength of the DVP was about 90 000, including 8 000 transport police and 1 500 members of the factory police.

During the 1970s, the surveillance work of the criminal police increased as part of a general expansion of surveillance activities in the GDR and was one reason why the *Vopo* was not trusted by the East German populace.

(MD)

Volkswagen (VW) The VW group is the third largest industrial enterprise in Germany. It consists domestically of VW and Audi, along with Seat (Spain), Skoda (Czech Republic), and international divisions in North America, South America, Africa and the Asia/Pacific region, plus Volkswagen Financial Services. The group was privatised in 1961, and NIEDERSACHSEN holds 40 per cent of its shares.

The Wolfsburg plant was built in 1938 to produce, among others, the 'people's car', which became known as the 'beetle'. This only entered full production after the war and quickly became an international best-seller. It epitomised Germany's industrial power and export-led growth as it was reliable, efficient, economical and relatively cheap. In spite of this success, however, the product range was narrow and heavily dependent on exports.

Audi and NSU were consequently acquired in the second half of the 1960s to facilitate a move up-market, while the stagnant VW was forced to successfully innovate in the early 1970s by the introduction of new models, notably the Golf. By 1995, the Group had 240 000 employees who produced 3.5 million units. Sales were DM88 billion. Profits were DM340 million, following a loss of nearly DM2 billion in 1993.

As with any other major player in the motor industry the need for environmental protection, the rapid increase in global population and production with resultant new markets have demanded innovative responses from the VW Group. The most notable indications are, first, the strategic location of production facilities in Mexico, Brazil, South Africa and China. Second, product developments were introduced. Third, volume and productivity planning indicated in 1993 that VW AG had around 30 000 employees more than actually required. In response to this, total working time was reduced by introducing a flexible four-day (28.8 hour) week. Similar working-time adjustments, with corresponding pay cuts, were introduced at Audi AG.

See BMW; DAIMLER-BENZ.

(EOS with ROS)

Vorschulische Erziehung   Pre-school education in Germany is supported in a number of ways. In the first three years of a child's life its mother or father can take unpaid leave from their jobs for up to three years in order to look after the child (*Erziehungsurlaub*). This applies to every single child in a family. During at least the first six months and up to 2 years after birth parents also receive increased child benefits (*Erziehungsgeld*), the level of which is set by each BUNDESLAND no matter whether the parents work or not.

A number of organisations provide full-time care for babies (*Krabbelstube, Kinderkrippe*). Mother-and-toddler groups and play groups are provided by local councils and the churches. Formal pre-school education starts at age 3 or 4 in the *Kindergarten*. These are maintained privately or by the state and their fees are low. Their aim is to provide care whilst developing the child's personality. Children normally attend *Kindergarten* either in the morning or in the afternoon. There is a shortage of places even though in some *Bundesländer* all children have a constitutional right to a place. Full-time care is provided in day-care centres ((*Kinder)tagesstätten*), but there is a shortage of places there as well.

See GRUNDSCHULE.

(AW)

W

Wahlkampf Election campaigning in Germany generally takes longer to gather momentum and never quite reaches the fever pitch of its British or American equivalents. During the campaign, parties will make use of television commercials, time for which is allocated according to party strengths, posters and information stands in shopping areas. However, British-style canvassing is unknown, and election meetings are frequently combined with a social element, typically involving prodigious quantities of beer.

Elections are always held on Sundays. The so-called 'hot phase' of the campaign begins about a month before the election. As yet, TV debates are not features of campaigns. As in many western democracies, the focus of German electoral campaigns is increasingly shifting away from issues and towards personalities. Normally, election counts in Germany hold few surprises, as the opinion polling institutes provide highly accurate forecasts around 15 minutes after the polls close.

BUNDESTAG elections are interspersed with LANDTAG elections in Germany's 16 BUNDESLÄNDER. If periodic local and European elections are also taken into account, electoral campaigning is almost a permanent feature of German politics. This was especially the case in 1994, the so-called 'super election year' (*Superwahljahr*), when, in total, 19 elections were held. Worries about a consequent 'electoral fatigue', in particular in light of falling turnout levels, have led to calls for the 'bundling' together of *Landtag* elections.

(SG)

Wahlrecht Germany's federal election law employs a modified form of proportional representation. Any German over 18 has the right to vote (although since 1 January 1996, EU citizens may vote in local and European elections) and to stand for election.

In the federal electoral system, each voter has two votes, one for a constituency MP, elected by simple majority, and a second for a party list, which determines the overall allocation of seats in the BUNDESTAG according to proportionality. If a party's total number of seats is greater than the number of constituencies it has won (the normal case), the party's remaining MPs are determined by party lists. However, if a party wins more directly elected seats than it is entitled to by proportional representation, it is allowed to keep these seats as 'surplus mandates' (*Überhangmandate*).

A key feature of the German system is the 5 per cent clause (FÜNFPROZENTKLAUSEL), which provides parties with parliamentary representation only if they win over 5 per cent of the vote. However, at federal level parties can circumvent this rule by winning 3 or more constituency seats. In 1994, the PDS entered the *Bundestag* by this method, even though it won only 4.4 per cent of the vote.

Since the 1970s, there has been a gradual drop in turnout at elections, from a high of 91 per cent in 1972 to 79 per cent in 1994, with turnout in the East considerably lower than in the West. The drop has been more marked at LANDTAG elections and is especially low in the eastern BUNDESLÄNDER. Indeed, an all-time low of 54.9 per cent was reached in 1994 at the SACHSEN-ANHALT *Landtag* election. While turnout at elections may still be high in an international comparison, the falling levels in Germany have been linked to a growing feeling of POLITIKVERDROSSEN-HEIT (political apathy).

(SG)

Währungsreform   The currency reform was the introduction of a new central banking system and the DM in Western Germany in 1948. Although the economy had been recovering since the end of the war, hoarding led to trading in black markets. The Allies therefore founded the *Bank deutscher Länder* in March, followed by the draconian introduction of the DM in June. In essence, old currency holdings and bank deposits were reduced to 6.5 per cent of their original value and public-sector debt was virtually eliminated. Similarly, mortgages and other private debts were converted at the rate of DM 1: RM 10. Owners of real assets fared extremely well whereas those who had tried to save money lost most of it. On the other hand, money was worth something again. Everybody received 60DM to start with.

German exporters benefited from a devaluation of the DM exchange rate in 1949. At the same time, European Payments Union credits resolved a foreign exchange crisis and a little later the London Treaty reduced West Germany's external debt to manageable proportions. These factors, along with the 'big bang' of the currency reform, facilitated the rise of the Social Market Economy during the 1950s. The DM moved to convertibility within a decade and export surpluses became the order of the day. Such rational explanations of economic take-off undermine the mythical element in the terminology of the 'economic miracle' (WIRTSCHAFTSWUNDER) – a myth which was to adversely affect the incorporation of East Germany where a similar 'miracle' was widely expected to happen.

In 1990, a further major currency reform occurred with the Monetary, Economic and Social Union of the GDR with the Federal Republic. The introduction of the DM into the GDR was motivated by the short-run expediency of giving consumers there access to the currency at an extremely favourable exchange rate.

See WIRTSCHAFTS-, WÄHRUNGS- UND SOZIALUNION.

(EOS)

Waigel, Theo Theo Waigel is Federal Finance Minister and leader of the CSU. Born near Augsburg in 1939, Waigel became an MP in 1972, rising quickly through the ranks of the CSU to lead his party's MPs from 1982–89. Following Franz Josef STRAUß, death in 1988, Waigel became leader of the party and was appointed Federal Finance Minister in 1989, a post he has held ever since. As Finance Minister, Waigel has been responsible for the financing of German reunification and was also one of the German signatories to the Maastricht Treaty.

In mid-1993, Waigel was involved in an acrimonious battle with Edmund Stoiber, then Bavarian Interior Minister, for the post of Bavarian Minister-President, which had been vacated by the previous incumbent, Max Streibl, following a financial scandal. Waigel was unable to shore up sufficient support within the CSU and consequently lost.

Since 1993, Waigel has been repeatedly undermined in his position as party leader by Stoiber, who is widely held to harbour ambitions for the party leadership. He has been blamed for the drastic increase in the tax burden since unification. Stoiber's Eurosceptic opinions have also conflicted with Waigel's firm support for European Economic and Monetary Union.

See BAYERN.

(SG)

Warschauer Pakt The Warsaw Pact was the security pact of the Soviet bloc. The GDR was one of the founder members of the Warsaw Pact or Warsaw Treaty Organisation (WTO) in May 1955, although its formal entry did not take place until January 1956. The Pact provided a system of collective security in the Soviet sphere of influence. It was, however, not only a mechanism whereby the Soviet Union could control and manage members' armed forces but also a means to ensure ideological compliance and, by threatening or using force, political loyalty, too. Although the process of integration made some headway in the 1960s and 1970s with the development of multinational institutions and exercises, the Pact was not strictly speaking an organisation geared to warfare. The main body of the organisation was the Political Consultative Committee. Other organs included the Permanent Commission and the Joint Secretariat. The Joint Armed Forces were placed under the control of a Soviet commander-in-chief.

The geopolitical importance of the GDR was reflected in the GDR's forces forming, together with Polish and Soviet units, the Pact's first-echelon military force directed against NATO as well as the stationing in 1983 of Soviet missiles in the GDR in response to NATO's missile deployment. The GDR was unique for the level of integration of its forces in the Pact and its dependence on the Soviet Union. The GDR army, the NATIONALE VOLKSARMEE , for example, was the only East European military establishment under the direct command of the Warsaw Pact Supreme Command in peacetime; the commander-in-chief of the Soviet forces in Germany could in theory declare a state of emergency in the GDR; and the navy was under the operational command of the fleets of the Warsaw Pact.

The collapse of Soviet power in the later 1980s culminated in the dissolution of the Pact as a military alliance in 1991.

See BRESCHNEW-DOKTRIN.

(MD)

Wehrhafte Demokratie 'Militant democracy' is a term associated with the balance which needs to be struck between the basic rights guaranteed in the GRUNDGESETZ and the limits which need to be placed on those rights in order to ensure that the *Grundgesetz*, as a democratic constitution capable of upholding basic rights, is not undermined.

The problem of striking such a balance is faced by all democratic systems of government. It has had, however, a particular resonance in the Federal Republic for a number of historical reasons: (a) the way in which anti-democratic parties like the National Socialists and the Communists were able to use the rules and rights of democracy in the Weimar Republic in their attempts to overthrow the democratic order; (b) the subsequent abuse of basic rights in the Third Reich; and (c) the existence in the GDR of a system of government on German territory which failed to uphold basic rights.

Two examples of the 'militant' protection of democracy by limiting the scope of basic rights have been given in the Federal Republic. The first is the constitutional provision for proscribing political parties which threaten the 'free democratic order'. The second is the presumption that public employees must be supportive of the free democratic order. Use was made of the former twice in the 1950s in the banning of parties of the extreme Right and Left. The latter became a controversial issue with the so-called Radicals' Decree (RADIKALENERLAẞ) of 1972, which sought to shield public service from the new forms of radicalism which emerged from the students' movement and extra-parliamentary opposition of the late 1960s.

The problem of such conceptions of militant democracy is that of drawing a line between taking necessary measures to uphold the democratic order and displaying unnecessary intolerance of unconventional political beliefs. It was widely felt that the implementation of the Radicals' Decree veered too much into the realms of intolerance.

This issue has re-emerged in muted form since unification in the unwillingness of some *Bundesländer* to consider employing members of the PDS in public service.

See APO; DRITTES REICH; GRUNDRECHTE; ÖFFENTLICHER DIENST; POLITISCHE PARTEIEN; STUDENTENBEWEGUNG; WEIMARER REPUBLIK.

(CJ)

Wehrpflicht   Compulsory military service and conscription into the BUN-DESWEHR (Federal Armed Forces) was introduced for all males in July 1956. Conscription was needed to raise the size of the army to 500 000 now that German rearmament had been permitted through West German membership of the West European Union and NATO. More importantly, the creation of a conscripted army was a device to legitimise the existence of West German armed forces at home and abroad. Conscription broadened the social base of the armed forces as well as anchoring the *Bundeswehr* within West Germany's new democratic institutions and society. Drawing on the lessons of German military history and the privileged position it had held in society, conscription aimed at preventing the emergence of a military 'state within a state'. This was attempted through the notion of *innere Führung*, or inner leadership, central to which is the idea of *Bürger in Uniform*, or citizens in uniform. Germany's conscripts are subject to civilian law and conscientious objection (*Wehr-* or *Kriegsdienstverweigerung*) is a principle upheld in the Basic Law. As an alternative to military service German men can opt for community service (ZIVILDIENST).

The end of the Cold War and German unification have challenged the principle of conscription. Germany is currently debating as to whether a professional army may suit its needs more. *Wehrpflicht*, has, however played an important role in the internal process of German unification with citizens from the new *Bundesländer* serving their military service in the *Bundeswehr*. A further issue under discussion is the possibility of allowing women to serve in the military.

(KL)

Weimarer Republik   The Weimar Republic was the first democratically governed German state. Established in 1918 amid the upheavals of German defeat in World War I, it was dismantled 15 years later following the National Socialist accession to power in 1933. The Republic took the prefix of Weimar when its first elected assembly met in 1919 in the city of Weimar in order to escape the political tensions and violence at the time overshadowing the capital city of Berlin.

The Weimar Republic was proclaimed on 9 November 1918 after a series of strikes and mutinies, sparked by war-weariness, had undermined the authority of the German Empire and its military command. The new democratic Republic was faced by two immediate problems: gaining control of the revolutionary momentum of the workers' and soldiers' protests; and negotiating the terms of Germany's defeat in the war. The former was dealt with by military force. The latter remained a perpetual burden for the Republic. The Versailles Peace Treaty (VERSAILLER FRIEDENSVERTRAG) was almost universally regarded in Germany as unfair and over-punitive, while the new democratic politicians who had done their best to negotiate its terms were seen as traitors who had 'stabbed Germany in the back' at Versailles.

The association of the 'stab-in-the-back-myth' (*'Dolchstoßlegende'*) with the democratic Republic provided a constant rallying point for anti-democratic forces of the nationalist and extreme Right in their aim to restore some form of authoritarian system of government. The National Socialist Party (NSDAP) emerged, from the end of the 1920s, as the most powerful of these. Just as there were anti-establishment forces on the Right, however, equivalent forces existed on the Left. Inspired by the revolutionary movement of 1918–19, and resentful of the way in which the movement had been violently suppressed, a strong Communist Party (the KPD) emerged, committed to the establishment of Soviet-style communism in Germany. Both these anti-establishment forces acted as a millstone around the neck of the Weimar Republic, less so in their violent attempts to overthrow the Republic in the period 1919–23, which were relatively easily put down, but more in their influence on the parliamentary situation.

The Weimar parliament, the REICHSTAG, was elected by a form of pure proportional representation, which gave a platform to even small anti-establishment parties (as were the Nazis before 1930). This squeezed the room for manoeuvre of the pro-democratic parties, at their forefront the SPD and the Catholic Centre Party, which in any case steadily lost support throughout the Weimar years. As a result, it became increasingly difficult to put together and maintain in office coalition governments prepared to work constructively within the Weimar system of government. This difficulty was heightened by two constitutional provisions: first, a simple majority of the *Reichstag* could unseat the sitting Chancellor (and his government) without having any alternative in mind; second, the President (REICHSPRÄSIDENT) had the power to appoint and dismiss Chancellors (and to rule by decree irrespective of Chancellor and *Reichstag* under wide-ranging emergency powers) in a curious overlapping of executive powers. Governmental turnover was as a result high (with 15 different governments from 1919–33), depriving the Republic of political stability.

The problem of instability was exacerbated by the economic weakness of the Republic, which endured two catastrophic economic crises in its 15-year life: the Great Inflation of 1923 and the Great Depression from 1929. The inability of the Republic to secure stable economic conditions produced resentment which fed into support for anti-establishment parties: from 1928–32 the KPD vote increased by more than a half, and that of the NSDAP *twelvefold*. Given the hostility of the KPD and NSDAP to each other, it became difficult to form any kind of government with majority support in the *Reichstag*. Chancellors and their governments were as a result increasingly appointed by the *Reichspräsident* and governed through his emergency powers rather than by parliamentary vote.

The last Chancellor to be appointed by this method was Adolf HITLER, leader of what had become the largest party in the Republic, the anti-republican NSDAP, in January 1933. The passing of Chancellor Hitler's 'Enabling Law' (ERMÄCHTIGUNGSGESETZ) on 23 March 1933, empowering him to rule by decree, signalled the demise of the Weimar Republic.

Although short-lived, the Weimar Republic remains tremendously important today. The reasons for its failure to establish enduring democratic government in Germany and for the accession to power of the NSDAP were some of the key factors taken into account when the constitution (GRUNDGESETZ) of the Federal Republic of Germany was drawn up. The Weimar experience provided an object lesson which the Federal Republic purposefully – and, as it turned out, successfully – set out to avoid.

See BUNDESKANZLER; BUNDESPRÄSIDENT; CDU/CSU; DEUTSCHES REICH; DRITTES REICH; KONSTRUKTIVES MIßTRAUENSVOTUM; NATIONAL-SOZIALISMUS; NOTSTANDSGESETZE; WAHLRECHT.

(CJ)

Weiterführende Schulen   *Weiterführende Schulen* are the schools following on from primary school. There are the *Hauptschule* (five years), *Realschule* (six years) and the *Gymnasium* (nine years), the *Gesamtschule* (five, six or nine years) and as the most recent addition the *Regionalschule*. It is compulsory to go to school for nine years (including the four years of primary school). The first two years following primary school are meant to serve as orientation (ORIENTIERUNGSSTUFE) for pupils before they make a definite choice for one or other type of school. Years five to ten are called *Sekundarstufe I*, years 11 to 13 are called *Sekundarstufe II*.

The *Hauptschule* provides an academically sound education combined with an introduction to modern working life. The school-leaving certificate is a *Qualifizierter Hauptschulabschluß* and enables pupils to take up an apprenticeship. English is generally taught through all years. The *Realschule* was formerly called *Mittelschule* (middle school) and provides an education which is more oriented towards the practical needs of industry and administration. Pupils can still go on to the *Gymnasium* after year ten when they have obtained their school-leaving certificate (*Mittlere Reife*). The *Gymnasium* developed from the medieval (Latin) grammar school. In the nineteenth and twentieth centuries new disciplines were brought in and *Gymnasien* specialising in classics, foreign languages, sciences, performing arts and economics developed. Students need to go to the school of their catchment area unless they want to specialise in subjects a particular school does not offer. The school-leaving certificate is the *Abitur* or *Allgemeine Hochschulreife* allowing students to study at university. In *Sekundarstufe II* students specialise in two or three subjects (depending on the *Bundesland*) and also study five or more minor subjects which must include mathematics, German and a foreign language. *Gesamtschulen* are comprehensive schools which either work more towards integration of pupils of all skills or more towards streaming. There are *Gesamtschulen* in nearly every *Land* now but particularly in HESSEN and NORDRHEIN-WESTFALEN. The *Regionalschule* is a kind of comprehensive school up to year ten in areas of low population density. Children who want to go on further will then have to travel to the nearest *Gymnasium* after obtaining the *Mittlere Reife*.

See GRUNDSCHULE; ÖFFENTLICHE SCHULEN; ORIENTIERUNGSSTUFE; SCHULPFLICHT.

(AW)

Weizsäcker, Richard von   Richard von Weizsäcker was Federal President from 1984–94. Weizsäcker's father was a senior diplomat during the Third Reich; indeed, Weizsäcker defended him during the Nuremberg trials in 1946. He joined the CDU in 1956 and was a member of the BUNDESTAG from 1969–81. From 1981–84, he was governing mayor of West Berlin. He was elected Federal President in 1984.

Richard von Weizsäcker was one of the most popular and respected politicians in the history of the Federal Republic. This was largely due to his willingness to confront Germany's uncomfortable past, rather than forget it and his speech marking the 40th anniversary of Germany's defeat in 1985 remains a landmark of post-war history.

As well as being the first Federal President of unified Germany, Weizsäcker is famous for the blistering attack he lauched on the role of political parties in society in 1993. Criticising them as 'power crazy' and expressing concern about the degree of influence they wield in society as a whole, his remarks are widely considered to have raised awareness of the problem of POLITIKVERDROSSENHEIT (political apathy) in Germany.

See BERLIN; BUNDESPRÄSIDENT; BUNDESVERSAMMLUNG.

(SG)

Wende   The term *Wende* literally means a 'change-around', and has been used to decribe important political turning points in Germany. It referred initially to a change of government in 1982. This was brought about because the FDP left their then coalition partner, the SPD to side with the CDU/CSU and help form a conservative-led government. *Wende* both refers to the FDP's defection and the change from a social democratic to a conservative government proposing, initially at least, a change in political direction similar to that of Thatcher's Great Britain and Reagan's USA.

More recently *Wende* has been used to describe the events which took place over the fall of the Berlin Wall in 1989, ensuing reunification and the integration of the GDR into the Federal Republic. In this context, *Wendehals* describes a person who had a position of influence or privilege in the GDR system and then switched quickly and without scruples to establish him/herself in the new system.

See BERLINER MAUER; VEREINIGUNG.

(RW)

Wertewandel   '*Wertewandel*' is the term used in the Federal Republic to describe a shift in values among the electorate. Social scientists first noticed a process of value-shift amongst the German electorate in the 1960s. Two decades of liberal democracy and rising living standards had led to reduced authoritarian and/or nationalist values amongst all but the oldest Germans, a process which was reflected in a decline in religious observance and a more permissive attitude towards authority, work and personal morality. It was regarded almost without exception as a benign symptom of the 'normalisation' of German democracy. In the 1970s, however, social scientists came to use the phrase 'value-shift' to describe a more profound shift towards 'post-materialist' values, marked by a concern for 'quality of life' issues.

Today, the term '*Wertewandel*' is used as shorthand to describe the integration of post-materialist themes (such as environmentalism and feminism) into mainstream values. It is also used to explain the rise of the GRÜNE and the slow decline in the share of the popular vote enjoyed by the larger VOLKSPARTEIEN.

See APO; NEUE SOZIALE BEWEGUNGEN; POSTMATERIALISMUS; VOLKS-PARTEI.

(CL)

Wessi   '*Wessi*' is a post-unification designation for a West German. German unification revealed considerable differences between East and West Germans. After an early bout of enthusiasm after the collapse of the Berlin Wall, *Wessis* proved to be more lukewarm on German unity. Many resented the burden of higher taxes and accused OSSIS (easterners) of a subsidy mentality and lacking in initiative. An Emnid Institute survey in 1992 found that 62 per cent of *Wessis* regarded the cost of unification as a high burden on West Germans and 28 per cent were of the opinion that a majority of Westerners would have preferred unification not to have taken place.

See MAUER IM KOPF; STEUERLÜGE.

(MD)

WestLB (Westdeutsche Landesbank)   West LB is the third largest bank in Germany with a group balance sheet total in 1995 of DM430 billion, 10 000 employees in banking and post-tax profits of DM520 million. It is not to be confused with the *Landeszentralbanken*, the regional branches of the DEUTSCHE BUNDESBANK.

WestLB is owned by NORDRHEIN-WESTFALEN and four regional savings bank associations. Like other *Landesbanken*, its original role was acting as a central clearing bank to the savings banks. From the 1970s, however, WestLB was the pacemaker for several LB developments. It became a fully fledged universal bank, with interests in securities trading, capital markets and corporate finance just as the large private-sector banks were attempting to scale down their non-financial activities. It is the largest shareholder in PREUSSAG and took over Thomas Cook in 1989. It also acquired stakes of almost 40 per cent in the *Landesbanken* of RHEINLAND-PFALZ and SCHLESWIG-HOLSTEIN and has co-operation agreements with SüdwestLB. Its plans to merge with Helaba (now Hessen-Thüringen LB) did, however, not come to fruition. More recently, WestLB has also developed a strong presence in central and East Europe.

Until early 1996, it appeared that the WestLB would resemble the COMMERZBANK by relying on organic growth to expand its London operations. However, it has since followed the Deutsche and Dresdner Banks by acquiring its own London-based investment bank, Panmure Gordon.

The private-sector banks are critical of the *Landesbanken* generally because their guarantors (BUNDESLÄNDER governments) cannot become insolvent. This, it is argued, enables them to raise cheaper funding and use it to preserve employment in weak enterprises and protect them from either liquidation or hostile takeover.

See DEUTSCHE BANK; DRESDNER BANK; FINANZWESEN.

(EOS)

Widerstand Resistance to National Socialist rule in the Third Reich was criminalised shortly after the Nazi accession to power in 1933. Anyone opposing the regime risked being imprisoned, tortured, sent to a concentration camp or executed and their families faced persecution. The scope for resistance was, however, inherently limited by the initial euphoria about HITLER's plans for Germany, a traditional belief that a strong government was called for in times of need and the early military victories in the first two years of World War II. There was no unified voice against Hitler from the Churches. However, there was opposition from the beginning in some schools, church parishes, individual clergymen (e.g. C.A. Graf von Galen, Dietrich Bonhoeffer) and a few dedicated circles of intellectuals such as the *Kreisauer Kreis* around Graf Helmuth Moltke and the *Weiße Rose* around the Scholl family. There were a number of attempts to overthrow the regime and even to kill Hitler. Groups of civilians (eg. C.F. Goerdeler, Mayor of Leipzig) and the military (e.g. Graf Stauffenberg) were involved in plans to overthrow Hitler following the outbreak of World War II. These groups saw no peaceful way to rescue Germany from military and political extinction other than through such a coup. The main coup plot, co-ordinated by Graf von Stauffenberg on 20 July 1944, failed. Those involved and many others besides (around 5 000 in all) were executed – even in the final few weeks before the German surrender.

Bearing in mind the experience of the Third Reich, the GRUNDGE-SETZ guarantees a right of resistance as a last resort in situations in which the basic principles of the *Grundgesetz* or the rule of law (RECHTSSTAAT) are being undermined.

See DRITTES REICH; ERMÄCHTIGUNGSGESETZ; GESTAPO; NOTSTANDS-GESETZE; WEIMARER REPUBLIK.

(RW)

Wirtschafts- und Währungsunion Economic and Monetary Union (EMU) is scheduled to be established among (some of) the Member States of the European Union (EU) in 1999. EMU has been a long-term goal of European integration and successive German governments have been involved in attempts to strengthen economic and monetary co-operation among Member States throughout the history of the European Community. The successful establishment of EMU is perceived as vital for the consolidation and future development of the Internal Market.

The Maastricht Treaty establishing the European Union adopted a three-stage process for EMU and laid down the economic criteria (the so-called convergence criteria) which had to be met by Member States wishing to participate.

The onset of EMU will lead to the introduction of a single currency for all EU Member States. The 'Euro', as it will be called, will be gradually phased in to replace national currencies. This development has been the source of much controversy, particularly for the German public, which remains strongly attached to the DM.

At present the greatest concern is that the convergence criteria will not be met in time for the timetable to be followed. In particular there are fears that Germany will not be able to fulfil all the criteria, which could put the future of EMU into doubt: the German economy is perceived to be the backbone of economic integration in Europe, and its absence from the EMU project is almost unthinkable. In response to these problems and fears, there have been a number of remedies suggested, including the postponement of the onset of EMU and a 'looser' interpretation of the convergence criteria, allowing those on the 'border-line' to participate.

See BINNENMARKT; EUROPAPOLITIK.

(PH)

Wirtschafts-, Währungs- und Sozialunion Economic, monetary and social union between East and West Germany was regulated by treaty with effect from 1 July 1990. This union was a necessary condition for later unification and therefore largely governed by political factors. It was a 'big bang' approach similar to the currency reform (*Währungsreform*) in 1948 but in wholly dissimilar conditions. Exchange rates favoured consumers but disadvantaged some savers and rendered the technologically backward East German industry completely uncompetitive in its major and hitherto captive central and East European markets. The treaty also included consequential convergence of pay between East and West.

There have been inevitable large fiscal flows to finance social policy and infrastructure reconstruction from West to East Germany. The privatisation, rationalisation and reconstruction of Eastern industry was spearheaded by the TREUHANDANSTALT which left considerable debts. Although the infrastructure has been transformed, West German goods

and companies dominate the East's markets. Living standards in the East will not reach Western levels until 2010 at the earliest.
See VEREINIGUNG.

(EOS)

Wirtschaftspolitik Economic policy involves the setting of macroeconomic policy goals by government. Ideally, an economy should operate at high levels of employment, displaying low inflation and a balance of payments equilibrium. Economic growth will then result from this scenario.

These four goals are difficult to achieve simultaneously. They were broadly achieved in the period of the so-called 'economic miracle' in the 1950s and early 1960s. However, as confidence in the macroeconomic theory of the Social Market Economy (SOZIALE MARKTWIRTSCHAFT) was shaken during the 1960s, a new framework emerged – culminating in the so-called 'magic square' (*magisches Viereck*). This notion embodied the four goals set out above. It was initially set out in the Act to Promote Economic Stability and Growth (*Gesetz zur Förderung der Stabilität und des Wachstums der Wirtschaft*, 1967). Several other Acts then introduced a new role for budgetary policy as an instrument for controlling employment levels. By 1982, however, the macroeconomic paradigm of the Federal Government was based on monetarism. This implied that the growth in the money supply would be strictly controlled by the DEUTSCHE BUNDESBANK while the Federal Government would make markets more efficient by deregulation, privatisation and decreasing taxation to encourage risk taking. Although the *Bundesbank* did not achieve the former goal, it continued to produce low inflation through its management of interest rates. However, while exports continued to grow rapidly, unemployment remained a major policy problem. Economic growth has also been sporadic. In the mid-1990s, rising unemployment and a current account deficit during a period of low inflation and low economic growth have characterised the German economy.

The main problems today are incorporating East Germany and meeting the convergence criteria for European Economic and Monetary Union.

See ARBEITSLOSIGKEIT; HAUSHALTSPOLITIK; PRIVATISIERUNG; WIRTSCHAFTS- UND WÄHRUNGSUNION; ZAHLUNGSBILANZ.

(EOS)

Wirtschaftswunder The 'economic miracle' refers to the period of rapid and stable economic growth in west Germany from 1949 through to the mid-1960s. Although the main economic indicators in this period – growth rates, inflation, unemployment and the balance of payments – were remarkably good, especially in international comparison, the terminology of a 'miracle' is unhelpful. It has given a near-mythological status, exaggerated legitimation and resistance to reform to a political approach to economic management – the 'social market economy' – which has proved rather less successful over the last 15–20 years. It also raised unrealistic expectations that the former GDR could also experience 'miraculous' economic take-off after 1990.

It is therefore important to note that the 'miracle' of the 1950s rested on the coincidence of a number of unrelated factors including: the US-financed Marshall Plan; relatively modest war damage to German industrial plant; the influx of millions of refugees from former German territories in eastern Europe and the GDR who were both highly mobile and helped to keep wage costs low; the boost to production of machinery and West German export performance caused by the Korean War of 1950–53; and an active role of the banks in supporting industrial investment. In addition, there was a general, popular urge to reconstruct the economy and secure prosperity following the privations of war, defeat and occupation: most West Germans were simply willing to work harder than others. One might argue that the role of government policy in spurring on and managing this 'miracle' was, against this background, rather marginal. The currency reform of 1948 and the associated relaxation of price and production controls along with various tax incentives to labour and investment certainly played a role. However, rather more of the 'miracle' was effectively beyond the control and influence of policy-makers.

See MARSHALL-PLAN; SOZIALE MARKTWIRTSCHAFT; WÄHRUNGSREFORM. (CJ)

Wohnungspolitik   Housing policy is the field of social policy (SOZIALPOLITIK) where the aim is to ensure that a sufficient housing stock is available and that individuals and families can afford the costs of adequate housing.

State intervention to ensure a sufficient housing stock is a major concern given the Federal Republic's long-standing housing shortage, especially in respect of lower income groups. Intervention may consist either of providing subsidies for the private sector (rented accommodation or owner occupation) or of public sector investment in social (i.e. council) housing, or *Sozialwohnungen*. The balance between support for private and public provision has changed periodically, but during Helmut KOHL's Chancellorship (1982–) the emphasis has been on the former. Intervention to secure the affordability of housing has also had different aspects. Rent controls were one mechanism, but these have been largely deregulated in the Kohl era in the attempt to stimulate the private rented housing market. Rental costs have, as a result, risen quite dramatically at a rate of around ten per cent per year in the late 1980s and (in the West) 5 per cent per year in the 1990s. This has placed the onus on the main alternative affordability mechanism, that of housing benefit, or *Wohngeld*. This can be secured, on application, if certain criteria on family size, family income and housing costs are met.

The level of housing benefit available has not, however, kept pace with rent rises, forcing many to move to smaller and lower quality accommodation or to live further away from their workplace, and feeding a growing problem of homelessness (*Obdachlosigkeit*).

The emphasis on private provision, and the associated deregulation of rent controls, predetermined the course chosen for housing policy in East Germany after unification. Market mechanisms and rent rises have been introduced as means of dismantling the former GDR system of public sector provision and extremely low rents (of a level typically insufficient to cover maintenance costs). The proportion of housing costs in total family expenditures has as a result risen considerably, producing problems similar to those in the West. As a result, throughout Germany, groups such as young families, single parents, those in receipt of social assistance (SOZIALHILFE) due to low incomes, and foreigners have significant difficulties in affording adequate housing.

See FAMILIENPOLITIK.

(CJ)

Z

Zahlungsbilanz The balance of payments is the standard method for recording external trade, services, payments and capital transactions. After a record foreign-trade surplus of DM135 billion in 1989, goods were diverted from exports to feed the new demand in Eastern Germany. But by 1995 the surplus was again high (DM90 billion). There is no better indication of Germany's continued export success. However, the deficit in services was DM50 billion. Contributory factors have been deficits on foreign travel, investment income and transfer payments such as net payments to the EU of DM26 billion and remittances by foreign workers. From 1991 the overall balance of payments was thus in significant deficit.

Following the early balance of payments crisis in 1950, West Germany gradually built up large foreign currency reserves. In 1995 they were DM107 billion – only DM10 billion less than the record year of 1992, when reserves were boosted by heavy speculative inflows as a result of currency instability in the EU.

(EOS)

ZDF See RUNDFUNK AND FERNSEHEN.

Zehn-Punkte-Plan The Ten-Point Plan was Chancellor Helmut KOHL's initial proposal for a gradual road to German unification presented to the BUNDESTAG on 28 November 1989. The key point was the Federal Government's willingness to take a decisive step 'to develop confederative structures between the two states in Germany with the goal of creating a federation, a federal state order in Germany'. Concrete aid was promised to the GDR if 'fundamental change of the political and economic system of the GDR' was put into effect. This included the holding of free elections in the GDR and the creation of a legitimate democratic government. With regard to the external aspects of the plan, Kohl offered reassurances of fitting German unity into the future architecture of Europe and the European Community. No clear timetable was set by Kohl and it was anticipated that unification would require several years to complete.

Although the only opposition in the *Bundestag* to the plan came from the GRÜNE, the reception abroad, including the French and British governments, was far from enthusiastic. One notable exception was the American administration, the only foreign government to have been informed in advance.

See VEREINIGUNG; ZWEI-PLUS-VIER-VERTRAG.

(MD)

Zeitungen und Zeitschriften   All German newspapers and magazines were closed down following Germany's capitulation in 1945. Months later the Western Allies granted licences to publishers who were not suspected of having been Nazis as they saw newspapers as a means to re-educate the German people in democracy. A free press was guaranteed in the GRUNDGESETZ in 1949. The press is respected in the Federal Republic as a kind of fourth element (alongside the executive, legislature and judiciary) in the separation of powers (GEWALTENTEILUNG). Newspapers are financed through their advertising sections (two-thirds) and sales (one-third).

Despite a concentration of publishers, there are more than 400 daily and around 30 weekly papers as well as around 8 000 magazines. Newspapers can be classified by their geographical coverage. *Lokal-* or *Regionalzeitungen* (97 per cent of all papers) are widespread. These papers have sections on national affairs as well as on local/regional topics. Berlin, for example, has four city papers (selling around 800 000 copies daily), the *B.Z*, the *Berliner Zeitung*, the *Berliner Morgenpost* and the *Tageszeitung* (*TAZ*). National papers are broadsheets such as the *Frankfurter Allgemeine Zeitung* (*FAZ*) (conservative), the *Frankfurter Rundschau* (centre-left), *Die Welt* (conservative), and the *Süddeutsche Zeitung* (centre-right), and publish between 220 000 and 400 000 copies daily. The tabloid *Bild-Zeitung* is available nationwide and sells over 4 million copies daily. The Swiss broadsheet *Neue Zürcher Zeitung* is also widely available.The weekly papers with the biggest print runs are *Bild am Sonntag* (more than 2 million copies), *Die Zeit* with around 400 000 copies and *Welt am Sonntag*. Broadsheets have extensive coverage of foreign affairs. Foreign language papers are also widely available.

In the former GDR the press was controlled by the state. NEUES DEUTSCHLAND had 90 per cent of the dailies' market share. Since unification, the paper has changed into a respected, politically independent broadsheet.

Magazines have a significant share of the press market. The politically centre-left news magazine *Der Spiegel* is the market leader (over 1 million copies every week). *Capital* and *Wirtschaftswoche* dominate the market in the area of economics. *Der Stern* and *Die Bunte* are the biggest magazines investigating both current affairs and human interest stories. In addition, there are radio and TV magazines as well as a wealth of special interest magazines, often published by interest groups (VERBÄNDE), the

biggest one being *Motorwelt* (9 million copies per month), published by the automobile club ADAC.
(RW)

Zentralstelle zur Vergabe von Studienplätzen See NUMERUS CLAUSUS.

Zivildienst Community service is carried out by recognised conscientious objectors (*Wehr-* or *Kriegsdienstverweigerer*) instead of military service. Community service was developed as an alternative to military service to guarantee the right given in the GRUNDGESETZ that no-one should have to serve in the armed forces if they object on grounds of conscience. The period of community service fulfilled by the objectors is currently 13 months and can be spent in a number of different occupations, primarily within hospitals, youth hostels, retirement homes, etc. The Federal Office for Women and Youth is responsible for administering community service.

There is currently a lively political debate on the future shape of the German armed forces and one of the current proposals under discussion concerns the abolition of an obligation to serve in the army or fulfil community service.

See BUNDESWEHR; WEHRPFLICHT.
(PH)

Zwei-plus-Vier-Vertrag The 'Two-plus-Four' Treaty regulated the external aspects of German unification and embodied the restoration by the four post-war occupying powers of full sovereignty to Germany.

It was agreed in February 1990 that 'two-plus-four' talks should commence on the external aspects of German unification. The *two* German states were to deal not only with each other but also to negotiate simultaneously with the *four* former occupying powers, France, the Soviet Union, the USA and Great Britain. The talks commenced in May and were concluded in September 1990. The United States had fewer reservations than the other three powers and throughout the negotiations gave firm support to unification. The French, though initially worried about the dangers of an enlarged Germany, committed themselves to a policy of anchoring Germany by deepening European integration. This contrasted with the policy of a more sceptical British government which preferred a looser Europe and wanted to slow down the pace of unification. Although President Gorbachev had accepted German unification in late January 1990, the Soviet Union proposed that a united Germany should neither be a member of NATO or the WARSCHAUER PAKT. Soviet weakness obliged Gorbachev to concede German membership of NATO during his July meeting with Chancellor KOHL in the Caucasus. The pill was sugared by German promises of financial aid and economic co-operation and by placing a ceiling on the size of the German armed forces.

The 'Two-plus-Four' Treaty, which was signed on 12 September 1990, restored full sovereignty to Germany and defined the territory of Germany as that of the former GDR and Federal Republic plus Berlin. The Germans agreed to renounce the development of nuclear, chemical and biological weapons and to reduce their armed forces to 370 000 within three to four years. Soviet troops were to withdraw from Germany by the end of 1994. During this period, NATO military structures were not to be extended to GDR territory. The only forces stationed on the latter would be German units of territorial defence which were not to be integrated into the alliance to which united Germany would belong. Finally, the Federal Republic's right to join any alliance was confirmed, thus allowing her to remain in NATO.

See VEREINIGUNG; ZEHN-PUNKTE-PLAN.

(MD)

Zweiter Bildungsweg   The 'second educational path' is for students who want to study for higher school-leaving certificates after they have finished apprenticeships following the *Hauptschule* or *Realschule*. They can do this by following courses for mature students.

The *Abendgymnasium/Abendschule* (evening school) is for people who have successfully finished an apprenticeship and want to study in their spare time to obtain the qualification required for going to university (*Abitur*). *Abendgymnasien* are private schools which have been recognised by the state. They are non-fee-paying. Students take a three-year programme which includes German, history, geography, two foreign languages, mathematics and physics.

Kollege offer full-time education (over five semesters) to achieve the *Abitur*. Further institutions are *Berufsaufbauschule* and *Fachoberschule* for working people. Entrance requirements and curricula are determined by each BUNDESLAND.

See BAFÖG; VOLKSHOCHSCHULE.

(AW)

Zwischenprüfung   See GRUND- UND HAUPTSTUDIUM.